MARY KELLY

October Files

Richard Serra, edited by Hal Foster with Gordon Hughes
Andy Warhol, edited by Annette Michelson
Eva Hesse, edited by Mignon Nixon
Robert Rauschenberg, edited by Branden W. Joseph
James Coleman, edited by George Baker
Cindy Sherman, edited by Johanna Burton
Roy Lichtenstein, edited by Graham Bader
Gabriel Orozco, edited by Yve-Alain Bois
Gerhard Richter, edited by Benjamin H. D. Buchloh
Richard Hamilton, edited by Hal Foster with Alex Bacon
Dan Graham, edited by Alex Kitnick
John Cage, edited by Julia Robinson
Claes Oldenburg, edited by Nadja Rottner
Louise Lawler, edited by Helen Molesworth with Taylor Walsh
Robert Morris, edited by Julia Bryan-Wilson
John Knight, edited by André Rottmann
Isa Genzken, edited by Lisa Lee
Hans Haacke, edited by Rachel Churner
Michael Asher, edited by Jennifer King
Mary Kelly, edited by Mignon Nixon

MARY KELLY

edited by Mignon Nixon

essays and interviews by Mary Kelly, Paul Smith, Helen Molesworth, Laura Mulvey, Hal Foster, Parveen Adams, Emily Apter, Margaret Iversen, Griselda Pollock, Rosalyn Deutsche, and Mignon Nixon

OCTOBER FILES 20

The MIT Press
Cambridge, Massachusetts
London, England

This book was set in Bembo by New Best-set Typesetters Ltd.

Library of Congress Cataloging-in-Publication Data

Names: Nixon, Mignon, editor.
Title: Mary Kelly / edited by Mignon Nixon.
Description: Cambridge, MA : The MIT Press, 2016. | Series: October files | Includes bibliographical references and index.
Identifiers: LCCN 2016000494 | ISBN 9780262034784 (hardcover : alk. paper) | ISBN 9780262529327 (pbk. : alk. paper)
Subjects: LCSH: Kelly, Mary, 1941—Criticism and interpretation. | Kelly, Mary, 1941- Post-partum document. | Feminism and art.
Classification: LCC N6537.K42 M37 2016 | DDC 709.2—dc23 LC record available at http://lccn.loc.gov/2016000494

149353161

Contents

Series Preface vii
Acknowledgments ix

Mary Kelly — **Notes on Reading the *Post-Partum Document* (1977)** 1

Paul Smith and Mary Kelly — **No Essential Femininity: A Conversation between Mary Kelly and Paul Smith (1982)** 9

Helen Molesworth — **House Work and Art Work (2000)** 23

Laura Mulvey — **Impending Time: Mary Kelly's *Corpus* (1986)** 53

Hal Foster and Mary Kelly — **That Obscure Subject of Desire: An Interview with Mary Kelly by Hal Foster (1990)** 65

Parveen Adams — **The Art of Analysis: Mary Kelly's *Interim* and the Discourse of the Analyst (1991)** 79

Emily Apter — **Fetishism and Visual Seduction in Mary Kelly's *Interim* (1991)** 99

Margaret Iversen and Mary Kelly **Mary Kelly in Conversation with Margaret Iversen (1994)** 115

Griselda Pollock **Mary Kelly's *Ballad of Kastriot Rexhepi*: Virtual Trauma and Indexical Witness in the Age of Mediatic Spectacle (2004/2010)** 131

Rosalyn Deutsche **Not-Forgetting: Mary Kelly's *Love Songs* (2006)** 153

Mignon Nixon **Mary Kelly's *Mimus*: Feminism's Waves (2015)** 167

Index of Names 193

Series Preface

OCTOBER Files addresses individual bodies of work of the postwar period that meet two criteria: they have altered our understanding of art in significant ways, and they have prompted a critical literature that is serious, sophisticated, and sustained. Each book thus traces not only the development of an important oeuvre but also the construction of the critical discourse inspired by it. This discourse is theoretical by its very nature, which is not to say that it imposes theory abstractly or arbitrarily. Rather, it draws out the specific ways in which significant art is theoretical in its own right, on its own terms and with its own implications. To this end we feature essays, many first published in *OCTOBER* magazine, that elaborate different methods of criticism in order to elucidate different aspects of the art in question. The essays are often in dialogue with one another as they do so, but they are also as sensitive as the art to political context and historical change. These "files," then, are intended as primers in signal practices of art and criticism alike, and they are offered in resistance to the amnesiac and antitheoretical tendencies of our time.

The Editors of *OCTOBER*

Acknowledgments

Mary Kelly's "Notes on Reading the *Post-Partum Document*" was first published in *Control Magazine* 10 (1977), pp. 10–12. It was prepared for a seminar titled "Psychoanalysis and Feminism" at the ICA, London, in 1976, held during the exhibition of *Post-Partum Document (PPD) I–III*. This text was reprinted in Mary Kelly, *Imaging Desire* (Cambridge, MA: MIT Press, 1996), pp. 20–25. "No Essential Femininity: A Conversation between Mary Kelly and Paul Smith" first appeared in *Parachute* 26 (1982), pp. 31–35. This discussion was initiated during the exhibition of *Post-Partum Document* at the Anna Leonowens Gallery, Nova Scotia College of Art and Design, Halifax, in 1981. It was reprinted in Mary Kelly, *Imaging Desire*, pp. 63–76. Helen Molesworth's "House Work and Art Work" was published in *October* 92 (Spring 2000), pp. 71–97. An earlier version of this essay was published in *Rewriting Conceptual Art*, edited by Michael Newman and Jon Bird (London: Reaktion Books, 1999). Laura Mulvey's "Impending Time: Mary Kelly's *Corpus*" (1986) was written as the catalog text for "Corpus," an exhibition held at Riverside Studios, London, and at Kettle's Yard, Cambridge, in 1986. The essay was reprinted in Mulvey's *Visual and Other Pleasures* (Bloomington: Indiana University Press, 1989), pp. 148–155. "That Obscure Subject of Desire: An Interview with Mary Kelly by Hal Foster" was originally published in *Mary Kelly: Interim* (New York: New Museum of Contemporary Art, 1990), pp. 53–62, and was reprinted in Mary Kelly, *Imaging Desire*, pp. 165–179. Parveen Adams's "The Art of Analysis: Mary Kelly's *Interim* and the Discourse of the Analyst" originally appeared in a special issue of *October* edited by Parveen Adams: "Rendering the Real," *October* 58 (Fall 1991), pp. 81–96. It was republished in Parveen Adams, *The Emptiness of the Image: Psychoanalysis and Sexual Differences* (London: Routledge, 1996), pp. 70–89. Emily Apter's "Fetishism and Visual Seduction in Mary Kelly's *Interim*" was also published in *October* 58 (Fall 1991), pp. 97–108. "Mary Kelly in Conversation with Margaret Iversen" originally appeared in *Talking Art* (London: ICA Documents, 1994), pp. 101–117. This was a transcript of the seminar held in conjunction with the exhibition *Gloria Patri* at the Institute of Contemporary Art, London, 1993. The conversation was later published in Mary Kelly, *Imaging Desire*, pp. 187–202. The version of Griselda Pollock's "Mary Kelly's *Ballad of Kastriot Rexhepi*: Virtual Trauma and Indexical Witness in the Age of Mediatic Spectacle" reprinted here was published in *Digital and Other Virtualities: Renegotiating the Image*, ed. Antony Bryant and Griselda Pollock (New York: I. B. Tauris, 2010). Earlier versions appeared in *Parallax* 10, no. 1 (2004) and in the catalog for the exhibition *Mary Kelly: The Ballad of Katriot Rexhepi* at EspacioAV, Murcia, 2006. Rosalyn Deutsche's "Not-Forgetting: Mary Kelly's *Love Songs*" was published in *Grey Room* 24 (Summer 2006). Mignon Nixon's "Mary Kelly's *Mimus*: Feminism's Waves" is published here for the first time.

I warmly thank Mary Kelly for her advice and collaboration on this File. It has been a privilege to work with her. I am grateful to all the authors for allowing their texts to be included in this volume. Special thanks are due to Rachel Churner for her expert and invaluable editorial support. I also thank Jonathan Horrocks of Pippy Houldsworth Gallery, London, for his meticulous care in assembling photographs of Mary Kelly's work. The cooperation of the institutions that have allowed us to reproduce images of a number of pivotal exhibitions is greatly appreciated. I am, as ever, indebted to Karin Kyburz of the Courtauld Institute of Art, London, for picture research. I also thank Judy Chicago, Mierle Laderman Ukeles, and Martha Rosler for allowing photographs of their work to be reproduced in "House Work and Art Work." For editorial advice and constant encouragement, I thank Adam Lehner, managing editor of *October*, and the editorial board.

Notes on Reading the *Post-Partum Document*

Mary Kelly

The Discourse of the Women's Movement

The *Post-Partum Document* is located within the theoretical and political practice of the women's movement, a practice which foregrounds the issues of subjectivity and ideological oppression. More specifically, the *Document* is identified with the tendency that bases the notion of ideological oppression on a psychoanalytic theory of subjectivity, that is, the unconscious.[1] Freud's discovery of the unconscious had crucial implications for theorizing the process by which human subjects become constituted in ideology. If there is no ideology except in practice and by a subject, then ideological oppression is not merely false consciousness. The ideological refers not only to systems of representation but also to a nonunitary complex of social practices which have political consequences. Moreover, these consequences are not given as the direct effect of the means of signification employed in a practice. They depend on a political analysis of what is signified.[2]

For the purposes of such an analysis, the *Post-Partum Document* is the product of a practice of signification, and as such, it does not reflect but reworks the feminist ideology in which it was founded. This is primarily the ideology of consciousness-raising groups that still form a major part of the women's movement. The *Document* reiterates, at one level, the unique contribution that consciousness-raising made to political practice in general by emphasizing the subjective moment of women's oppression.[3] But, at another level, it argues against the supposed self-sufficiency

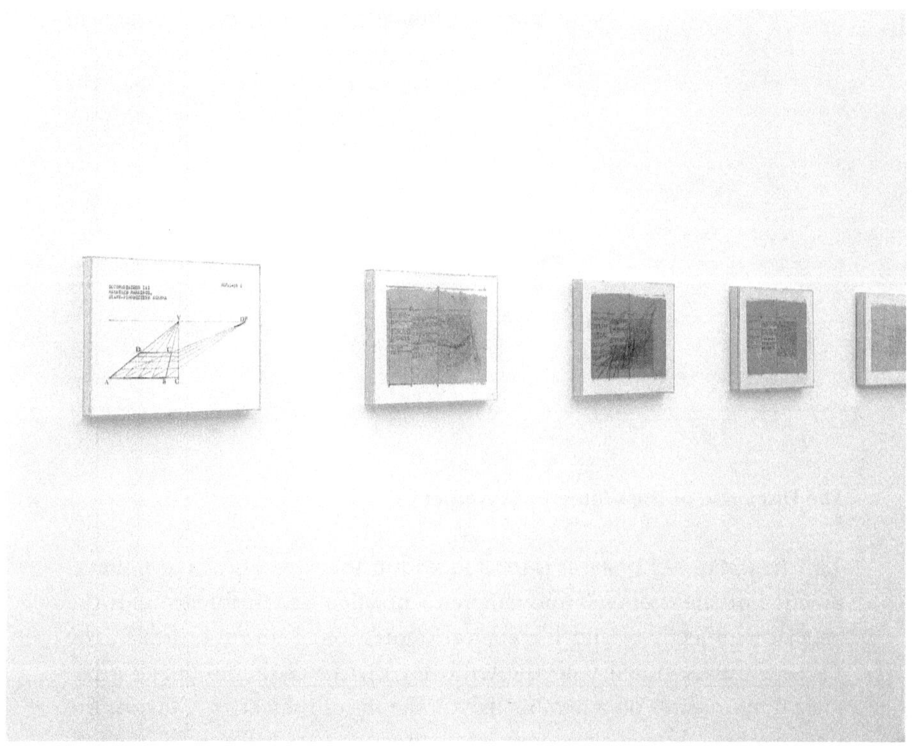

Mary Kelly, *Post-Partum Document: Documentation III, Analysed Markings and Diary-perspective Schema*, 1975. Perspex units, white card, sugar paper, crayon, 13 units; each 11 × 14 in. Collection of Tate, London. Installation view, Generali Foundation, Vienna, 1998. Photo by Werner Kaligofsky. Courtesy the artist and Pippy Houldsworth Gallery, London.

of lived experience and for a theoretical elaboration of the social relations in which femininity is formed. In this sense, the *Post-Partum Document* functions as part of an ongoing debate over the relevance of psychoanalysis to the theory and practice of both Marxism and feminism. Furthermore, the debate includes a critique of the patriarchal bias underlying some of the theoretical assumptions on which the *Document* is based.[4]

The Discourse of the Mother-Child Relationship

The *Post-Partum Document* describes the subjective moment of the mother-child relationship. An analysis of this relationship is crucial to an understanding of the way in which ideology functions in/by the material practices of childbirth and child care. Feeding or dressing a child depends as much on the interchange of a system of signs as teaching him/her to speak or write. In a sense, even the unconscious discourse of these moments is "structured like a language."[5] This underlines the fact that intersubjective relationships are fundamentally social. More precisely, every social practice offers a specific expression of a general social law and this law is the symbolic dimension which is given in language.[6]

In patriarchy, the phallus becomes the privileged signifier of this symbolic dimension.[7] Although the subject is constituted in a relation of "lack" at the moment of his/her entry into language, it is possible to speak specifically of the woman's "negative place" in the general process of significations or social practices that reproduce patriarchal relations within a given social formation. In childbirth, the mother's negative place is misrecognized insofar as the child is the phallus for her.[8] This imaginary relation is lived through, at the level of ideology and in the social practice of child care, as proof of the natural capacity for maternity and the inevitability of the sexual division of labor.[9]

The documentations of specific moments such as weaning from the breast, learning to speak, and entering a nursery demonstrate the reciprocity of the process of socialization, that is, the intersubjective discourse through which not only the child but also the mother is constituted as subject.

The Discourse of Women's Practice in Art

The *Post-Partum Document* forms part of the "problematic" of women's practice in art. The problematic includes a symptomatic reading of the visual inscriptions of women artists. Such a reading, based as much on absences as presences, suggests the way in which the realm of "the feminine" is bounded by negative signification in the order of language and culture. Because of this coincidence of language and patriarchy, the feminine is, metaphorically, set on the side of the heterogeneous, the unnameable, the unsaid. But the radical potential of women's art practice lies precisely in this coincidence, since, insofar as the feminine is said, it is profoundly subversive.[10]

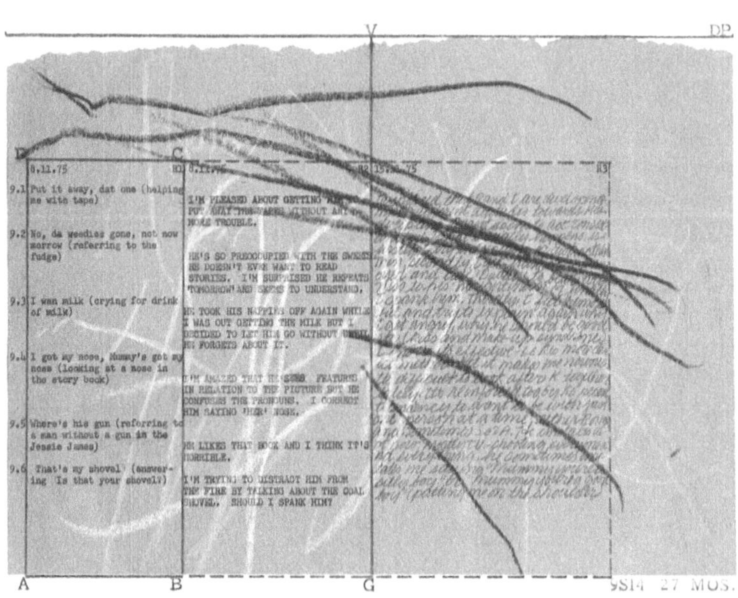

Mary Kelly, detail of *Post-Partum Document: Documentation III, Analysed Markings and Diary-perspective Schema*, 1975. Perspex unit, white card, sugar paper, crayon; 11 × 14 in. Collection of Tate, London. Courtesy the artist and Pippy Houldsworth Gallery, London.

However, the *Post-Partum Document* is not an excavation of female culture, or a valorization of the female body or of feminine experience as such. It is an attempt to articulate the feminine as discourse, and therefore places the emphasis on the intersubjective relationships which constitute the female subject.[11] Currently in women's art practice, there is a proliferation of forms of signification where the artist's own person, in particular her body, is given as a signifier, that is, as object. In the *Document*, as a means of distantiation, the figure of the mother is not visibly present. Although it is a self-documentation of the mother-child relationship, here between myself and my son, the *Post-Partum Document* does not describe the unified, transcendental subject of autobiography, but rather, the decentered, socially constituted subject of a mutual discourse. Moreover, this subject is fundamentally divided. There is a conscious/unconscious split which has operations characteristic of both sides: the signifying processes or drives on the one hand, and the social constraints such as family structures or modes of production on the other.[12] The means of signification used in the *Document* are scriptovisual in order to articulate the gap left by this split, that is, to show how the unconscious processes irrupt into a signifying practice and cut across the systematic order of language and, also, to show the difficulty of the symbolic order for women.

In the *Post-Partum Document*, the art objects are used as *fetish objects*, explicitly to displace the potential fetishization of the child and implicitly to expose the typically fetishistic function of representation.[13] The stained liners, folded vests, child's markings, and word imprints have a minimum sign value in relation to the commodity status of representational art, but they have a maximum affective value in relation to the libidinal economy of the unconscious. They are "representations," in the psychoanalytic sense, of cathected memory traces.[14] These traces, in combination with the diaries, speech events, and feeding charts, construct the discourse of the mother's lived experience. At the same time, they are set up in an antagonistic relationship with the diagrams, algorithms, and footnotes which construct the discourse of feminist analysis. In the context of an installation, this analysis is not meant to definitively theorize the *Post-Partum* moment, but rather to describe a process of secondary revision. In a sense, this text is also included in that process not as a topology of intention, but as a rewriting of the discourse of the *Document* which is at once a repression and a reactivation of its consequences.

Notes

1. The *Post-Partum Document* is most closely associated with the debate that surfaced after the publication in 1974 of Juliet Mitchell's book *Psychoanalysis and Feminism*, and in particular with a Lacanian reading of Freud, which was in strong evidence as a theoretical tendency at the Patriarchy Conference in London in May 1976. A seminar titled "Psychoanalysis and Feminism" was organized during the showing of the *Post-Partum Document* at the ICA New Gallery in October 1976. The relevance of psychoanalysis to ideology, feminine psychology, and art practice was discussed by a panel on which I was a participant along with Parveen Adams, lecturer in psychology, Brunel University;

Susan Lipshitz, psychologist, The Tavistock; filmmaker Laura Mulvey; and writer Rosalind Delmar.

2. Paul Q. Hirst, "Althusser's Theory of Ideology," *Economy and Society* 5 (November 1976): 396; see also section on "Representation," pp. 407–411.

3. Rosalind Coward, "Sexuality and Psychoanalysis," unpublished paper, 1977.

4. For a useful outline of the debate see the Editorial Collective's article on "Psychology, Ideology, and the Human Subject" in *Ideology and Consciousness* 1 (May 1977): 5–56. The critique concerns Lacan's acceptance of the "universality of language," c.f. Luce Irigaray, *Speculum de l'Autre Femme* (Paris: Editions de Minuit, 1974). See also "Women's Exile: An Interview with Luce Irigaray," trans. Couze Venn, *Ideology and Consciousness* 1 (May 1977): 62–76.

5. See Jacques Lacan, "The Insistence of the Letter in the Unconscious," in *Structuralism* (New York: Anchor Books, 1970), pp. 287–323.

6. Julia Kristeva, "The System and the Speaking Subject," *Times Literary Supplement*, October 12, 1973.

7. For an elaboration of the consequences in terms of sexual difference, see Jacques Lacan, "La Signification du phallus," *Écrits* (Paris: Editions du Seuil, 1966), pp. 685–695.

8. Misrecognition here refers specifically to Lacan's sense of the term as in "the function of misrecognition which characterizes the ego in all its structures," and not to ideological "misrecognition." See Jacques Lacan, "The Mirror Phase as Formative of the Function of the I," *New Left Review* 51 (September–October 1968): 71–77.

9. The sexual division of labor is not a symmetrically structured system of women inside the home, men outside it, but rather an intricate, most often asymmetrical, delegation of tasks which aims to provide a structural imperative to heterosexuality. Mary Kelly, "Footnotes and Bibliography," *Post-Partum Document* (London: ICA New Gallery, 1976), p. 1.

10. See Julia Kristeva, "Signifying Practice and Mode of Production" in *La Traversée des Signes* (Paris: Editions du Seuil, 1975), trans. and intro. Geoffrey Nowell-Smith, *Edinburgh Magazine* 1 (1976).

11. In "Art and Sexual Politics" I defined the forms/means of signification employed in women's art practice in terms of the underlying structures of "feminine narcissism," based metaphorically on Freud's description of narcissistic object choice in "On Narcissism: An Introduction" (1914), in Sigmund Freud, *Collected Papers*, ed. Ernest Jones, trans. Joan Riviere (London: Hogarth Press and Institute of Psychoanalysis, 1950), p. 47. See also "Women's Practice in Art," Susan Hiller and Mary Kelly in conversation, *Audio Arts* 3 (1977), and "Women and Art," *Studio International* 3 (1977).

12. Julia Kristeva, "The System and the Speaking Subject," *Times Literary Supplement*, October 12, 1973; c.f. the splitting of the subject, Marcelin Pleynet, "de Pictura," trans. Stephen Bann, *20th Century Studies* (December 1977).

13. See Stephen Heath on fetishism and "representation" in classic cinema and popular photography, "Lessons from Brecht," *Screen* 15 (Summer 1974); see also Laura Mulvey, "Visual Pleasure and Narrative Cinema," *Screen* 16 (Autumn 1975).

14. J. Laplanche and J.-B. Pontalis, *The Language of Psychoanalysis* (London: Hogarth Press, 1973), p. 200. For Freud, the idea presentation/representation is to be understood

as what comes from the object and is registered in mnemic systems, and not as the act of presenting an object to consciousness; memory trace/mnemic trace is used by Freud to denote the way in which events are inscribed upon the memory, they are deposited in different systems and reactivated only once they have been cathected (p. 247); cathexis is an economic concept pertaining to the fact that a certain amount of psychical energy is attached to an idea or group of ideas, a part of the body, or an object (p. 62).

No Essential Femininity: A Conversation between Mary Kelly and Paul Smith

Paul Smith and Mary Kelly

PAUL SMITH: Would you begin by describing your *Post-Partum Document*?

MARY KELLY: Speaking quite generally, it's an extended documentation which I began in 1973 of the mother-child relationship. It took about six years to complete and is divided into six sections including, in all, about one hundred thirty-five pieces. I suppose I should also say that it was conceived as a piece for the conventional gallery space; that is, specific modes of presentation are employed. The plastic frames, for instance, parody the whole iconography of the museum "display"—not just the art museum but something like the natural history museum as well (which I've always thought of as a vast metaphor for the exploration of the mother's body). I wanted to put this archaeology of everyday life into that kind of framed space—an unexpected place—which would set up certain conditions for a critical reading. I felt it was crucial to consider how the work intervened in a particular institutionalized context. So, in a sense, the way it looks in the gallery is an important consideration. On the one hand, it appears to be a record of external events, but on the other, it doesn't function in that space as simply a document; the installation is intended to construct several readings or ways through the text. These are indicated first by the objects and the narrative texts which accompany them; second, by a series of diagrams which refer elsewhere to a kind of explication of the empirical procedures in the work; and third, by another set of diagrams which refer specifically to

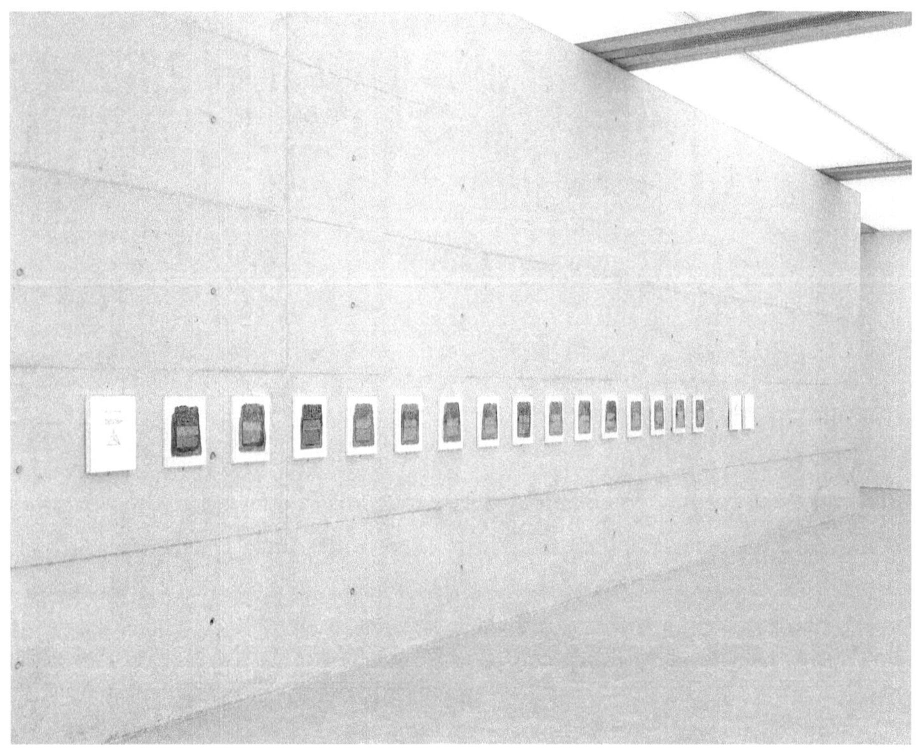

Mary Kelly, *Post-Partum Document: Documentation VI, Pre-writing Alphabet, Exergue, and Diary,* 1978. Perspex unit, white card, resin, slate, 18 units; each 14 × 11 in. Collection of Arts Council, UK. Installation view, Generali Foundation, Vienna, 1998. Photo by Werner Kaligofsky. Courtesy the artist and Pippy Houldsworth Gallery, London.

the work of Lacan and which suggest another possible reading based on psychoanalysis.

So, at one level the spectator is caught up, as it were, in a first-person narrative which traces the events specifically related to moments in the child's—that is, my son's—relationship with me: for instance, weaning from the breast, learning to speak, starting school, the first questions about sexuality, and finally, learning to write. Each one of these moments "develops" in an empirical sense, and this might indicate that the piece had a definite beginning and end; but, of course, at another level, the space of the diagrams that refer to the Lacanian readings places much less emphasis on a literal document or on a notion of, say, developmental stages, than on the construction of the relationship in terms of the mother's fantasies.

PS: I'd like to pick up on a lot of those points, but would you start by talking about the notion of narrative here? As I see it, the story of the mother-child relationship *is* specifically a story, chronological and linear, working on the level of traditional narrative in the sense that there's a problem posed and a resolution reached (which, here, is the final imposition of the social and symbolic upon the child). And also, isn't the spectator obliged to move around the work in the linear way that narrative traditionally entails?

MK: Certainly I didn't see it as a narrative in the traditional sense. I suppose that the diaries give a place to the mother in terms of the subject "I"; she speaks in the first person. But that's displaced by the metadiscursive style, which enters by way of the footnotes and which uses the third person as the dominant mode of address. So I'm not really privileging the autobiographical discourse—I'm always attempting to disrupt it.

As to what you say about a sort of development and resolution: I think that movement is thwarted in the work as well. In a traditional narrative one would perhaps expect a central point at which the heroine makes the decisions which produce a certain effect or dictate her fate. That's not the case here. The diaries just prolong and extend the description of events at the same level—so that when you talk about a resolution, I'd reply that resolution refers in a much more general way to the theoretical implications of the work, which are presented in the footnotes. That's to say, when I describe the mother-child relationship in the postpartum period as a confrontation between the Real and the Imaginary, which is always structured within the *primacy* of the Symbolic, that can be referred to in a certain sense as a resolution. It's less to do, though, with the narrative structure of the work and more with the theoretical perspective, which always sees the positioning of the subject and the construction of femininity as framed within the limits of language and culture. Some feminists, I know, might not agree. But then you have to ask yourself a question: if you don't subscribe to that notion of the universality of language, if you say that men and women don't enter into the same order of language and culture and that it's essentially different for the woman, that she can discover something outside, as it were, in opposition to that order, then doesn't that also effect a kind of closure—perhaps one that's even more dangerous in its implications for feminism? In its most extreme form, it would imply that femininity is tied to essential biological differences; or, alternatively, it would place emphasis on the experience of the pre-Oedipal moment as privileged for the woman, maintaining that the passage she makes through the Oedipus complex is somehow incomplete, or that she occupies a position "outside" in relation to representation. This would ultimately suggest that all women are in some sense neurotic as the necessary effect of their psychic positioning within the Symbolic.

PS: I suppose that, traditionally, one of the most effective ways of imposing a closure through a visual means of representation is to use the biographical or autobiographical image, always given as a wholeness. You've very deliberately left out of the *Post-Partum Document* your own body, your own image. What's involved in forgoing that temptation, and what kind of image of yourself do you think finally emerges from the work?

MK: When I placed emphasis on the fact that the work wasn't a reiteration of child development but an attempt to give a place to the mother's fantasies, this was also relevant in terms of the modes or forms of representation which I chose for underlining that decision. For me it was very important not to use filmic or photographic means—that is, nothing which would suggest the notion of documentation as a "slice of life"—not because that's actually the function of film or photography but rather, strategically, it was important to avoid any implication of that sort. The decision was also crucial because I feel that when the image of the woman is used in a work of art—that is, when her body or person is given as signifier—it becomes extremely problematic. Most women artists who have presented themselves in some way, visibly, in their work have been unable to find the kind of distancing devices which would cut across the predominant representations of woman as object of the look, or that would question the notion of femininity as a pregiven entity. I'm not exactly an iconoclast, but perhaps historically, just at the moment, a method needs to be employed which foregrounds the construction of femininity as a representation of difference within a specific discourse.

In the *Post-Partum Document* I'm concerned to see how femininity, within the discourse of the mother-child relationship, is produced as natural and maternal. Of course, the practices that are implied in that process, such as feeding or dressing a child, are as dependent on a system of signs as are writing or speaking. In a sense, I see all social practices as expressions of a general social law (of a symbolic dimension, as Kristeva puts it), which is given in language. This means that the formal emphasis on written and spoken words in my work simply stresses the fact that the production of the subject is primarily a question of positionality in language.

But I'm also aware of another implication: what I've evacuated at the level of the look (or the representational image) has returned in the form of my diary narrative. A kind of capture of the viewer occurs within the first-person narrative of the diary texts. For me, it's also absolutely crucial that this kind of pleasure in the text, in the objects themselves, should engage the viewer, because there's no point at which anything can become a deconstructed critical engagement if the viewer is not first—immediately and affectively—drawn into the work. I also think that narrative can function differently in an artwork because it is unexpected and controversial in that space.

PS: Working in this manner, you're cutting across a certain type of women's art practice which, in the last ten or so years, has been concerned to alter woman's given image by exactly the opposite mode you've chosen. I wonder if there's not something important going on in such work, which treats the woman as the object of the look but where she is redefined in some way.

MK: I suppose I'd like to broaden the question into a consideration of how the construction of femininity is viewed within differing art practices by women artists. Since the early seventies you could probably point to at least four different categories of work.

First, we have what we think of as cultural feminism, an attempt to excavate a separate order of language and culture for women. This work usually inscribes itself as either an appropriation of earlier forms of traditional women's crafts or as a reinvention and exploration of those means in terms of a contemporary practice—say, for instance, the emphasis on pattern painting in New York. Perhaps the most important example of that tendency was the early work of Judy Chicago and the project *Womanhouse*, and more recently its triumphant finale, as it were, with *The Dinner Party*. Chicago suggests that this valorization of women from the past is taking place precisely because history has tended, as she puts it, "to devour women." There, interestingly, you have a kind of inversion of the totem-meal: what's forbidden on the one hand—the devouring of the mother—is permitted on this one ritual occasion where the historical mother figures are put in the position of the father, their name and status ingested, as in the totem-meal, by the female viewers of this visual feast.

Second, you have work which actually uses the body itself, such as Suzanne Santoro's well-known book, *Towards New Expression*. Here, exploration of the female genitals becomes a means of appropriating a specifically feminine relation to language, which is given in the body. Theoretically, I imagine, the most effective exposition of that position would be in the work of Luce Irigaray: she talks very poetically about the female sex as two lips kissing one another. For her, any kind of intervention in that primal autoeroticism is seen as a sort of violence against the woman.

Then there's a more varied third category which revolves around what could be loosely described as feminine experience. These women artists feel that there is, not necessarily a biologically determined femininity, but an essentially feminine experience of the body, or rules under which women are dominated by *representations* of the body. This is the case with most performance work. Hannah Wilke, for instance, refers to the eroticism of the woman's body. She presents herself very typically as the object of the look, and in doing so I suppose she is acting out the feminine position—the position of being the phallus for the other. But there is a contradiction. That image of totalization, the mirror image as it were, is always subject to fragmentation, disarray, or disavowal. So you have with Gina Pane, for example, the signs of self-mutilation that could be interpreted as the other side of the mirror image, or Adrian Piper, in her *Guerrilla Theatre*, where she makes herself as despicable as possible—a kind of inversion of what she sees as the stereotypical desired object.

What I think emerges as a kind of underlying contradiction is that, while the woman sees her experience in terms of the "feminine" position as the object of the look, she also has to deal with the fact that she's the subject of desire, or that she is, as artist, in the masculine position as subject of the look. The difficulty she finds in being in those two places at once seems to me to demonstrate through the actual practice something about the insistent bisexuality of the drives. You find this in the practice of most of the women artists right through these categories; you find there's some way in which a fundamental negation of the notion of an essential femininity nonetheless appears. Even in work which is overtly derived from the female body you can find a kind of superimposition of phallocentric and concentric imagery—Louise Bourgeois's sculpture is an interesting example. I could go on endlessly citing examples, but the point I'm trying to make in general is that the work itself, in spite of what women say about it, demonstrates that masculine and feminine positions are never fixed.

The question of sexuality which I feel is emerging (partly as a consequence of that other work) is posed neither in terms of a reduction to the body nor in terms of an essential feminine experience, but precisely in the realm of the social construction of masculine or feminine identities. This new tendency is by no means homogeneous. It turns, on the one hand, toward a kind of economic determinism in, say, the work of Martha Rosler, or perhaps, on the other hand, toward a theory of subjectivity—I might use my own work as an example, but I would say that the emphasis should be placed on the intersection of those two instances, the social and the psychic, as they meet in constructing the sexed subject.

PS: You're talking somewhat in psychoanalytical terms and you've also indirectly brought up the question of Marxism. Maybe this is the place to propose my sense of your work as characteristically European, insofar as one of the firm bases of North American feminism has been exactly a repudiation of Freud, a refusal to accept certain of his ideas and, in some cases, a foreclosure of the very idea of the unconscious. This hasn't been true in Europe, so do you see your work at all in that dialectical opposition to such a tendency in North America?

MK: Certainly one of the conspicuous differences in the European women's movement is that socialist feminism has remained alive and well. In America the development of the movement seems to have been circumscribed by radical feminism on the one hand and traditional Marxism on the other; only very recently has there been any real attempt to mediate these positions in terms of art practices. Lucy Lippard's organization of the exhibition *Issue* at the ICA in London last year was the first real initiative of that kind. But one could still sense there in most of the work by American artists that any emphasis on the "personal" appeared to detract from what they would consider "wider social issues."

Now, in the way that much European feminist work has developed, I don't think that's been the case—the social and the psychic haven't been seen as necessarily antagonistic or contradictory. But one would have to add that within the socialist feminist groupings, say in Britain, it's only a smaller tendency that's been involved in work on psychoanalysis. Certainly the debates around psychoanalysis and Marxism in the movement have been very productive, although the intended marriage of the two never took place. The outcome has been more on the order of discovering that one can only use certain methods of analysis in relation to their specific objects: there's no single theoretical discourse which is going to offer us an explanation for all forms of social relations or for every mode of political practice.

The *Post-Partum Document* found its inspiration, if you can call it that, within the socialist feminist tendency of the women's movement in Britain. I identify very much with those who have been doing work in the field of psychoanalysis—initially the History Group, then the Lacan reading group, and more recently the journal *m/f.* In 1976 there was an important conference on the topic of patriarchy where the issues of psychoanalysis were raised within a wider context. There were workshops discussing Lacan's rereading of Freud. It was very controversial but nevertheless it was debated within the movement; that hasn't been the case in North America. My work grows directly out of those debates and is almost concurrent with their every stage. I started out with an emphasis on the psychology, the feminine psychology of the mother being sealed in the division of labor and child care—a position which one could say is reflected in Mitchell's book *Woman's Estate*, which I then modified and reworked so that by the last section of the *Post-Partum Document* in 1979 I wasn't talking so much about patriarchy in terms of the division of labor, but rather with reference to the construction of sexual difference.

PS: Implied there, and in those debates, is the necessity of inserting into political considerations a theory of the speaking subject: your work does seem to me to highlight one of the problems that much of this kind of work has had to face, namely, that it can be accused of a certain patriarchal bias because of its reliance on Lacan and his definition of woman in relation to the phallus. Also, there is in your work a sort of recourse to rational structures (diagrams, graphs, theoretical discourse, and so on) which I'd characterize here as patriarchal, as male. Do you accept, on the one hand, that there is this recourse to rationality as an authority in your work, and, on the other hand, do you accept this view of Lacan as being irredeemably patriarchal?

MK: Taking up your question in relation to the art practice itself, one would have to see the theoretical work primarily as "writing" or as a mode of representation rather than as any form of final explication. When I employ something like the Lacanian diagrams, they, too, are cathected as images of the difficulty of the Symbolic, or perhaps as emblems of a kind of love-hate relationship with the father—which is not exactly a recourse to rationality as authority. At one level you could say the work itself, particularly the reworking of that experience of maternity in the footnotes, expresses a fundamental desire to know and to master. Now, in regard to the actual theoretical examples cited—say the articles by Lacan which I used to analyze the various moments of separation—another level of questioning is raised about whether I should be using any kind of "male discourse" as some feminists might say—why Freud, why Lacan? I must admit that I did really want to find alternatives in the beginning. I read Maud Mannoni, Françoise Dalto, Melanie Klein; but Lacan's work, particularly his notion of the two end points of the mirror phase, was crucial for my first three works, "Weaning from the Breast," "Weaning from the Holophrase," and "Weaning from the Dyad"; that material required a rather more complicated analysis of separation and entry into the order of language than could be afforded by either Klein (who pushes the Oedipal moment so far back that we can't get a clear picture of those early distinctions) or Dalto (who places it too schematically at two-and-a-half years old). But in sections IV and V ("On Femininity" and "On the Order of Things"), which are centrally concerned with the representation of loss, not only as loss of the child but also as loss of the maternal body, I rely very heavily on Montrelay's reading of Lacan, her definition of the "feminine" unconscious as the imposition of *concentricity*, an archaic oral-anal schema, upon the phallocentric organization of the drives. Then in the final section, "On the Insistence of the Letter," a definite theoretical shift takes place, initiated by the analysis of the child's prewriting, which raises questions concerning the phonocentric and perhaps logocentric bias of Lacan's position. (By that I mean his dependence on Jakobson's linguistics.)

PS: For me, though, one of the most interesting parts of the whole work is its double inscription of fetishism; on the one hand, the mother fetishizing the child as phallus, and on the other, the sense that the work itself, once installed, becomes a further fetish, replacing the dangers of the fetishization of the child. Underneath that, however, is a discomfort arising from the idea that fetishism is always a surrender to the law of the father, to patriarchal order—and Freud, of course, ascribes fetishism specifically to the masculine domain. So what is fetishism for a woman, and how does it work?

MK: In fantasy, castration anxiety for the man is often represented as the loss of the penis, the arms, the legs, or some other bodily substitute. When we talk about this imaginary scenario for the woman, we say that her castration fears take the form of losing her loved objects, especially her children. They are going to grow up and leave her, reject her, perhaps die. To delay, disavow, the separation she has already in a sense acknowledged, she tends to fetishize the child in some way: for example, by dressing him up, by continuing to feed him no matter how old he gets, or simply by having another one. Perhaps then, in relation to pornography, we could talk about the mother's memorabilia: the way she saves things, like the first shoes, photographs, locks of hair, and so on. My work takes off from that point. In place of the first shoes, we have the stained liners or the first words set out in actual typeface. When I used something like the plaster imprints of the child's hands, the fragments of his comforter, or the objects like insects or plants that were his gifts, they are intended to be read as transitional objects, but not in Winnicott's sense of surrogates, rather in Lacan's terms as, say, emblems of desire.

So I've displaced the fetishization of the child at one level onto the artwork. But I've made it explicit in the work so that I think this also functions at another level which questions the fetishistic nature of representation itself. All the objects are framed and fixed in a way which defines them as precious objects, things to be seen or sold. Yet they're commonplace or ordinary. What's more, because they're found objects, they're not properly invested with creative subjectivity, in other words, with the kind of authenticating mark, or authorship, which is so essential to the art market.

But the question of fetishism gets us into some difficulties about the work. One of the clinical definitions of fetishism is that it doesn't concern any specific object: it's simply a question of how the original cathexis is displaced from one idea or object or part of the body to something often totally unrelated. As Freud points out, art is a kind of nonneurotic variation on the theme of fetishism, so there's a sense in which we're not actually talking about the same thing in *Post-Partum Document*, because it's something which is sublimated in a socially acceptable form and therefore generalizable as a discourse and as a practice. But the work is also a case history—it is *my* experience of those events. It has sometimes been frightening, but I don't think the implications of this are really accessible to me for analysis.

PS: I'd like to ask you about writing and language in the work. Because you're overlaying different types of discourse, mapping out various linguistic terrains, and adding one voice to others, there seems to me to be implicitly some kind of hierarchy of discourse established at certain points. This perhaps comes out of my sense that the discourse of psychoanalysis is being privileged, but also on a more local level (as in "Documentation III" where you have your voice, your inner speech, and the child's original discourse all inscribed over the child's scribblings), there does seem to be some sense of a hierarchy pointing to some position of power and suggesting that someone somewhere could be using the "right" language: this brings up the question for the whole work as to what kind of language you're aspiring toward.

MK: Hopefully, the work is a continual displacement rather than a hierarchization of certain forms of language. The way it works through different levels of language is certainly seen to be unraveling the sense in which representation is always a representation of loss. The piece that illustrates this most clearly is "Documentation IV," where the imprints

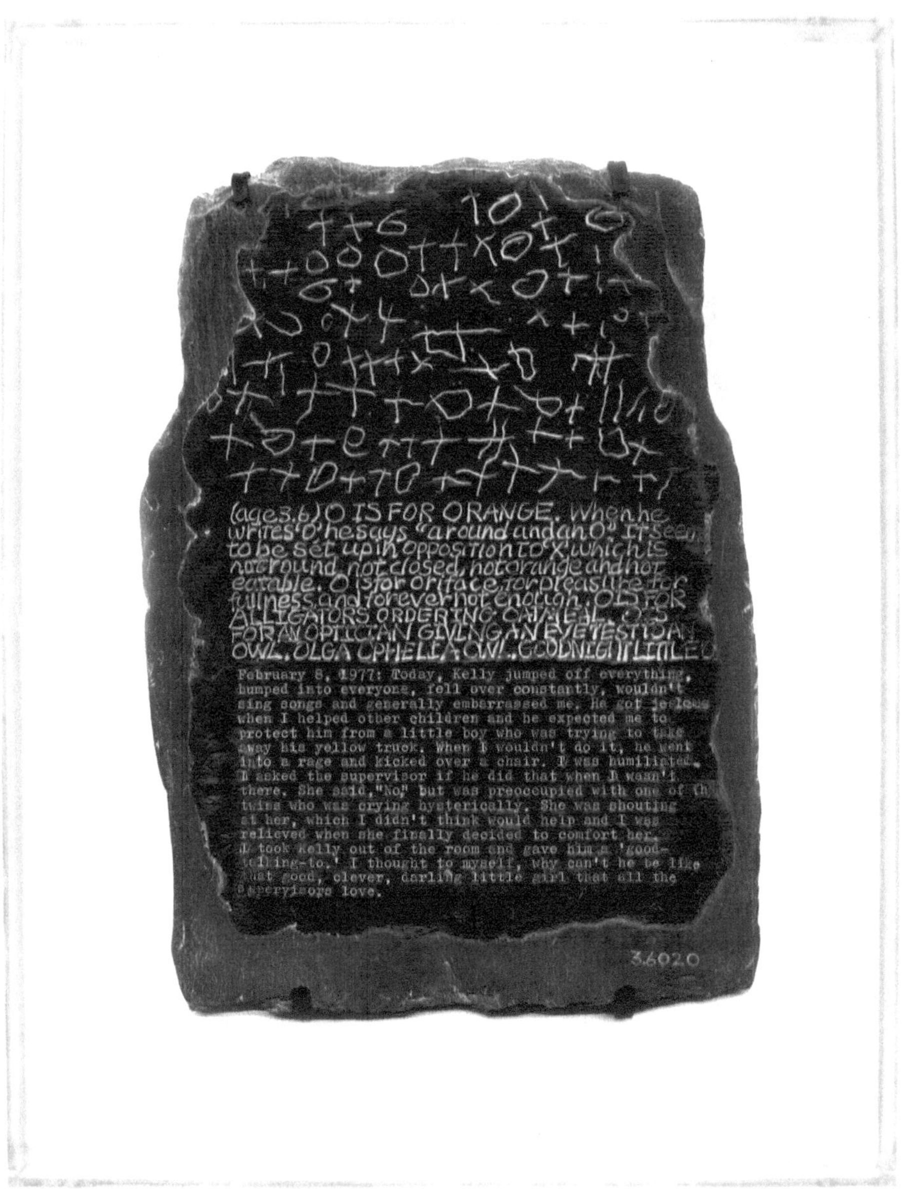

Mary Kelly, detail of *Post-Partum Document: Documentation VI, Pre-writing Alphabet, Exergue and Diary [O Is for Orange]*, 1978. Perspex unit, white card, resin, slate; 14 × 11 in. Collection of Arts Council, UK. Courtesy the artist and Pippy Houldsworth Gallery, London.

of the child's hands disappear and a diagrammatic representation of the relationship appears. Throughout the work, while I'm speaking about it and trying to understand it, I'm also in the process of recognizing that something has already been lost. So in that particular part, where I talk about the pleasure of the child's body and the problem of the incest taboo for the mother, I'm also trying to see what's at stake beyond the representation of the child's body itself. What emerges, I think, is (as usual) the mother's body. By saying that the representation of femininity is constructed as maternal, I mean that in this relationship the woman experiences that closeness to the mother's body which she imagined in those first identifications with her own mother. In that sense, too, when I use the writing on the slates in "Documentation VI," I'm referring to the child's marks as a kind of anagram of the maternal body. The whole project, not only the visible artwork but the process itself, is about the relation of writing to the mother's body. But this has been said often enough. What I've emphasized in that relation is a moment of transgression where separation threatens the woman's representation of herself as essentially and naturally maternal and creates a kind of chasm which resounds with questions. The woman questions the socially given meanings for the feminine. So I guess the kind of language I'm aspiring to is one which will prolong that rupture.

PS: In some way, you've just answered the question I'm about to ask. If that transgressional moment of loss does open up a new space, it might nonetheless still be read with a certain pessimism regarding women's condition since, even though it gives the impulse to change and to make different things happen, it can surely be a moment that's repeatable only at certain junctures in your life (and for most women not very often at that). Doesn't it suggest finally that the symbolic realm imposed and reimposed upon us is constricting and unchangeable?

MK: On the contrary, I see it as very optimistic because it shows exactly that the symbolic realm is not really fixed and homogeneous, but that it's riddled with contradictions. Precisely because what we call "ideology" is a complex arrangement of social practices and systems of representations which are always inscribing their difference from one another, we can find a space for change. It's the totalizing view of culture that leads to pessimism. When you say either that we're absolutely constrained by patriarchy or that it's only a matter of false consciousness to be shaken off, that, for me, is when you come up with a much more constricting view. I think that what's discovered in working through the *Post-Partum Document* is that there is no preexisting sexuality, no essential femininity, and that to look at the processes of their construction is also to see the possibility of deconstructing the dominant forms of representing difference and justifying subordination in our social order.

House Work and Art Work

Helen Molesworth

> Laughter in the face of serious categories is indispensable for feminism.
>
> —Judith Butler, *Gender Trouble* (1990)

The much-noted eclecticism of 1990s art practice appears to have been countered only by a steady fascination with and revival of art from the 1970s. This interest, shared by artists, critics, historians, and curators, generated numerous exhibitions and publications dedicated to the feminist work of the period.[1] That such interest in 1970s feminist practice is long overdue perhaps goes without saying, although for many it has emerged as either a mysteriously forgotten moment or the return of the repressed. In both guises many of these stagings have continued, unfortunately, to consolidate a logic of "us" and "them," a structure of bitter binary opposition, an intellectual disjuncture between feminist work based in "theory," poststructuralism, or social constructionism, and work derived from the so-called principles of "essentialism."[2] Far from an attempt to set the record straight, or to ascertain definitively what did or did not happen, this essay is motivated by a need to rearticulate the current reception's account of the relations between these two bodies of work. More precisely, it seeks to reconsider four artists at work in the 1970s—Judy Chicago, Mary Kelly, Mierle Laderman Ukeles, and Martha Rosler—artists whose works have been caught in an interpretive blind spot created by the current reception's perpetuation of the antagonism between feminist art of the 1970s and '80s.[3]

Despite the breadth and complexity of the issues—the diversity of practices within each, somewhat loosely defined, "camp"—a certain reduction has taken place in the current reception of 1970s feminist work, an intellectual fault line broadly described in generational terms. And as the disjuncture between feminist practices from the 1970s and '80s is repeatedly historicized as a permanent rupture, we currently receive these strained relations in the form of a caricature. This situation is perhaps most problematic and prevalent in the classroom, where the debate is often hypostatized into an art-historical compare-and-contrast, iconically represented by two seemingly antithetical art works: Judy Chicago's *The Dinner Party* and Mary Kelly's *Post-Partum Document*, works taken to be exemplary of an essentialist approach in Chicago's case, and a theory-based feminist practice in Kelly's case. Although both works were completed in 1979, they have been rendered crudely oppositional and hierarchized, and are often asked to bear the weight of a generational split—from the 1970s to the '80s—as well as presenting, equally self-evidently, the "progression" in feminist art *from* essentialism *to* theory.[4] The language of progress is used across the board; listen as Lisa Tickner argues that the "adolescent vitality of 1970s feminism matured successfully into a body of rigorous 1980s art and criticism."[5] Similarly, Griselda Pollock demarcates a shift from a politics of "liberation" to a "structural mode of analysis."[6] And Faith Wilding, a member of *Womanhouse*, described some 1970s artistic experiments, particularly cunt imagery, as "crude … precursors for a new vocabulary for representing female sexuality and the body in art."[7]

The logic of progress has done much to codify this classic pairing of post-1960s art into a stale binarism: all contrast, no comparison. Yet perhaps we can loosen the starched opposition of essentialism "versus" theory, by acknowledging that the model of compare-and-contrast need not *only* produce dismissive hierarchies, or generational or oppositional binarisms. It is a model equally well designed to elaborate on moments of affinity and shared concerns (not yet acknowledged), *as well as* moments of contestation and difference (which have been insisted on more forcefully).

Despite various challenges to this generational/progressive frame, it has stiffly endured. The tenacity of the division occludes a more pedestrian question: Why is this particular art-historical debate so problematic? For instance, why don't we simply say, "Both sides have strong and weak points," and pluralistically be done with it? As unproductive as this debate has been, merely to paper over significant aesthetic, ideological, and philosophical differences would be to run the risk of consolidating the category heading "feminist art." As a codified "movement" (however internally fractured), feminist art is stripped of its transformative power.[8] Rendered separate and distinct, and hence easier to marginalize, it is unable to challenge and modify our definitions of other artistic categories, the result of which has been to prohibit articulations of the connective tissue between these works and the putatively "dominant" conversations simultaneously being held in the art world.[9] One way, perhaps, to reread the theory/essentialism split is to see artists during the 1980s—in the Pictures group, for instance—as consciously working with ideas such as the theory of representation precisely as a way to avoid the problems of the marginalization of "feminism."[10] So, too, we could see that it was clearly important for feminists to be able to disagree, and even fight with, previous generations of feminists, as a way both to open the field of inquiry and to proliferate its influence. Currently, however, the continual rehearsing of the theory/essentialism debate, only to choose sides at the end, has disallowed other interpretive formations to arise. For instance, the division may serve to maintain, rather than expand, the rather limited range of feminist theory that operates in the art world. There currently exist critical feminist discourses other than Anglo-American empiricism and continental theory; and the chasm between them has been navigated, most notably, by political philosophers. In other words, we need not only be bound to the interpretive models that have traditionally accompanied each body of work, but we can also look to the tools and interpretive possibilities offered by the feminist critique of political philosophy.

In *Feminism and Philosophy*, Moira Gatens has staged the feminist debate in terms of those who privilege a model of equality and those who think in terms of difference.[11] These terms are analogous to the essentialism/theory split, and Gatens astutely problematizes both positions. First, she sets out to dismantle the idea of equality. She argues that the problem with the model of "equality in the public sphere" is that

> the public sphere is dependent upon and developed around a male subject who acts in the public sphere but is maintained in the

> private sphere, traditionally by women. This is to say that liberal society assumes that its citizens continue to be what they were historically, namely male heads of households who have at their disposal the services of an unpaid domestic worker/mother/wife.[12]

These services have become so naturalized that "clearly, part of the privilege accorded to members of a political body is that their needs, desires, and powers are converted into rights and virtues."[13] In other words, Gatens suggests that the political realm within which women struggle for equality, such as democracy, must be disarticulated, not presumed a priori to be a "neutral" system, except for *its inability to grant women equality.* The system is founded on inequality; hence "equality in this context can involve only the abstract opportunity to become men."[14] Democracy's dependence on inequality has been naturalized as the public and private spheres have been used to shore up distinctions and inequities between men and women, particularly in that the private sphere has been "intricate[ly] and extensive[ly] cross-reference[d] … with the body, passions, and nature."[15] This critique of equality (as found in much Anglo-American feminist theory) reveals the very notion of equality and its symbolic representation in the public sphere to be historically dependent on the unacknowledged (and unequal) labor of the private sphere.[16]

Gatens is also suspicious of the discursive move from equality to difference. Noting that feminist writing and art practice, after freeing itself from the tyranny of nature, took up explorations of female sexuality, she cautions that such a move runs the risk of reducing women's subjectivity to their sexuality. While Gatens is sympathetic to critical feminist explorations of psychoanalytic models of subjectivity fundamentally rooted in sexuality, she counters the ahistorical logic of psychoanalysis by submitting it to a Foucauldian analysis that conceives of the body as "an effect of socially and historically specific practices."[17] She argues that "bodies are turned into individuals of various kinds" by "discourses and practices [which] create ideologically appropriate subjects" and "practices [which] construct certain kinds of bodies with particular kinds of power and capacity."[18] Furthermore, "to insist on sexual difference as *the* fundamental and eternally immutable difference would be to take for granted the intricate and pervasive ways in which

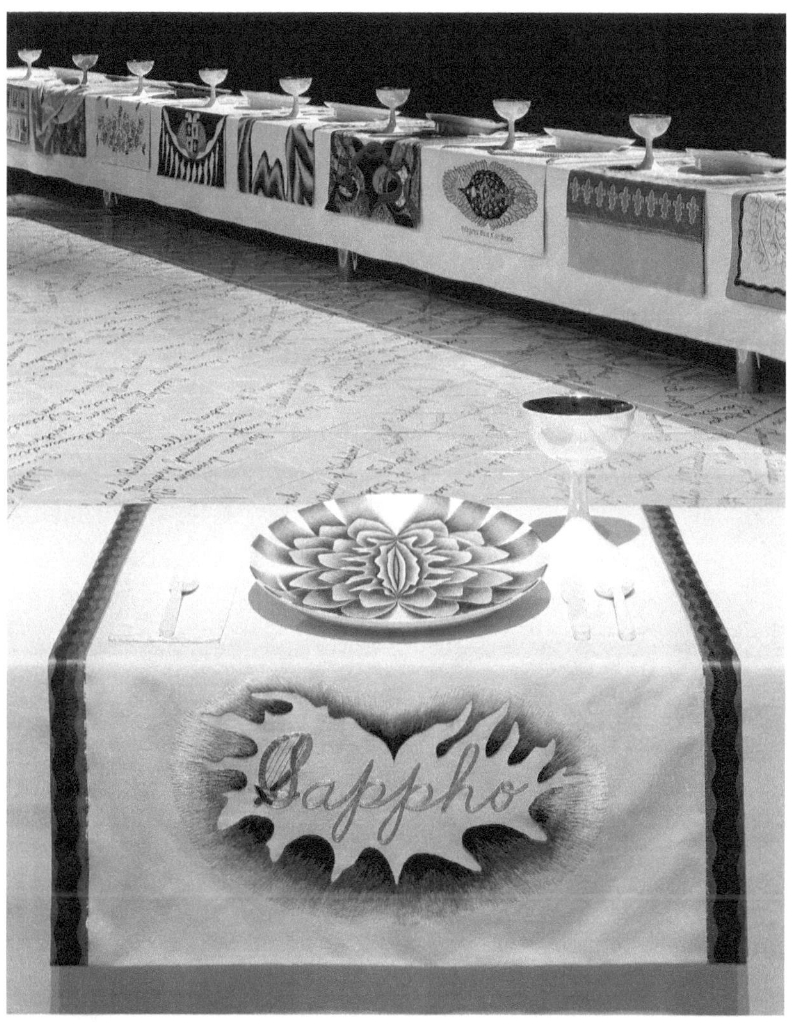

Judy Chicago, Sappho place setting from *The Dinner Party*, 1974–1979. Ceramic, porcelain, textile. Collection of the Brooklyn Museum, Gift of the Elizabeth A. Sackler Foundation, 2002.10. Photo by Donald Woodman. © 2016 Judy Chicago/Artists Rights Society (ARS), New York.

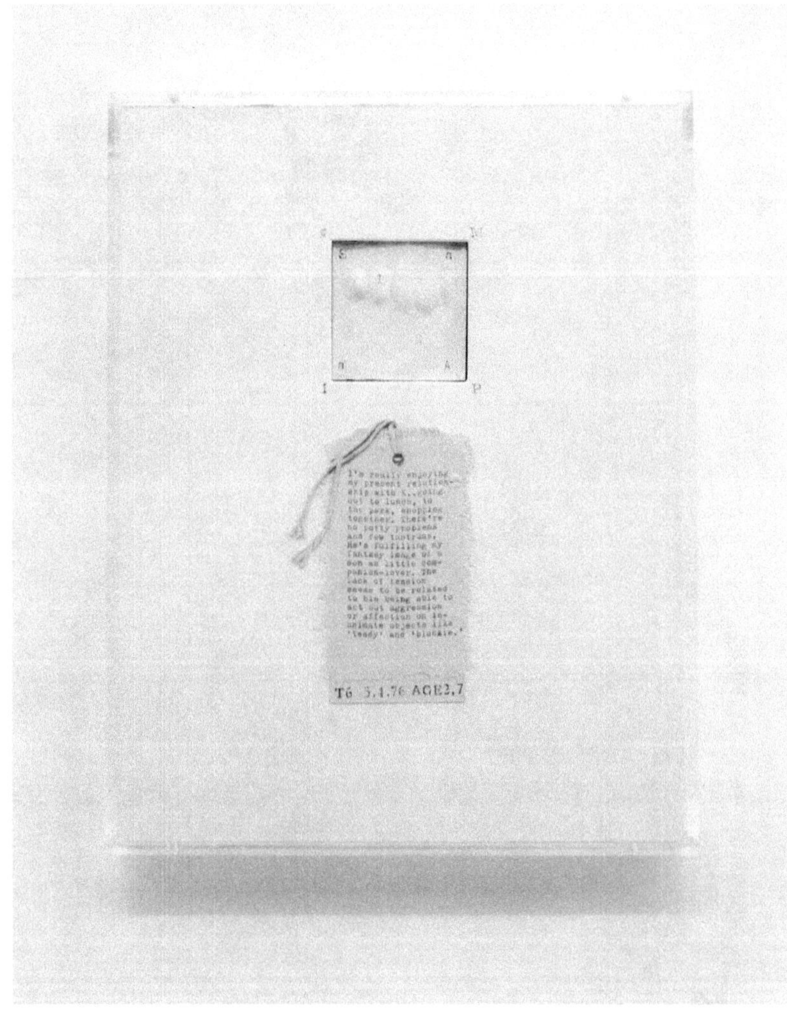

Mary Kelly, detail of *Post-Partum Document: Documentation IV, Transitional Objects, Diary, and Diagram*, 1976. Perspex, white card, plaster, cotton, ink, string, wood; 14 × 11 in. Collection of Zurich Museum. Courtesy the artist and Pippy Houldsworth Gallery, London.

patriarchal culture has made that difference its insignia."[19] She is wary, then, of feminists who place sexuality (as the extension of or outcome of sexual difference) at center stage, theoretically or aesthetically. One effect of Gatens's critique is to register the extent to which *both* groups of feminist work explored issues of sexuality to the exclusion of other attributes of subjectivity and also to the exclusion of political philosophy's critique of the role of the private sphere in the democracy-capitalism covenant.

As Gatens problematizes the equality/difference dichotomy through a feminist analysis of political philosophy, so, too, a similar operation can be performed on the iconic pairing of the *Post-Partum Document* and *The Dinner Party*, by considering them in conjunction with Mierle Laderman Ukeles's *Maintenance Art Performances* (1973–74) and Martha Rosler's videos *Semiotics of the Kitchen* (1975) and *Domination and the Everyday* (1978)—works produced around the same time and under similar cultural pressures. Ukeles's and Rosler's works are explicitly concerned with how "ideologically appropriate subjects" are created, in part, through the naturalizing of unpaid and underpaid domestic labor. By placing the *PPD* and *The Dinner Party* within this expanded interpretive field, labor, particularly domestic or maintenance labor, emerges as a thematic shared by these four artists (as well as many others of the period). The introduction of the problem of such labor leads, in turn, to a consideration of the relations between public and private, which emerges as a defining issue in the discussion of 1970s art and the legacy of feminism's intervention in it. The problematic of public and private spheres is, of course, present in both *The Dinner Party* and *Post-Partum Document*, but the essentialism/theory debate has occluded its importance, disallowing the debate to be framed in terms of a *political* economy as well as a bodily or psychic one.[20]

In her 1969 "Maintenance Art Manifesto" Ukeles divided human labor into two categories: development and maintenance. She writes:

> Development: pure individual creation; the new; change; progress; advance; excitement; flight or fleeing. Maintenance: Keep the dust off the pure individual creation; preserve the new; sustain the change; protect progress; defend and prolong the advance; renew the excitement; repeat the flight.[21]

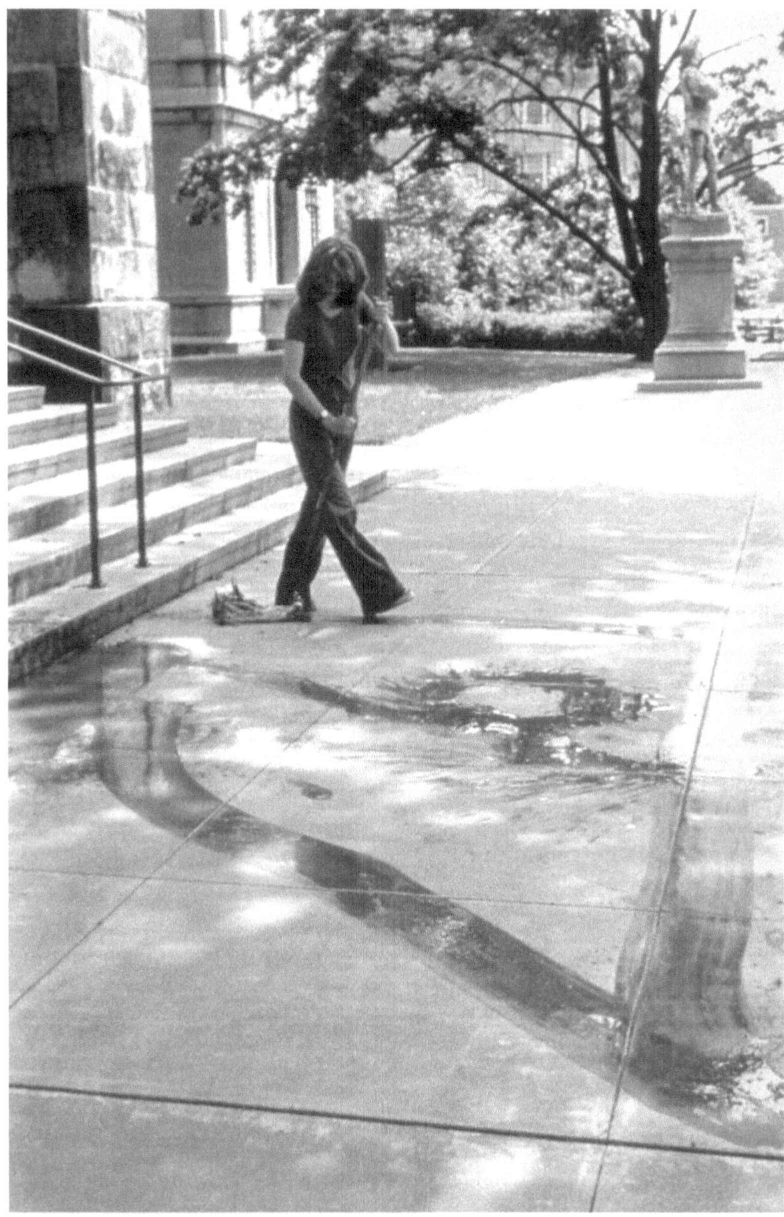

Mierle Laderman Ukeles, *Hartford Wash: Washing, Tracks, Maintenance: Outside,* 1973, part of *Maintenance Art* performance series, 1973–1974. Performance at Wadsworth Atheneum, Hartford, Connecticut. Courtesy Ronald Feldman Fine Arts, New York.

Ukeles's manifesto insists that ideals of modernity (progress, change, individual creation) are dependent on the denigrated and boring labor of maintenance (activities that make things possible—cooking, cleaning, shopping, child rearing, and so forth). Incisively, Ukeles does not refer to maintenance as domestic labor, or housework, for it is evident that such labor is not confined solely to the spaces of domesticity. Included in this manifesto was a proposal that Ukeles live in the museum and perform her maintenance activities; while the gallery might look "empty," she explained that her labor would indeed be the "work."[22] Her offer went unaccepted.

In 1973, however, the Wadsworth Atheneum agreed to the *Maintenance Art Performances*. In *Hartford Wash: Washing Tracks, Maintenance Inside*, Ukeles scrubbed and mopped the floor of the museum for four hours. In *Hartford Wash: Washing Tracks, Maintenance Outside,* she cleaned the exterior plaza and steps of the museum. She referred to these activities as "floor paintings." In *Transfer: The Maintenance of the Art Object,* she designated her cleaning of a protective display case as an artwork—a "dust painting." Normally this vitrine was cleaned by the janitor; however, once Ukeles's cleaning of the case was designated as "art," the responsibility of the cleaning and maintenance of this case became the job of the conservator. The fourth performance, *The Keeping of the Keys,* consisted of Ukeles taking the museum guards' keys and locking and unlocking galleries and offices, which when locked were subsequently deemed to be works of "maintenance art." In each performance Ukeles's role as "artist" allowed her to reconfigure the value bestowed upon these otherwise unobtrusive maintenance operations, and to explore the ramifications of making maintenance labor visible in public.

Martha Rosler's videos *Semiotics of the Kitchen* and *Domination and the Everyday* also critically engaged the problem of housewifery. In the relatively new medium of video, *Semiotics of the Kitchen* humorously skewered both the mass-media image of the smiling, middle-class, white housewife and theories of semiotics, suggesting that neither was able to provide an adequate account of the role of wife/mother/maintenance provider. Informed by Marxist and feminist critique, *Domination and the Everyday* considers the everyday household labors of women in tandem with global politics. Like the *Maintenance Art Performances*, *Domination* suggests that the domestic chores of cooking and child rearing are not exclusively private, but, instead, that such labors are intimately

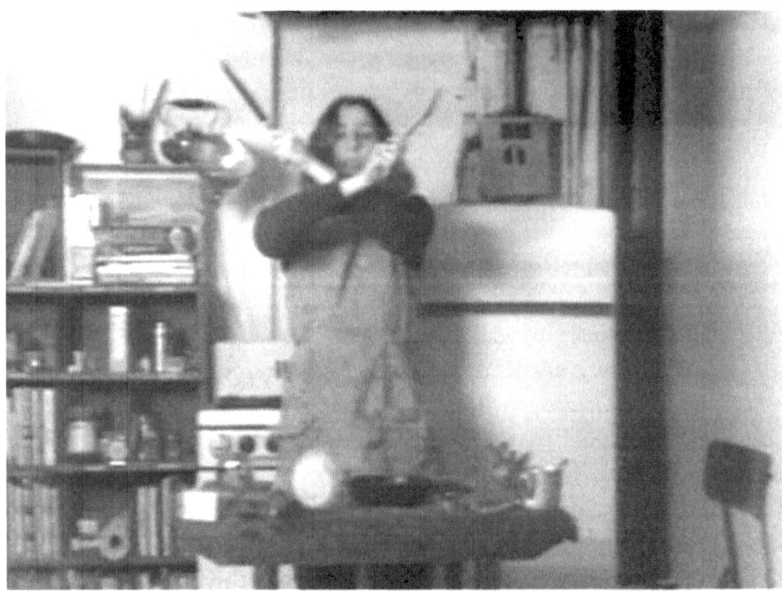

Martha Rosler, still from *Semiotics of the Kitchen*, 1973–1974. Courtesy the artist and Mitchell-Innes & Nash, New York.

connected to public events, and furthermore that unpaid and underpaid maintenance labor needs to be thought of as equivalent to other forms of oppression.

What happens if the *Maintenance Art Performances* and Rosler's early video work are insinuated into *The Dinner Party* and *Post-Partum Document* binarism, creating a four-way compare-and-contrast? Might such an expanded field allow us to see previously unacknowledged aspects of each of the works? For instance, as well as seeing the stark contrast between Chicago's cunt-based central core imagery and Kelly's pointed refusal to represent the female body, we might also see that all four artists deal in varying degrees with putatively "private" aspects of women's lives and experience: motherhood, cleaning, cooking, and entertaining. Similarly, as opposed to the intractable contrast between the lush tactile quality of *The Dinner Party* and the diagrammatic aspect of the *Post-Partum Document*, we might see the importance of text in each of the works. The women's names that cover the floor and place settings mean that reading is also integral to viewing *The Dinner Party*. Rosler's *Domination and the Everyday* contains a running text at the bottom of the screen, and Ukeles's works contain charts, posted announcements, and the "Maintenance Art" verification stamp. Each artist participated in the assault on the privileged role of vision in aesthetics, as did so many of their 1970s contemporaries. When the binarism is undone we can see that these works were directly engaged with the most "advanced" artistic practices of the day—Minimalism, Performance, and Conceptual art—and that they were also in the process of forming the practice of Institutional Critique.[23] This is, again, to insist on the linkages between art informed by feminism and most of the advanced or critical artistic practices of the 1960s and '70s that took as part of their inquiry the institutions within which art is encountered. The artists who worked in this manner—whose work's content was bound up with domesticity or maintenance and its structural relation to the public sphere—have been by and large neglected by the historians and archivists of Minimalism, Conceptual art, and Institutional Critique.[24] Their omission was caused not by active suppression but rather a fundamental *misrecognition* of the terms and strategies they employed. The overtly domestic/maintenance content of such works was read as being equivalent to their meaning. Therefore, little or no attention was paid to these works' engagement with the Duchampian legacy of art's investigation of its own meaning, value, and institutionality. What has not been fully appreciated are the ways in which this usually "degraded" content actually permits an engagement with questions of value and institutionality that critique the conditions of everyday life as well as art. Hence, when we compare *The Dinner Party*, *Semiotics of the Kitchen* and *Domination and the Everyday*, and the *Post-Partum Document* with Ukeles's explicit feminist address of the museum, we are able to reframe them in such a manner as to see that they were each bound up with a critique of the institutional conditions of art. Among the four artists this critique manifested itself in varying degrees and was shaped by different concerns. There is no denying that Chicago's work may seem to us now the most problematic of the four, in that her work supports a notion of genius and "artist" in keeping with the ideal model of bourgeois subjectivity offered by the Western art museum. Yet, despite the differences between the works (or because of them), the feminist critique of the institutions of art should no longer be misrecognized, for its understanding of the relations between "private" acts and public institutions will reframe the work of contemporaneous figures in the field. Such a comparison will ultimately expand our notion of Institutional Critique, precisely because the feminist critique differs so markedly from the paradigmatic works of figures such as Marcel Broodthaers, Daniel Buren, or Hans Haacke. For as we will see, it insisted on the reciprocity and mutual dependence of the categories of private and public.

***

Ukeles's performances, by establishing domestic (read private, natural) labor as "maintenance," help to articulate the structural conditions of the relations between the public and private sphere. It is the "hidden" and unrecognized nature of this labor that permits the myth that the public sphere functions as a self-contained and independent site, a site devoid of interest (in classic Habermasian terms). However, by staging such labors in the museum, a traditional institution of the bourgeois public sphere, Ukeles's work establishes maintenance labor as a subject for public discussion. For, as Rosalyn Deutsche has argued, "what is recognized in public space is the legitimacy of debate about what is legitimate and what is illegitimate."[25] It is the very publicness of art, art's traditional reliance on a public sphere for its legibility and value, that makes art such a rich terrain for feminist critique. Hence Ukeles's performance of maintenance activities, in full view of the museum and its visitors, opens public space to the pressures of what it traditionally excludes, or renders invisible. The work of Chicago, Kelly, and Rosler does this too, each at the level of explicit content (although Kelly and Rosler do considerably more work at the level of form, as well). But when Ukeles renames domestic labor "maintenance," she uses ideas and processes usually deemed "private" to open institutions and ideas usually deemed "public." This gesture is in obvious sympathy with the 1970s feminist slogan "the personal is political," but, more incisively, it supports political philosopher Carole Pateman's contention that "the public sphere is always assumed to throw light onto the private sphere, rather than vice versa. On the contrary, an understanding of modern patriarchy requires that the employment contract is illuminated by the structure of domestic relations."[26] In other words, one legacy of feminist criticism is to establish that it is the private sphere that can help us to rearticulate the public sphere, as opposed to the other way around. Ukeles's exposure of this problematic animates the content of labor in both *The Dinner Party* and the *Post-Partum Document,* pulling these works away from their more familiar interpretations.

To position this work as negotiating the terrain of public and private is to establish its links to, as opposed to its separation from, other postwar art practices.Chicago's early sculptural activity—in works such as *Pasadena Lifesavers* (1969–70)—took the form of repetitive modular units fabricated from industrial materials, objects clearly in dialogue with Minimalism and its West Coast variant, "finish fetish."[27] Chicago's repetitive formal structure, her use of the triangular shaped table, her fetishism of surface and texture suggest that *The Dinner Party* continued her dialogue with Minimalism. However, by the mid-1970s, Chicago had imported explicit content into these otherwise generic structures. Specifically sexed bodies are offered as opposed to the nonspecific or universal body posited by Minimalism's understanding of phenomenology, and the "private" nature of genitalia, especially the vagina, is rendered spectacularly public. Likewise, historically under-recognized forms of domestic and decorative craft replace the lure (and perhaps just barely veiled decorative aspects) of industrial production. Minimalism also asked for a consideration of the logic of repetition; consider Donald Judd's oft-quoted "one thing after another." Reading *The Dinner Party* through a hermeneutics of maintenance suggests that the logic of repetition is not exclusively bound to industrial production but exists as well—although with vastly different effects—in the perpetual labors of cooking, eating, and cleaning up: the women's work that is never done; work that is conspicuously absent in *The Dinner Party,* effaced as it was by its Minimalist counterparts.[28] And if Minimalism asked its viewers to distinguish what in the room was not sculpture, what in the room constituted institutional space, then *The Dinner Party* potentially asked viewers to articulate what in the room existed in the realm of the private and what belonged in the realm of the public.[29]

By tweaking and pinching Minimalism's suppression of the particularity of gendered bodies, *The Dinner Party* suggested that the (impossible) idea of a generic body helped to enable the historical bourgeois public sphere as a site of (fictional) disinterest, a site bound by the terms of patriarchy. Kelly's *Post-Partum Document* similarly critiqued the terms of Conceptual art. Kelly's early work, done in Britain during the 1970s, was collaborative in nature and focused largely on the struggle for women's equality in the workplace. Two works stand out: the co-curated exhibition *Women and Work* (1975) and the collaboratively made film *Nightcleaners* (1975), which documented the organizing of a women's cleaning union but refused the traditional methods of agitprop or documentary, opting for Brechtian strategies of distanciation.[30] *Women and Work* depicted two years of research into the sexual division of labor in a metal-box factory. By conceiving of the exhibition as the artwork itself, *Women and Work* questioned both the autonomy of the art object and the fiction of the disinterested gallery space. The show's refusal of visuality, its negation of the art object as a commodity, and its challenge to the traditional role of the gallery within the distribution system all partook of Conceptual art's assault on art.

It would be *Post-Partum Document*, however, that would launch a more thorough critique of Conceptual art. Following on Minimalism's investigation of the public quality of art, much Conceptual art sought to replace a spatial and visual experience with a linguistic one, or what has been called "the work as analytic proposition."[31] This meant that the art object could be radically de-skilled, potentially democratizing art's production. However, Frazer Ward has argued that while Conceptual art "sought to demystify aesthetic experience and mastery ('Anybody can do that'), [it] maintained the abstraction of content crucial to high Modernist art," hence, "if Modernist painting was just about painting, Conceptual art was just about art."[32] Just as Chicago exposed Minimalism's abstract viewer, similarly the explicit content of the *Post-Partum Document* complicated Conceptual art's hermeticism.[33]

The *Document*'s numerous graphs and charts, in their standardized frames (a repetition that rhymes with Chicago's), represent the labor of childcare, labor normally obscured in Western capitalist culture. One effect of the category of the mother as essential and biological is to naturalize this labor, placing it outside of social conditions. (It is telling that the *PPD* emerges around the time of the idea of the "working mother," as if mothering weren't already a form of work.) Kelly's refusal to image the mother impedes the naturalization of the labor of motherhood (in Gatens's words, "cross-referenced with the private"). By submitting this labor to the public and social languages of work and science, the *Document* countermands Conceptual art's maintenance of abstract relations between public and private realms, revealing its continuation of a modernist paradigm of art for art's sake. (Indeed, if one of the primary responses to modernist painting is "My kid could do that" or "What is that crap on the walls?" then Kelly's inclusion of her son's soiled diapers could be seen as a joke at the expense of both Conceptual art

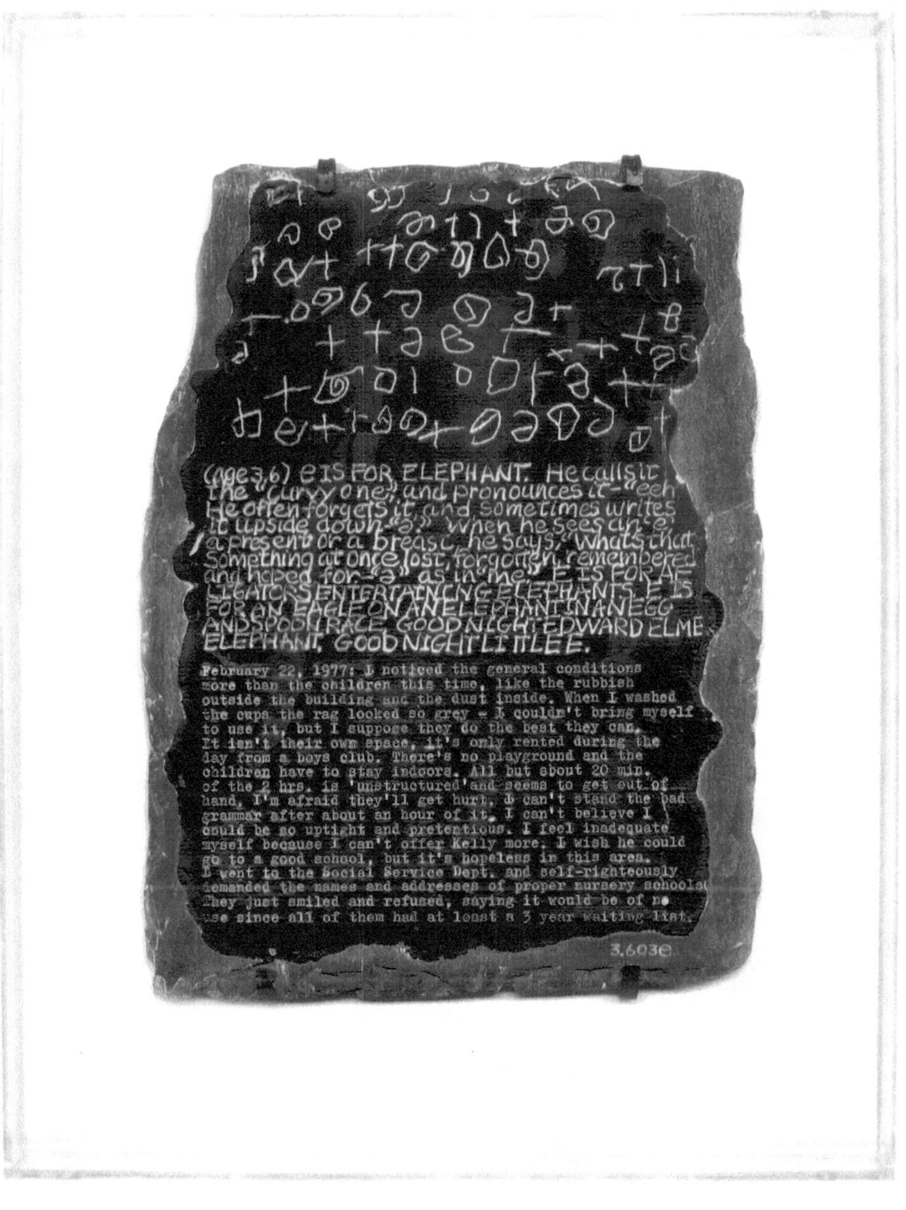

Mary Kelly, detail of *Post-Partum Document: Documentation VI, Pre-writing Alphabet, Exergue, and Diary [E is for elephant]*, 1978. Perspex unit, white card, resin, slate; 14 × 11 in. Collection of Arts Council, UK. Courtesy the artist and Pippy Houldsworth Gallery, London.

and modernist painting.) Kelly's inclusion of maintenance labor also functions as an address to the institution of the museum. She has said of the work, "As an installation within a traditional gallery space, the work subscribes to certain modes of presentation; the framing, for example, parodies a familiar type of museum display in so far as it allows my archaeology of the everyday to slip unannounced into the great hall and ask impertinent questions of its keepers."[34] This "archaeology of the everyday" permitted Kelly to represent two forms of labor—artistic and domestic—both of which debunk the myths of nonwork that surround both forms of reproduction (artist as genius, mother as natural). *PPD* stages the relations between artistic and human creation as analogous, and by doing so interrogates the boundaries between public and private realms of experience. And if one premise of Conceptual art is that "anyone can do it," then Kelly's work suggests that the same is true of the labor of mothering, for to de-naturalize such labor is to make it non-gender-specific.

While Chicago and Kelly were extensively engaged with the public discursive fields of Minimalism and Conceptual art, Ukeles's explicit address of the museum makes her work an early instance of Institutional Critique.[35] By taking the normally hidden labor of the private sphere and submitting it to public scrutiny in the institutions of art, *Maintenance Art* explored the fictional quality of the distinction between public and private. The performances demonstrated that the work of maintenance is neither exclusively public nor private; it is the realm of human activities that serves to bind the two. Ukeles's use of performance—her insistence that her "private" body perform "private" activities in public space—seems to suggest that maintenance is a key component of subjectivity. Yet it is one that often goes unrecognized, and instead is naturalized through repetition into the status of "habit," as opposed to being constitutive of identity. So one effect of Ukeles's performances is to show how institutions such as the museum unconsciously help to maintain "the category of artistic individuality that emblematizes bourgeois subjectivity" through its suppression of its dependence on the labors that keep the white cube clean.[36]

However, when the bonding between public and private realms is exposed, or when an identity delineated by maintenance, as opposed to artistic expression, is foregrounded, the "proper" functioning of the public institution is compromised. Ukeles's performances dramatize that when maintenance is put front and center, made visible, given equal value with art objects, the museum chokes and sputters. For instance, *The Keeping of the Keys* wreaked havoc on the museum's normal workday. The piece so infuriated the curators, who felt that their office and floor should be exempt, that when Ukeles announced that their office was to become a piece of "maintenance art," all but one curator ran out of the office, fleeing both the artist and their own work. The work stoppage that resulted from the systematic privileging of maintenance work over other forms of work is a vivid instance of Carole Pateman's argument that it is absolutely structural to patriarchy and capitalism that the labor of maintenance remain *invisible.* When made *visible*, the maintenance work that makes other work possible arrests and stymies the very labor it is designed to maintain.

This work stoppage was not isolated. In *Transfer: The Maintenance of the Art Object*, Ukeles selected a female mummy housed in a glass case from the museum's collection. Traditionally, it was the janitor's job to keep this case clean. In a ceremony staged for the camera, the janitor relinquished his rag and cleaning fluid to Ukeles, who then cleaned the case as a "Maintenance Artist," as opposed to a maintenance person, making what she called a "dust painting." After the mummy case was cleaned she stamped both it and the cleaning rag with a rubber stamp certifying their new identities as "Maintenance Art Works." The stamped rag and the cleaning fluid were then offered to the museum conservator, in the same ceremonial manner; for the cleaned case, now a work of "Maintenance Art," could only be cleaned (or maintained) by the conservator.

The photographs of *Transfer* are accompanied by a hand-drawn diagram that resembles a low-tech flow chart and details the ramifications of the transfer, mapping how one job (cleaning) had been made the province of three different professionals (janitor, artist, conservator). The goofiness of the chart is a send-up of the clinical "aesthetic of administration" put forth by many Conceptual artists and practitioners of Institutional Critique, although here the diagram mimes managerial concerns with the division of labor as well.[37] This performance highlights the division of labor that supports the aura of the artist's signature, an aura the museum is dependent on for its legitimacy (and which it in turn legitimates), but in *Transfer*, anyone can use the maintenance art stamp, compromising the value of the artist's signature as a guarantor of art.

More importantly, though, by insisting that everyone clean the mummy case, the performance intimates that anyone can perform maintenance. Once again the public exposure of maintenance gums up the work of the museum, complicating the smooth, seamless, efficient functioning of the institution.

Ukeles's *Maintenance Art Performances* combine slapstick humor and serious critique. This aesthetic mixture (Karl Marx meets the Marx Brothers) is also found in the works of Martha Rosler. Rosler is perhaps best known for her two influential Conceptual pieces, *The Bowery in Two Inadequate Descriptive Systems* (1974–1975) and *Vital Statistics of a Citizen, Simply Obtained* (1977), both of which exposed the limits of representation and imported charged political content into the field of Conceptual art. Her early collages and video works are less familiar. Many of these works focused on various aspects of cooking: the disparity between starvation and gourmet meals; the cultural value placed on cooking, and the complicated hierarchies of who cooks and who serves what food. Several works transpose the language of cooking and the language of art, forming a composite that alludes to the similarity between the terms "artwork" and "housework." In all of these early works—be they videos, film scripts, or postcard pieces—Rosler frames the conviviality of food as a bodily necessity and pleasure that binds all human beings. Yet lest such commonality give rise to humanist myths (as is the case with Chicago's work), she also casts the production of food as a form of maintenance labor, and hence subject to the inequities of race, class, and gender, that cannot be merely swept away under the guise of things "private" or "domestic." Similar to Ukeles's performances in both their rejection of traditional artistic media and their focus on various aspects of maintenance labor, video works such as *Semiotics of the Kitchen* and *Domination and the Everyday* turn a critical eye toward the relations between public and private that shape our daily lives.

Both videos employ various strategies of distanciation, yet, as in Ukeles's performances, such strategies are combined with a sometimes caustic, sometimes slapstick sense of humor. In *Semiotics of the Kitchen*, Rosler stands in a kitchen and names various cooking utensils in alphabetical order and then mimes their uses ("bowl," she declares, and stirs an imaginary substance). Rosler "performs" the role of cook as if the stage directions were written by Bertolt Brecht; straight-faced and purged of emotion, she discourages any identification on the part of the viewer. (However, in the background we can see a large book whose binding reads "MOTHER," suggesting a possible root cause for the character's bizarre behavior.) The tape also lacks a plot, offering a list instead of a story, further blocking "normative" identification. A broadly drawn spoof on television cooking shows, the tape further discourages identification in that there is nothing to cook, no recipe to complete, we are not asked to follow along with her activities. Yet Rosler's deadpan delivery is held in humorous relation to her slapstick-like performance of nonexistent activities (recalling Charlie Chaplin's *Gold Rush*, Rosler ladles an imaginary liquid and then tosses it over her shoulder; instead of "slicing" or "cutting" with the knife, she aggressively stabs at the air). The exaggerated sense of physical labor means that her everyday kitchen gestures border on the calisthenic. The work's humor and deliberate foiling of the maintenance labor of cooking (if the kitchen had any actual food in it the set would have resembled the aftermath of a food fight) recalls Ukeles's slapstick aesthetic. Indeed, to think of the two works in tandem is to heighten the way in which the works are designed in part to provoke an extremely ambivalent response on the part of the viewer. Should we giggle or shudder at the trapped quality of Rosler's slightly maniacal home cook? Do we laugh knowingly at Ukeles's "floor paintings," with their explicit evocation of the grand painterly gestures of Jackson Pollock, or do we feel a tinge of shame at the public display of a woman who cleans up after us? Responses are rendered ambivalent, in part because both Rosler and Ukeles have combined an aesthetic of identification (traditionally associated with second-wave feminism) with one of distanciation (usually affiliated with poststructuralist feminism); and they have done so, in large measure, by showing us the fault line between things considered private and things considered public.

Rosler deals with this problematic even more rigorously in *Domination and the Everyday*. Self-described as an "artist-mother's 'This is Your Life,'"[38] the tape begins with an image of Chilean dictator Augusto Pinochet. The image track quickly becomes layered, as a steady stream of disparate pictures—family snapshots, mass-media advertising, photographs of political leaders and artists—fills the screen. Scrolling along the bottom of the screen is a dense theoretical text analyzing the problem of class domination and the relation between those who make culture and those with political power, arguing that "the controlling class also

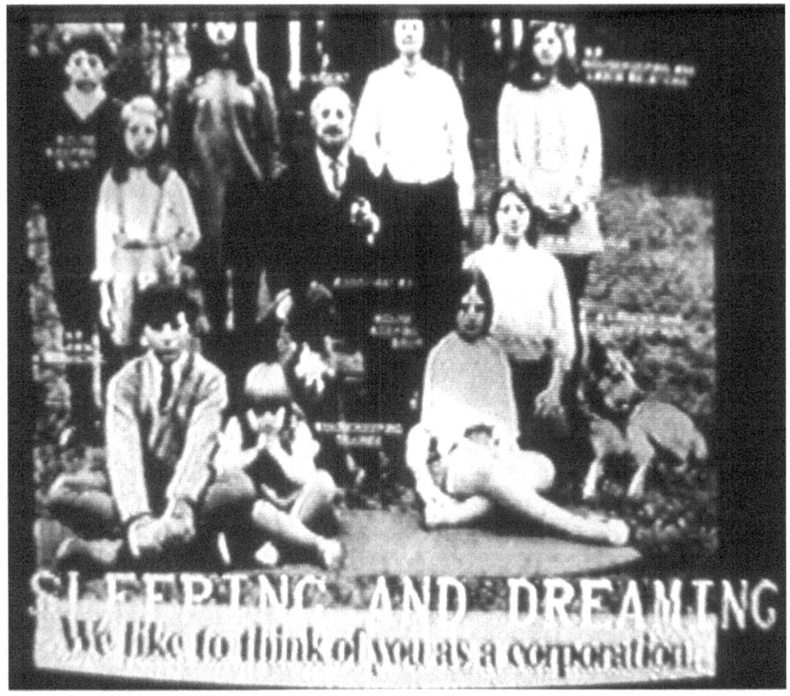

Martha Rosler, still from *Domination and the Everyday,* 1978. Courtesy the artist and Mitchell-Innes & Nash, New York.

controls culture." Deploying a classic strategy of filmic distanciation, the sound and image track are separate. Accompanying this already dense visual field is a similarly doubled soundtrack, as we hear, simultaneously, the real-time conversation between Rosler and her young son as she readies him for bed and a radio interview with the famous art dealer Irving Blum.

Here the everyday labor of mothering, of feeding, reading bedtime stories, and cleaning, is laid down next to humanist art discourse, Marxist analysis, and the cruel facts of political domination; their polyvalence renders them, if not entirely equivalent, at least impossible to hierarchize. As one track among many, it is hard to privilege the everyday labor of Rosler's mothering, as hard as it is to keep any one of the tracks in focus above the others, as each interrupts, overlaps, synchronizes, and seems incommensurate with the others. To this end *Domination and the*

Everyday does something slightly different from the *Maintenance Art Performances*. Rosler does not isolate the labor in order to show it, nor does she engage the literal public spaces of the museum. Rather, by placing maintenance labor as one competing factor among many, one ingredient among many that blend together to form the everyday, she shows it to be as structuring of our lives as other, seemingly invisible structures—political domination, for instance. For Rosler the question is how to make the connection between the brutal regime of Pinochet and the ideology of first world bedtime stories; how to understand the relays between Irving Blum's blather about the genius of Jasper Johns and the laconic address of mother to child, as she slowly persuades the boy to get ready for bed. What do all these things have to do with one another? The tape insinuates that they are related in our inability not only to recognize them (they are too layered; they compete too steadily for our individuated attention), but further, to draw any meaningful connections *between* them. A sentence scrolls by: "We understand that we have no control over big events; we do not understand HOW and WHY the 'small' events that make up our own lives are controlled as well."

Domination and the Everyday proposes that the public sphere is more than simply the space of the traditional institutions of the bourgeois public sphere (e.g., the museum). Instead, Rosler's work images a public sphere reorganized by, and shot through with, the effects of television (hence her use of video). Eschewing both the traditional venues and mediums of "art," she turned instead to mediums not sanctioned by the art establishment (video, postcards, and performance works), mediums that presented difficulty in terms of distribution—showing distribution to be as important an element in the art process as consumption or production.[39] While Chicago, Kelly, and Ukeles are explicit in their address of more traditionally defined public space, Rosler's work is an early instanciation of the changing parameters of such space, the very despatialization of public space. However, while notions of what constitutes the public may shift, the society of the spectacle hardly operates without the structural role of maintenance labor. And Rosler's works make clear that we not only have to value that labor as such, but that one way we might be able to do that is to articulate the relations among and between different forms of dailiness: the everyday for her being an ineluctable mixture of politics, culture, and maintenance activities. (This is one way Rosler refuses a fetishization of the everyday as a retreat from politics.)

To perform this articulation is to be willing to tear away at the layers and veils of ideology that not only separate people from one another but also render various aspects of daily life radically disjointed. And it is here that the function of maintenance as an activity that forms a bond between public and private realms becomes so important. Rosler's work refutes the either unknowing or unwilling acquiescence of people to systems of domination, be they ideological, cultural, or political. Yet such refusals do not operate strictly in the negative, as *Domination and the Everyday* ends on a decidedly utopian note:

> It is in the marketplace alone that we are replaceable, because interchangeable, and until we take control we will always be owned by the culture that imagines us to be replaceable. The truth, of course, is that NO ONE can be replaced … but there will always be more of us, more and more of us, willing to struggle to take control of our lives, our culture, our world … which to be fully human, we must do and we will.[40]

★★★

> My work is a sketch, a line of thinking, a possibility.[41]
>
> —Martha Rosler

I have been arguing that the aspect that binds these works together is their concern with the problems of labor and political economy and their address to the public institutions of art. By importing explicitly domestic or private content (Chicago and Kelly) or by substituting the notion of domestic labor with maintenance labor (Ukeles), or by insisting on the equivalence between maintenance labor and other forms of domination (Rosler), all four artists explore the interpenetration between public and private institutions. This is notable, for in each instance the various institutions of art have wanted precisely to suppress the public address of the works. This is why, for instance, *The Dinner Party* is accused of being too kitschy, for Chicago has smuggled the decorative and the domestic into the modernist museum.[42] So, too, the familiar disparagement of the *PPD*, that it "should be a book," is a desire to deny its place in the public space of the museum, to suppress the non-naturalness of motherhood as a legitimate public discussion.

Rosler's work has received the least "proper" art world attention (she was only recently the subject of a European-initiated museum retrospective). Her explicit desire to envision an art practice that addressed a more diffuse notion of the public sphere and a more expansive notion of art has meant that many of her early video works on food and cooking and her postcard pieces that deal with domestic labor remain difficult to see. Finally, and perhaps most telling of all, the Wadsworth Atheneum kept no records of Ukeles's *Maintenance Art Performances*, recalling Miwon Kwon's observation that when the work of maintenance is well accomplished it goes unseen.[43]

Another aspect that binds these works is that each participates in what Fredric Jameson calls the "laboratory situation" of art.[44] All four works submit various "givens" about the way the world works to a type of laboratory experimentation. For instance, the body and perception are questioned by Minimalism; the status of the art object is queried by Conceptual art; the medium of video places a strain on both art institutions (in terms of distribution) and the viewer (in terms of expectation); and the regimes of power embedded in the museum are articulated by Institutional Critique. Yet I would contend that these artists add yet another layer to these "laboratory experiments," for embodied in each work is a proposition about how the world might be *differently* organized. Woven into the fabric of each work is the utopian question, "What if the world worked like this?" Chicago offers us the old parlor game of the ideal dinner party, and suggests that the museum could be a site for conviviality, social exchange, and the pleasures of the flesh. Kelly's work intimates the desire for a culture that would bestow equal value on the work of mothering and the labor of the artist; so, too, the work's very existence points toward a different model of the "working mother." Rosler images a polyvalent and dialectical world where the demands of work and pleasure, and the seeming separation between culture and domination, are held in a constant tensile relation to one another. Ukeles's work, again, may be the most explicit in its utopian dimension, its literalness a demand beyond "equal time equal pay" or the "personal is political," for hers is a world where maintenance labor is equal in value to artistic labor—a proposition that would require a radically different organization of the public and private spheres.

Feminism has long operated with the power (and limitations) of utopian thought. It is telling, then, that these artists have dovetailed the "what if" potential of both art and feminism. Yet they have not collapsed the distinction between art and life; rather, they have used art as a form of legitimated public discourse, a conduit through which to enter ideas into public discussion. So while all of the works expose the porosity between public and private spheres, none calls for the dismantling of these formations. Fictional as the division might be, the myth of a private sphere is too dear to relinquish,[45] and the public sphere as a site of discourse and debate is too important a fiction for democracy to disavow. Instead, these pieces have articulated something similar to the utopian thought of feminists like Moira Gatens, and, more recently, Drucilla Cornell. As Gatens argues, "To effect the total insertion of women into capitalist society would involve the acknowledgment of the 'blind spot' of traditional socio-political theorizing: that the reproduction of the species, sexual relations and domestic work are performed under *socially constructed* conditions, not natural ones, and that these tasks are socially and economically necessary."[46] She suggests a new model of the body politic, one that would be able to account for the heterogeneity of its subjects and their *asymmetrical* relations to reproduction, sexuality, and subjectivity.

Such utopian language is vague, and for some time now such vagueness has produced frustration or dismissal. However, this is a utopian language without the problematic proscriptive nature of previous utopian thought. Similarly, it is not a theoretical language that ends with a description of a system or an ideology. Instead, it offers *speculation.* At the end of *Feminism and Philosophy*, Gatens calls for representations, both symbolic and factual, of future conceptions of sociopolitical and ethical life. And in *At the Heart of Freedom*, Drucilla Cornell writes, "There is a necessary aesthetic dimension to a feminist practice of freedom. Feminism is invariably a symbolic project."[47] It is within the tradition of art as a laboratory experiment that Chicago, Kelly, Rosler, and Ukeles engage in speculative feminist utopian thought, each attempting to rearticulate the terms of public and private in ways that might fashion new possibilities for both spheres and the labor they entail. But this is not a call for a utopian field in which all parties agree on the terms of the discourse, decidedly not. While all four artists are bound by their interest in labor, their address to questions of public and private, and their pointed complications of the (now) standard narratives of postwar advanced art practice, they clearly differ in contentious and important ways. While this essay has valorized a moment of obscured affinity, this is not to say that such affinities should be privileged as such. Difference is crucial for utopian thought, in that utopia (like democracy) has the potential to offer discourses marked precisely by disagreement and contestation. For some time feminism has labored under equally false ideals of harmony or superiority. What seems increasingly necessary in our putatively "post-feminist" age is a feminism vibrant enough to encourage dissension and conflict without closing off considerations of points of contact, moments of unexpected convergence. That 1970s art work informed by feminism is currently a site of intellectual energy is perhaps due to the problems of labor that shape our current public sphere: from the "end" of the welfare mother to home officing; from the new threats to privacy made possible by the ever-expanding role of the Internet in the lives of people in developed nations to the multinational corporate reorganization of public space. These issues seem to run through the fabric of our daily lives with astounding thoroughness. If the politics of the 1970s were marked by various battles for equality, and the politics of the 1980s were shaped by struggles over the politics of representation under the Reagan/Thatcher era, where the spectacle reigned supreme, then the core of contemporary politics may be shaped largely by the reciprocity and contested relations between the public and private spheres and the forms of labor that support them.

Notes

1. In the past few years numerous exhibitions have taken place, to name but a few: Mary Kelly's *Post-Partum Document* was reassembled in its entirety by the Generali Foundation in Vienna, Austria (September 25–December 20, 1998); Martha Rosler is the subject of a traveling retrospective organized by Ikon Gallery in Birmingham, UK; Mierle Laderman Ukeles's *Maintenance Art Series* was shown in its entirety at the Ronald Feldman Gallery, New York; Judy Chicago's *The Dinner Party* was the centerpiece of an exhibit curated by Amelia Jones at the Armand Hammer Museum, Los Angeles (April 24–August 18, 1996); *Division of Labor: Women and Work* was held at the Bronx Museum (1996); and the *Bad Girls* exhibition took place at the New Museum, New York (January 14–February 27 and March 5–April 10, 1994). So, too, books and journals have proliferated: *October* dedicated an entire issue to the question of feminism, replete with a questionnaire and a roundtable (*October* 71 [Winter 1995]); Laura Cottingham produced *Not For Sale* (1998), a video essay designed for teaching feminist art; *Feminism and Contemporary Art: The Revolutionary Power of Women's Laughter* by Jo Anna Isaak appeared in 1996 (London: Routledge); Mira Schor's award-winning *Wet: On Painting, Feminism, and Art Culture* (Durham, NC: Duke University Press, 1997) also appeared recently; and *The Power of Feminist Art* brought together in one volume a commanding overview of American feminist art of the 1970s (New York: Harry N. Abrams, 1994).

2. Under the umbrella of "essentialism," I am referring to artists and critics such as Norma Broude, Mary D. Garrard, Judy Chicago, Harmony Hammons, Suzanne Lacy, Lucy Lippard, Ana Mendieta, Faith Ringgold, Miriam Schapiro, Mira Schor, Faith Wilding, the artists involved in *Womanhouse* and the Feminist Art Program. And with regard to poststructuralism, I'm thinking here of the work of Victor Burgin, Mary Kelly, Silvia Kolbowski, Barbara Kruger, Kate Linker, Laura Mulvey, Griselda Pollock, Cindy Sherman, and Lisa Tickner.

3. For a more elaborated account of this debate, see my "Cleaning Up in the 1970s: The Work of Judy Chicago, Mary Kelly, and Mierle Laderman Ukeles," in *Rewriting Conceptual Art,* ed. Michael Newman and Jon Bird (London: Reaktion Books, 1999).

4. Given that the works were made during the same period, clearly this is not the case. However, they were made in different geographical locations within which extremely different types of feminist discussions were taking place. See Mary Kelly's remarks to this effect in "A Conversation on Recent Feminist Art Practices," *October* 71 (Winter 1995), pp. 49–69.

5. Lisa Tickner, *October* 71 (Winter 1995), p. 44.

6. Griselda Pollock, "Painting, Feminism, History," in *Destabilizing Theory*, ed. Michele Barrett and Anne Phillips (Stanford: Stanford University Press, 1992), p. 154.

7. Faith Wilding, "The Feminist Programs at Fresno and CalArts, 1970–75," in *The Power of Feminist Art*, ed. Norma Broude and Mary D. Garrard (New York: Harry N. Abrams, 1994), p. 35.

8. Mary Kelly has frequently argued against the category "feminist art." Arguing against the notion of a cohesive "style" of feminist art, she proposes instead the notion of art "informed by feminism." See the exchange between Kelly and Silvia Kolbowski in "A Conversation on Recent Feminist Art Practices" in *October* 71 (Winter 1995), pp. 49–69.

9. This is the effect of Laura Cottingham's video essay, designed for pedagogical purposes, *Not for Sale*. This tape's structure is based on that of the art history survey: it casts a wide net, includes a barrage of artists without explanation or justification for their inclusion (save their gender). The effect of which is that we are left with an alternative "canon." The separatist quality of the tape means that the practice of many artists is radically de-contextualized and the work of nearly all the artists is ghettoized. For more on this tape, see my "Not for Sale" in *frieze* 41 (Summer 1998).

10. My thanks to Janet Kraynak for a discussion of this point.

11. Moira Gatens, *Feminism and Philosophy: Perspectives on Difference and Equality* (Bloomington: Indiana University Press, 1991).

12. Moira Gatens, "Powers, Bodies, and Difference," in *Destabilizing Theory*, p. 124.

13. Gatens, *Feminism and Philosophy,* p. 38.

14. Ibid., pp. 124–125.

15. Ibid., pp. 122–123.

16. For an elaboration of this argument, see Carole Pateman's *The Sexual Contract* (Stanford: Stanford University Press, 1988). This critique elaborates on the problem of "equality" within liberal thought that is based in part on the inability of capitalism to function without the unpaid labor of maintenance. This subsequently permits a critique of democracy's historical dependence on slavery. Here the implications of political theory

are indispensable for thinking through the perennial blind spot of both Anglo-American and continental feminism, the problem of racial and ethnic difference.

17. Gatens, "Powers, Bodies, and Difference," in *Destabilizing Theory*, p. 131.

18. Ibid., p. 128.

19. Ibid., p. 135.

20. Additionally, the essentialism/theory debate may also have restricted feminist discourse to notions of the subject that reside (rhetorically) outside of the dominant structure of capitalism, hence further marginalizing the political potential of feminism, and art that operates within its concerns.

21. For a reprint of Ukeles's "Maintenance Art Manifesto" in its entirety, see "Artist Project: Mierle Laderman Ukeles Maintenance Art Activity (1973) with responses from Miwon Kwon and Helen Molesworth," *Documents* 10 (Fall 1997).

22. It is Ukeles's insistence on the structural aspect of everyday maintenance labor, as opposed to a fetishized notion of the "everyday," that distinguishes her performances from recent practices that merely represent or stage the everyday, such as Rirkrit Tiravanija's recent exhibition in which he placed a facsimile of his apartment in the gallery and allowed visitors to use the space as they saw fit. For instance, part of the "Maintenance Art Manifesto" included an exhibition proposal called "Care," in which Ukeles proposed to do the following: "live in the museum as I customarily do at home with my husband and my baby, for the duration of the exhibition, (Right? or if you don't want me around at night I would come in every day) and do all these things as public Art activities: I will sweep and wax the floors, dust everything, wash the walls (i.e., 'floor paintings, dust works, soap sculpture, wall paintings'), cook, invite people to eat, make agglomerations and dispositions of all functional refuse. The exhibition area might look 'empty' of art, but it will be maintained in full public view. MY WORKING WILL BE THE WORK." Needless to say no one ever accepted this proposal. For an account of Tiravanija's practice, see Janet Kraynak's "Rirkrit Tiravanija's Liability," *Documents* 13 (Fall 1998).

23. Griselda Pollock has argued that the "radical reconceptualization of the function of artistic activity—its procedures, personnel, and institutional sites—is the major legacy of feminist interventions in culture since the late sixties." See Griselda Pollock, "Painting, Feminism, History," in *Destabilizing Theory*, p. 155.

24. For instance, no women artists are discussed in Benjamin H. D. Buchloh's "Conceptual Art 1962–1969: From the Aesthetic of Administration to the Critique of Institutions," *October* 55 (Winter 1990), although Hilla Becher and Hanne Darboven are mentioned in passing. Ann Goldstein and Anne Rorimer, *Reconsidering the Object of Art 1965–1975* (Cambridge, MA: MIT Press, 1995) included only eight women out of a total of fifty-six artists. More recently, however, this seems to have changed. For example, Peter Wollen included numerous women artists in the North American section of the *Global Conceptualism* (2000) exhibition.

25. Rosalyn Deutsche, *Evictions: Art and Spatial Politics* (Cambridge, MA: MIT Press, 1996), p. 273.

26. Pateman, *The Sexual Contract*, p. 144.

27. For an account of Chicago's early work and *The Dinner Party*'s fetishism of surface, see Laura Meyer, "From Finish Fetishism to Feminism: Judy Chicago's *Dinner Party* in California Art History," in *Sexual Politics: Judy Chicago's Dinner Party in Feminist Art*

History, ed. Amelia Jones (Los Angeles: UCLA and Armand Hammer Museum with University of California Press, 1996).

28. *The Dinner Party*, it should be noted, is always exhibited accompanied by documentary photographs of the massive groups and collectives of women who worked on the project. In this regard the labor of making *The Dinner Party* is always registered, but in a peripheral, supporting role. *The Dinner Party* effaces the marks of labor within its boundaries, and in so doing presents itself like a traditional museum-oriented art object: the result of creative genius as opposed to manual labor (a distinction that perpetuates the power relations between the artist and those who work in his or her atelier), and, furthermore, the result of artistic labor only, not the maintenance labor that supports such labor.

29. For an account of Minimalism that argues that the sculptures pressured the terms of what is and is not sculpture, see Rosalind Krauss, "Sculpture in the Expanded Field," in *The Originality and the Avant-Garde and Other Modernist Myths* (Cambridge: MIT Press, 1985).

30. The exhibition *Women and Work* was curated by Margaret Harrison, Kay Hunt, and Mary Kelly; *Nightcleaners* was made by the Berwick Street Film Collective: Marc Karlin, Kelly, James Scott, and Humphry Trevelyn. For the best account of Kelly's early practice, see *Social Process/Collaborative Action: Mary Kelly 1970–75*, exhibition catalog, ed. Judith Mastsai (Vancouver, Canada: Charles H. Scott Gallery, Emily Carr Institute of Art and Design, 1997).

31. Buchloh, "Conceptual Art 1962–1969," p. 107.

32. Frazer Ward, "Some Relations between Conceptual and Performance Art," *Art Journal* 56, no. 4 (Winter 1997).

33. In this light Kelly's *PPD* can be seen as a direct attack against the Conceptual art of someone like Joseph Kosuth, for instance, but not, say, the work of Hans Haacke. However, Kelly's work also does serve to problematize the dominant reception of Conceptual art as defined by male artists. For more on the historical context of the *Post-Partum Document*, see Juli Carson, "(Re)Viewing Mary Kelly's *Post-Partum Document*," *Documents* 13 (Fall 1998).

34. Mary Kelly, *Post-Partum Document* (London: Routledge & Kegan Paul, 1985), p. xvi.

35. I do not want to place these artists so firmly within specific categories that their work is seen to be either only an instance of that "style" of work, nor do I want to suggest that these "styles" are in any way internally coherent. Rather, I want to emphasize the ways in which these works are in conscious and explicit dialogue with the predominant movements of critical art of their period.

36. Frazer Ward, "The Haunted Museum: Institutional Critique and Publicity," *October* 73 (Summer 1995): 83.

37. The phrase "aesthetic of administration" is taken from Benjamin H. D. Buchloh's definitive "Conceptual Art 1962–1969."

38. The tape is called this in the descriptive list of Rosler's works found in *Martha Rosler: Positions in the Life World*, ed. Catherine de Zegher (Birmingham, Vienna, and Cambridge, MA: Ikon, Generali, and MIT Press, 1998).

39. This is perhaps why *Vital Statistics* and *The Bowery* are her most well-known works, in that each could be disseminated more easily in the form of photography, and hence traveled better through the distribution network of art magazines, etc. (For instance, *Vital Statistics* is usually represented as a photograph, while the video is not often shown.).

40. Rosler in *Martha Rosler: Positions in the Life World,* p. 31.

41. Benjamin H. D. Buchloh, "A Conversation with Martha Rosler," in *Martha Rosler: Positions in the Life World,* p. 31.

42. For more on the charge of kitsch launched against *The Dinner Party*, see Amelia Jones's "The 'Sexual Politics' of *The Dinner Party*: A Critical Context," in *Sexual Politics: Judy Chicago's Dinner Party in Feminist Art History.*

43. Conversation with the artist, summer 1997. See Miwon Kwon, "In Appreciation of Invisible Work: Mierle Laderman Ukeles and the Maintenance of the White Cube," *Documents* 10 (Fall 1997).

44. Fredric Jameson, "Periodizing the 1960s," in *The Sixties without Apology* (Minneapolis: University of Minnesota Press, 1984), p. 79. Additionally, Martha Rosler has said of her own work: "Everything I have ever done I've thought of 'as if': Every single thing I have offered to the public has been offered as a suggestion of a work … which is that my work is a sketch, a line of thinking, a possibility" (Buchloh, "A Conversation with Martha Rosler" in *Martha Rosler: Positions in the Life World,* p. 31).

45. For more on the importance of privacy, see Drucilla Cornell, *At the Heart of Freedom: Feminism, Sex, and Equality* (Princeton: Princeton University Press, 1998). Cornell despatializes privacy by insisting on the idea of an imaginary domain. The imaginary domain is a site (both imagined and actualized), where persons are free to articulate their desires with the historical protections of the idea of "privacy." By despatializing privacy she is able to unhinge it from notions of private property, notions which have been legally disadvantageous for women (with regard to domestic violence, for instance).

46. Gatens, *Feminism and Philosophy,* p. 129.

47. Cornell, *At the Heart of Freedom: Feminism, Sex, and Equality,* p. 24.

Impending Time: Mary Kelly's *Corpus*

Laura Mulvey

Corpus, the first section of Mary Kelly's large project *Interim*, stirs up feelings that cannot quite be pinned down into words, images that are on the verge of being discovered and ideas that might be on the top of a collective tongue. This sensation is due to the exhibition's subject matter and to its visual presentation. Both are allied to the debates and experiments around women's relation to language and images that drew feminist aesthetics into "alliance" with avant-garde aesthetics during the 1970s. Mary Kelly's work as an artist and theorist, and my own work as a filmmaker and theorist, are identified with this movement; and we both gained a cultural identity and framework from its existence. But our common political origins go back further, to the early days of the Women's Movement in 1970. It is for this reason that writing the introduction to this catalog means more to me than the pleasure of discussing and celebrating the work of an artist I admire, and consider to have great political and poetic significance.

Paradoxically, our shared experience in the Women's Movement gives the exhibition a meaning for me that goes beyond the immediate level of commitment to feminist politics and aesthetics. The fact that now, from the perspective of 1986, we can look back to a common origin and involvement in a movement that has necessarily acquired a history, raises questions about how passing time becomes history and, then, questions about the political aspects of our concepts of time. And these speculations find an echo in the content of the exhibition: the crisis of the female body at a certain age, and the formal aspects of the exhibition: the crisis of an avant-garde at a certain age.

At first glance, *Corpus* might seem to be about endings. Woman's beauty is like a *memento mori,* suggesting by its very perfection the inevitability of human decay. In a similar fashion, an avant-garde must be synonymous with innovation, validated by a gloss of novelty, and is thus stalked from its inception by a threat of entropy and obsolescence. My own tendency, in the early to mid-1980s, was to acquiesce in the death of the avant-garde. The conjecture between radical politics and radical aesthetics that had been so important in the 1970s seemed to have outlived its usefulness. It should give way to the demands of time, following the same destiny as a woman who loses her ability to desire as she accepts the world's surface estimation of her desirability.

At second glance, *Corpus* specifically resists such a fatalistic closing-off of an epoch into an ending. The exhibition is not about the woman aged, but about an *Interim,* an intermediate time during which the "something" that might be pending can be transformed by changed understanding and perspectives so that it can be opened up to unexpected eventualities. Time is put "on hold," as it were, and stretched out for minute horizontal examination, not as a Canute-like resistance to the fact of passing time, but as a means of analyzing the images and mythologies that predestine and constrain our experience of lived time. Similarly, Mary Kelly's aesthetic position seems to have avoided the avant-garde's proclivity to swing like a pendulum between the Scylla of purism on the margins and the Charybdis of recuperation at the center. She also seems to have transcended the 1970s paranoia about visual pleasure. Although there are numerous references to theory, and particularly the notoriously difficult psychoanalytic theory, there are other means of entry into understanding and enjoying the work. It is itself unashamedly beautiful and satisfying to the spectator. Without losing principle or intellectual vigor, poetry and visual experience are now immediate, giving hope for an avant-garde that can live beyond the founding moment of negative aesthetics. There is something opportune about this exhibition, as though Mary Kelly had, with a sixth sense, suggested that in considering the crisis of the woman's body as a construction in discourse, the avant-garde needs to face its position in historical time and the critical, art-historical constructions that overlay its presence as a movement.

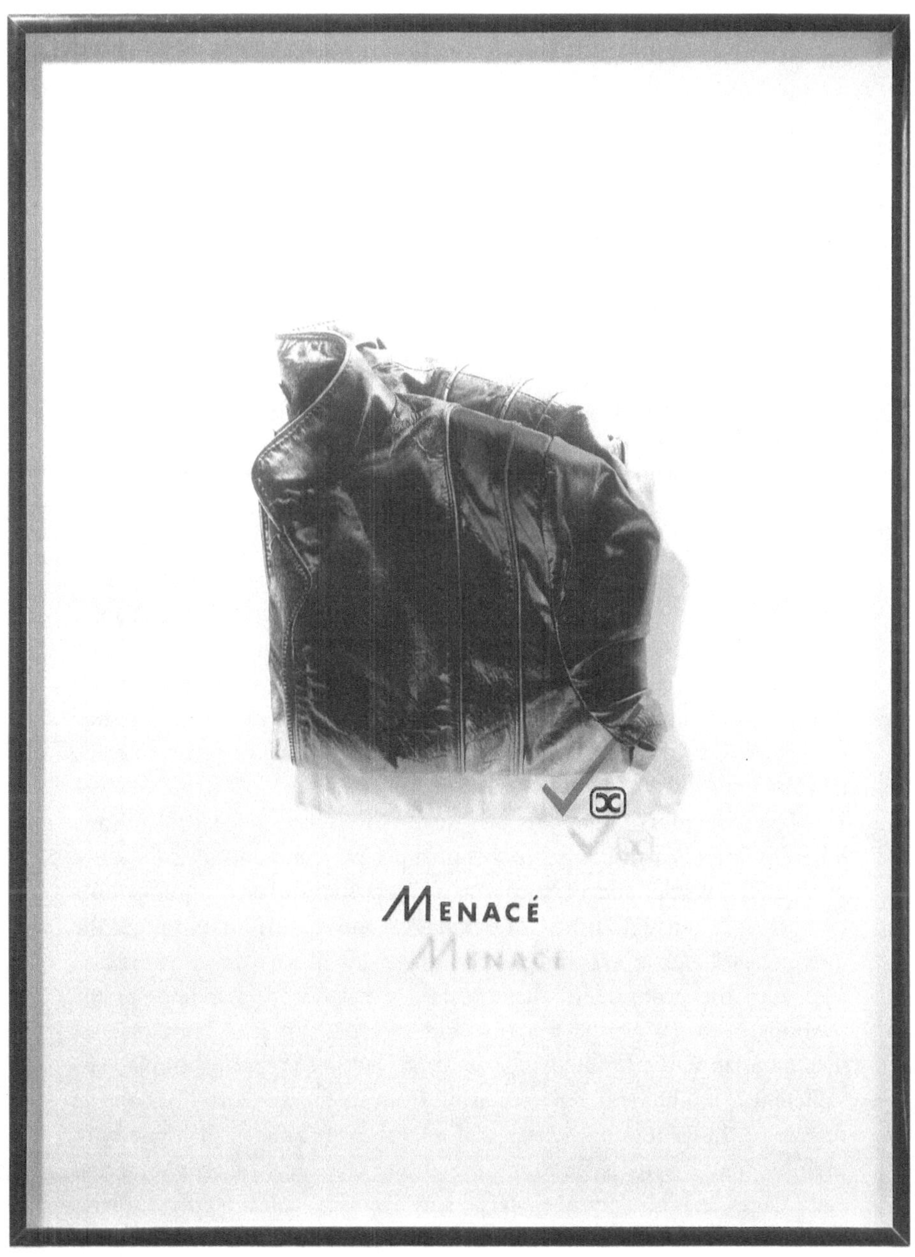

Mary Kelly, detail of *Interim, Part I: Corpus (Menacé)*, 1984–1985. Laminated photo positive, silkscreen, acrylic on Plexiglas; 48 × 36 × 2 in. Courtesy the artist and Pippy Houldsworth Gallery, London.

Quite apart from the problems raised by an avant-garde's "natural" life span, the transition from the 1970s to the 1980s has been particularly difficult. Feminist art and theory were born and became self-aware, articulate, political, and aesthetic projects for the first time. There was an important coincidence between this transformative moment and a widespread reaction against the aesthetics of realism, echoing many aspects of feminist positions on representation and imagery. In the wider social and economic sphere, the 1970s and 1980s are divided, with the effects of Thatcherism aggravating recession, unemployment, poverty, industrial crisis. It might seem more appropriate, faced with the exigencies of this situation, to turn away from the specialized issues of the 1970s avant-garde to the real social and economic problems at hand. But there is something to be learned, perhaps, from that other difficult and disastrous transition from the 1920s to the 1930s, when the politics of representation and concern with questions such as the representation of the unconscious fell from priority to irrelevance in the face of political and economic turmoil. Now it seems crucial not to abandon the feminist commitment to form and language as areas of struggle (since from a feminist perspective representation must be a political issue) while also reassessing the relation between art and politics at a time of historical change. And the feminist use of psychoanalytic theory has established that there is a reality of the psyche and collective fantasy that cannot be ignored.

The aesthetics of heterogeneity that evolved during the 1970s allows different levels of discourse to be juxtaposed, fragmenting a cohesive view of the world, and of history as a single strand that progresses on a vertical axis through time. The knight's move, detour through the unconscious, lack of synchronization, these are all strategies now associated with the postmodern that can also expand understandings of the relations between artistic practice and society. But there is a danger, that fascination with the image as such, with the simulacrum's self-sufficiency, might sever representation from its moorings to float on the surface of things in a passionate and relevant but isolated dialogue with itself. While *Corpus* is undoubtedly about problems of representation and images, it is also about material and historical reality. The woman's body is not presented simply as an item of discourse, but lived in time and sexuality and emotion. Mary Kelly uses heterogeneity as a means to arouse poetic curiosity, and there is rigorous uncertainty about the final answers to the problems she is raising.

There is also a problem of transition specific to this artist. The theme of time in *Corpus* can throw light back on to her previous work, *Post-Partum Document*, and the difficulties of moving on from there. Complicated and demanding, simultaneously monumental and as intricately woven as a tapestry, *Post-Partum Document* epitomizes the theoretical asceticism of its time. Kelly documented, from her own experience, the space of motherhood between birth and onset of the child's Oedipus complex. The trajectory through the Oedipus ends with a child's quasi-understanding of its place in the historical dimension and its first inklings of the continuous, progressive nature of conscious visualization of time. In contrast, the mother and child's dyadic relation is based on the experience of space in a continuous present tense.

> Infancy is a perpetual present. This could be linked with the small child's extraordinary memory—which is not a memory but a continuous actuality. So, too, because of the Oedipus and castration complexes, only humans have yesterdays. As far as we can tell animals nor pre-Oedipal human infants divide time into future, past and present. Time for them would seem to be nearer to spatial relationships: here, there; come, gone; horizontal, punctuated duration rather than a vertical, temporal perspective.[1]

In addition to making the crucial distinction between temporal and spatial relations, this point suggests that our understanding of time is generally dependent on a construction of images in space, such as a linear verticality as opposed to horizontal punctuating points. In recent work on narrative structure, it has been usual to describe the cause/effect temporal linearity of a story as a *horizontal* line of development. In the difficulty of grasping the idea of the passing of time, it is interesting to consider how significant the visualization of the process can be, and how limited our conceptual vocabulary seems when it is needed. Within the aesthetic dimension, Maya Deren, in a famous symposium held in New York in 1963, tried to use the images of horizontal and vertical to distinguish between her conception of poetry and narrative:

> The distinction of poetry is its construction (what I mean by a "poetic structure"), and the poetic construct arises from the fact, if you will, that it is a "vertical" investigation of a situation, in that it probes the ramifications of the moment, and is concerned, in a sense, not with what is occurring, but what it feels like or what it means. … Now it may also include action, but its attack is what I would call the "vertical" attack, and this may be a little clearer if you will contrast it to what I would call the "horizontal" attack of drama, which is concerned with the development, let us say, within a very small situation from feeling to feeling.[2]

It is not particularly important that Deren and Juliet Mitchell use their images of space/time differently. It is important that they both evoke an imaginative space (poetry on the one hand and fantasy on the other) that exists alongside or outside an image of sequential linearity, which only has space to acknowledge its inexorable movement into the future. (There is surely a place between these two quotations for Julia Kristeva's concept of the semiotic, in which she links the rhythms and patterns of poetry to the heterogeneity, the nonlinearity, of the pre-Oedipal.) Mitchell later comments:

> The great theorists of the nineteenth-century tradition—Darwin, Marx and Freud—explain the present by the past. The dominant sociological phenomenologies of the twentieth century in which Klein participated study lateral, horizontal, not vertical relationships.[3]

Feminist theory has mapped out another dimension to the "lateral," by drawing attention to the area of contact between the unconscious and its manifestation in collective fantasy, that is, roughly speaking, popular culture and its representations. Freud, too, saw layers and levels to the human psyche in which time is intricated and fossilized in the space of the unconscious. But the scars and traces that emerge symptomatically in language, images, and symbolizations, as well as cultural phenomena, were to him, primarily, a means of using the past to interpret and cure the individual in the present. Feminism, on the other hand, as a political movement must endeavor to unravel, to question, to reinvent the terrain of popular fantasy in which women's secondary status is sealed by the collective psyche.

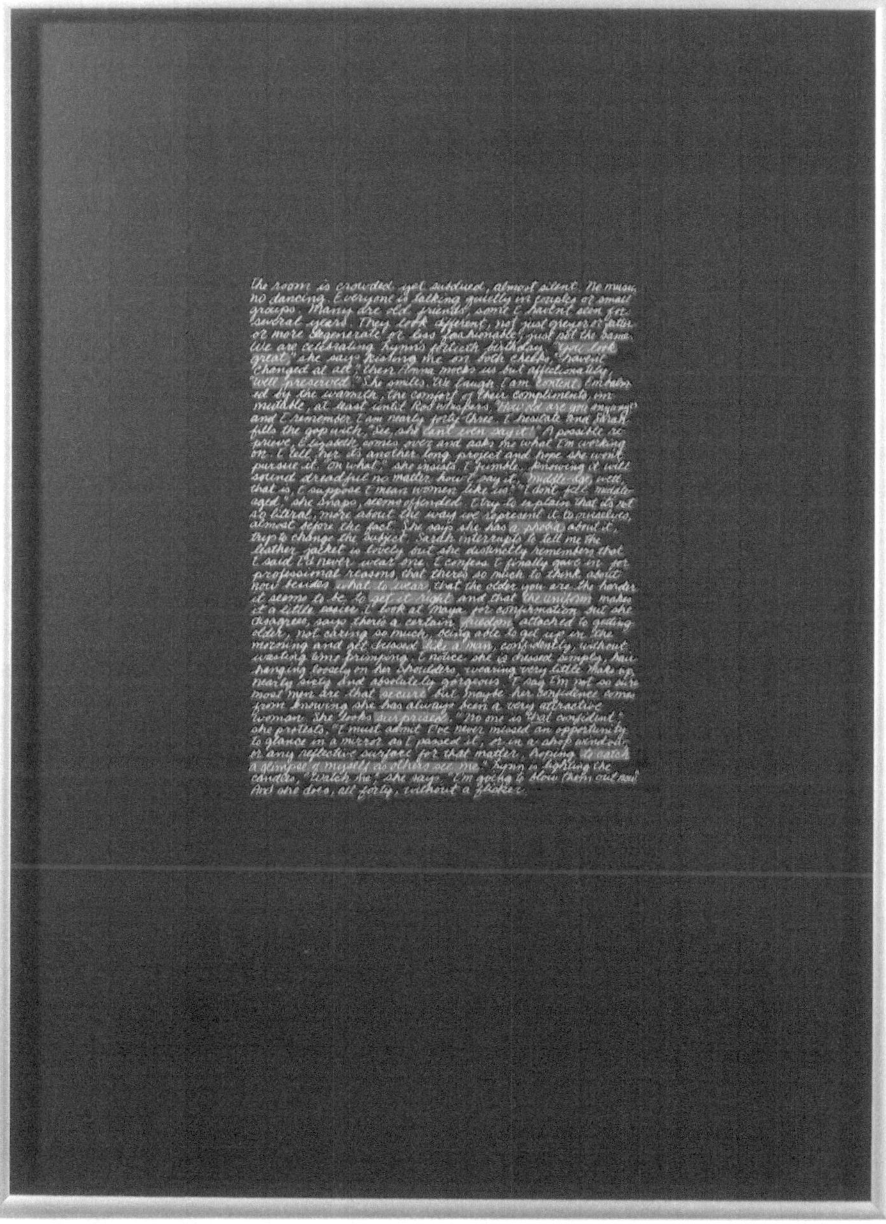

Mary Kelly, detail of *Interim, Part I: Corpus (Menacé)*, 1984–1985. Laminated photo positive, silkscreen, acrylic on Plexiglas; 48 × 36 × 2 in. Courtesy the artist and Pippy Houldsworth Gallery, London.

Interim focuses more on this area than does *Post-Partum Document*, especially in its reference to the discourses of advertising and popular medicine. In *Post-Partum Document*, an implicit narrative drive runs through the work, a line of development organized around the child's phase-by-phase progress toward the Oedipus complex. The artist/narrator/theorist Mary Kelly knows in advance that, at the end of the story, the mother Mary Kelly will have to accept the narrative's resolution and give place to the future in the Name of the Father. (As Lynne Tillman has pointed out to me: theory itself seems to occupy the place of the third term, an epitomized paternal presence.) On the other hand, almost at odds with this narrative drive, is a different depiction of time. *Post-Partum Document* takes place within minute modifications of real time as Mary Kelly used life's own dimension, the actual growth and development of her own child, to generate the different sections of the work. So the self-doubt, the questions, uncertainties, and anxieties of the mother's everyday hold the vertical linearity of time in suspense, spreading out into strands that branch alongside and in juxtaposition to each other. These conflicting concepts of time, space, and narrative are grounded in the mother's own contradictory desire. Her memorabilia are incorporated in the exhibition like a weight, or force of inertia, that tries to withstand the passage of time, but also like a sign of recognition that these memories will one day make a line with the past, across the Oedipal resolution and the end of the story. But the end of the story brings a strange reversal of roles in its wake. The artist/narrator/theorist has seen the mother's melodrama through to the end, but has in the process written herself out of existence. Monika Gagnon has pointed out that one of the final panels reads:

$$\frac{\text{What will I do?}}{\text{S}}$$

poignantly foreseeing the gap left by the end of work as well as the loss of the dyad.

Whereas *Post-Partum Document* had to accept narrative closure, *Corpus* makes an important contribution to opening out the question of endings, both in the word and image panels. One of the fascinating aspects of this work is its refusal to be pinned down or categorized. Although the written texts are not arranged as conventional stories, they contain many references to story-telling, swerving from antidote and recounting "personal experiences" to the fantastic world of fairy tales. The reader has to move from the register of real life and its unattainable desires to that of the imagination where those desires can be "lived out" in fantasy. In film, feminists have, by and large, refused to follow the extreme modernist repudiation of narrative. Stories, myths, and legends belong to the structure of our collective fantasy and cannot be ignored. But narrative also raises quite complex issues for feminism, particularly to do with the active/passive, male/female distribution of functions within a story and also the question of endings, of resolution of the story-line. Vladimir Propp has theorized the relation between character and narrative function in folk-tales. The hero's trials and tribulations have a specific, stable point of departure and move through a series of discrete points, a transformative process until he emerges triumphant into a new stability at the end, a moment of heroic transcendence and narrative resolution.

Mary Kelly builds on the history of debate and experiment that now exists as a body of work in this area, using it as a spring-board and reference point. Her central protagonist is drawn more from the melodrama, the women's genre, which centers on a heroine victim, and produces a particular kind of identification, based on sympathy rather that idealization. The overwhelming odds and real, unresolvable problems that the victim protagonist faces can only find a satisfactory "ending" by unlikely, privileged good fortune, a means of escape. This is the kind of narrative closure that Douglas Sirk cites as the "*deus ex machina*" or "tying the story together with pink ribbons." The artifice is clear to the spectator/reader. Mary Kelly draws unerringly on this tradition when she ends her series of written texts in Disneyland and "they lived happily ever after." She brings together the Proppian structure and its recognition of the importance of endings with the melodrama's ironic undermining of them. Both the fairy tale and the melodrama depend on transition from a state of misfortune to happiness. The misfortune is characteristically grounded in recognizable conditions of oppression, the world's injustice to those without power. The state of happiness is manifestly really only to be achieved through collective imagination. *Corpus* is both documentary and fantasy. Alongside the references to fairy tales, the discourses of advertising, popular medicine, and romantic fiction is the presence of the tape-recorder. The stories vividly reflect women's real dilemmas and the handwritten texts are reminiscent of a diary, but they are also images, textures, traces of the body in an emblematic sense.

At another level this combination of the real with fantasy refers to the analytic process itself, with its illusive double register that refers both to an individual's experience of real events and the invisible processes of the unconscious. References to psychoanalysis as a discourse and a history run through the whole work. The images, arranged in five sets of three, are named after the poses that J. M. Charcot identified as expressing the symptoms of sexual desperation in his hysterical female patients, and thus sets up two different historical traditions. First there is the history of psychoanalysis and its founding conversion from the study of physical symptoms (Charcot) to the study of word and language (Freud). Then there is also the history of psychoanalysis within feminism, and its origins in an intuitive fascination with hysteria as specific to women and their sexual oppression under patriarchy. (Freud's case-history "Dora" is a pivotal point for both these histories, and Mary Kelly refers to Dora's relation to her mother in the final set of texts.) Both psychoanalysis and feminism desire to be transformative. In terms of narrative, they would belong to the middle section of a story where changes, adventure, and traumas are acknowledged, within a time structure but one that questions the inevitability of closure and resolution, the stable point at the end of a "correct line" of development.

Corpus is made up of a series of pieces, each arranged in a triptych, each triptych organized around a woman's garment. The first two images in each triptych are closely linked together in a binary opposition. The first represents masquerade, the glossy finish of Hitchcock's blonde heroines, also the pervasive female presence in advertising that condenses women's relation to commodity consumption with the representation of woman's body as commodity. The second image tears off the mask to reveal a hidden disorder, representing the body's vulnerability—its wounds, as it were, and its actual uncontrollable symptoms. In the garments, their arrangement and their relationship to women's speech/writing and still unspeakable desire, *Corpus* achieves a very fine balance between the iconoclastic repression of the body during the 1970s which led to woman becoming unrepresentable and a recognition that such a reaction against the exploitation of women in images could lead to a repression of the discourse of the body and sexuality altogether. But it is wrong to overemphasize the dependent relations of the first two images. The presence of the third breaks into the neat duality that constructs our mythologies into polarizations such as public/private, inside/outside, voyeurism/exhibitionism, mother/whore, masculinity/femininity, and so on. The third image, with its explicit sexual reference to a discourse of perversion, opens up the question, beyond the balance between surface attraction, desirability, and inner physical and emotional feeling to the problem of female sexual desire. Mary Kelly implies that desire cannot be expressed without an image that can represent it. This third panel, then, speaks to the future, to the common need to redefine women's relation to their image, beyond the question of male appropriation of their image for masculine pleasure, to discover a feminine desire and understand female sexuality. The question, the gap, therefore, is addressed to "us."

Notes

1. Juliet Mitchell, "Introduction," in *The Selected Melanie Klein,* ed. Juliet Mitchell (New York: The Free Press, 1986), p. 26.

2. Maya Deren, "Poetry and the Film: A Symposium," in *Film Culture Reader,* ed. and with an introduction by P. Adams Sitney (New York: Praeger, 1970), p. 174.

3. Mitchell, "Introduction," p. 29.

That Obscure Subject of Desire: An Interview with Mary Kelly by Hal Foster

Hal Foster and Mary Kelly

HAL FOSTER: The conceptual structure of *Interim* is delineated in its section titles: *Corpus, Pecunia, Historia,* and *Potestas*. As well as your inquiry into psychoanalysis, they suggest different discourses—Marxist, Foucauldian—even different disciplines—anthropology, history. Why these four terms, and in this relationship?

MARY KELLY: In the five years before I began the production of *Interim*, I developed an archive of informal conversations with women on the subject of aging, and these were the recurring themes. There is obviously a Foucauldian methodology implied in the notion of archive. That is, I wanted to know how the various themes of this interim moment in a woman's life were constituted as discourses and, more ambitiously, I wanted to look at the formation of these discourses within the historical field of feminism. So, I guess *Corpus* recapitulates the debates of the 1970s, which resulted in a move away from an emphasis on positive images to a psychoanalytically informed concern with spectatorship. Then, *Historia* provides an overview, and reflects a preoccupation of the early 1980s with the question of "agency," or—from a political perspective—the problem of deciphering the relationship between social and psychic moments of oppression. *Pecunia* revives the topic of commodity fetishism—woman-as-consumer, and all that—which originated in the 1960s, but it transforms it into a question of her desire. This reflects my interest in the psychoanalytic concept of fetishism and its implications for women. And *Potestas,* I think, acts again as an overview by placing

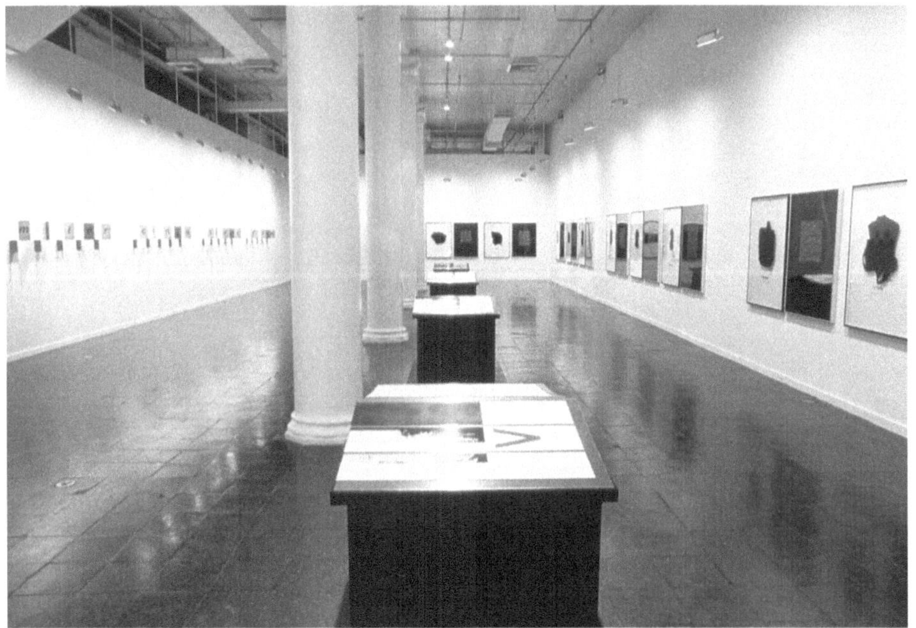

Mary Kelly, *Interim*, 1984–1989. Installation view, New Museum of Contemporary Art, New York, 1990. Courtesy New Museum, New York. Photo by Fred Scruton.

questions of money, property, or position in a wider context. It parodies a kind of biological, sociological, even psychological, binarism in Western culture—a schema of difference which perpetuates sexual or social division. What I wanted to look at, in particular, was the way power reproduces this division in language—in visual representation. I hope this section takes the debate into the 1990s by reassessing what we have or, as it seems, what we haven't achieved in terms of empowerment.

HF: Visually, *Interim* is a complex work, not only in its play of image and text, but in its repertoire of sign systems. You make references to popular culture, though not in the guise of catatonic representations of commodity images. Instead, you engage the different discursivities of everyday forms. *Corpus* alludes to fashion images, medical diagrams, [and] romance fiction, and its Plexiglas panels have the scale of small billboards; *Pecunia* plays on the language of classified ads, genres of personal fiction, and the kinds of riddles and puns found in greeting cards (these also seem to have suggested the size and display of its galvanized steel units). What other languages of everyday life are figured in *Interim*, especially in *Historia* and *Potestas*?

MK: You've covered *Corpus* and *Pecunia* so, to continue, *Historia* refers to generic newspaper or magazine layouts—galleys, paste-ups ... the metaphor of "making history." It takes the form of very large stainless steel pages, with images and texts screened on oxide panels. Laura Trippi suggested a reference to Kiefer which was interesting because it is precisely the heroic notion of a nation which I'm contesting here, with this critical history of an oppositional movement. Perhaps it's my version of his *Women of the Revolution. Potestas* is an extended pun on the sociological jargon of measurement. Its three-dimensional graph may be comic in its familiarity at one level—actually, at first glance it probably looks like minimal sculpture—but on another, it refers to the graph in a Derridian sense, a visual parallel to the schema of phonemic oppositions, as well as a trope for sexual difference.

HF: In *Post-Partum Document*, you visualized and analyzed the mother-child relationship. In *Interim*, you address a particular stage in the lives of women, a stage beyond reproduction, and putatively beyond desire (the given positions of femininity, you suggest), when the aging process comes to the fore. There is, then, a return to the body here, as announced directly in *Corpus,* and, indeed, the posing of the apparel in its image panels refers to the "passionate attitudes" of hysteria defined by J. M. Charcot. Now, in a 1987 text on *Interim*, you implied that the female body was elided in the shift from the visual theater of Charcot to the talking cure of Freud, a shift from looking to listening which marked the beginning of psychoanalysis.[1] Was the female body elided again in the critical focus on the patriarchal unconscious in feminist discourse of the 1970s? In *Interim*, do you relate this moment of elision to the foundational one of psychoanalysis? And, if *Interim* is involved in a return to the body, how are we to think of this?

MK: First, it's primarily within the medical discourse that the visible body was eclipsed, as you say, by new sciences like biophysics. But Freud's own discovery of the unconscious can be included in that process, too. I would say that in our time, the repressed—that is, the body—has returned as spectacle in the form of advertising. This is the new theater where the hysterical posturing of women proliferates. In both *Post-Partum Document* and *Interim,* I've problematized the image of the woman not to promote a new form of iconoclasm but to make the spectator turn from looking to listening. I wanted to give a voice to the woman, to represent her as the subject of the gaze. And, second, *Interim* proposes not one body but many bodies, shaped within a lot of different discourses. It doesn't refer to an anatomical fact or to a perceptual entity, but to the dispersed body of desire. I think of Lacan's description of erotogenic zones as including the phoneme, the gaze, the nothing, and, in this sense, I feel that the installation should be an event where the viewer gathers a kind of corporeal presence from the rhythm or repetition of images, rather than views the work from the fixed vantage point of traditional perspective. Finally, people often say that the body as a visual image is absent in my work. I would argue against such a limited definition of image. The visual field, after all, includes not only the register of iconic signs, but the index and symbol, as well. This heterogeneity of the sign—Norman Bryson calls it the "aniconic image"—is crucial for me because it can have the effect of displacing the female spectator's "hysterical" identification with the male voyeur. So, writing for me is obviously more than what is said. It's also a means of invoking the texture of speaking, listening, touching—Lacan suggests that the invocatory drives are, in a sense, closer to the unconscious—a way of visualizing, not valorizing, what is assumed to be outside of seeing. This is done in order to distance the spectator from the anxious proximity of her body—ultimately, the mother's body—the body too close to see, which is linked at the level of the unconscious to an archaic organization of drives and which bars the woman's access to sublimated pleasure.

HF: The primary focus of feminist-psychoanalytical film practice and theory in the last decade has been on the question of feminine spectatorship. Theoretically, this has suggested a move away from questions of voyeurism and fetishism, the staples of the patriarchal unconscious, toward questions of hysteria, masochism, and melodrama. Your work has been associated with a related trajectory in art practice and theory. In particular, what is your aim in this archaeological recovery of hysteria? Why is it theoretically important at a time when it is clinically almost nonexistent? Incidentally, the Surrealists were also interested—though obviously in a different way—in hysteria; Breton and Aragon called it the greatest poetic discovery of the end of the nineteenth century.

MK: Well, it's exactly the continuing romance of hysteria that interests me. Lacan—who was, at one time, very close to the Surrealists—talked about psychoanalysis as the "hystericization of discourse," and poses analysis against mastery, and hysteria against knowledge. And then, there are the women who were expelled, not from Charcot's theater, but from Lacan's *école freudienne*—I'm thinking here of Luce Irigaray. For them, the hysteric exposes the institution's fundamental misogyny; that is, woman founds the theory of psychoanalysis and sustains it by making the exchange of ideas between male theorists possible. So, hysteria, marginalized in one domain, becomes central in another … which is, of course, feminist theory. Just to give you some examples besides Irigaray: someone like Monique Plaza says hysteria is the revolt against patriarchy; Michèle Montrelay calls it the blind spot of psychoanalysis; Jacqueline Rose points to the problem of sexual difference: and Dora's film collective claims that the hysteric reveals the analyst's symptom and so becomes, in effect, the basis for a critique of Freud. I don't think *Interim* is an archaeological attempt to recover the hysteric-as-poet or dissident, but to see her more as a theoretical symptom within contemporary work.

HF: In *Interim,* as in *Post-Partum Document,* you point to gaps or soft spots in psychoanalysis—if these are not too problematic as metaphors—and yet you are generally perceived to be devoted to the work of Freud and Lacan. How would you characterize your negotiation of their theories?

MK: Devoted would not be the appropriate term as far as I'm concerned. I have a rather mercenary attitude toward these texts and use their insights—usually into male fantasy—to articulate their "lack" … problematic metaphor intended … of ability to deal with feminine sexuality. Their work on fetishism is a prime example. Also, I don't rely on Freud and Lacan exclusively. In *Corpus*, the central thesis revolves around Montrelay's work on the feminine body and [Catherine] Millot's paper, "The Feminine Superego." *Pecunia*'s logo, "Pecunia Olet," is taken from [Sándor] Ferenczi's work of the same title on the psychoanalysis of money. And Kristeva's influence seems to me evident everywhere.

HF: In different ways and to different degrees in *Corpus* and *Pecunia*, as in the *Document*, the feminine is located in the positions of mother, wife, sister, and daughter. (*Mater, Conju, Soror,* and *Filia* are, in fact, the section titles of *Pecunia.*) These positions are no more separable in your work than they are in social life, yet you seem to privilege the maternal term. Could you comment on this dominance in relation to your theoretical interests?

MK: Certainly *Post-Partum Document* is a work that deals explicitly with the mother-child relationship. In a way, maternal femininity seems almost synonymous with the notion of womanliness. It's what I'd call the "ideal moment," in that the woman, in relation to her child, is constituted as the actively desiring subject, without transgressing the socially accepted definition of her as "mother." But this poses an immediate contradiction. Maternity is not passive and consequently not "feminine." Also, what happens when the child grows up? Is "being a woman" just a brief moment in her life? Clearly, there is a fundamental instability in the category *woman,* which *Corpus* takes up in exchanges between men and women and among women themselves in the narratives. In a way, I suppose they repeat the hysteric's question: Am I a man or am I a woman? Even when the figure of the mother appears, for example, in *Extase,* she is seen to be masquerading; the happy family is really a farce. In *Pecunia,* I've decentered the maternal paradigm quite noticeably with the sections' titles. The emphasis here is on the whole set of social relations implicated in the designations: mother, daughter, sister, wife. I was thinking of the way Foucault describes the family as conveying "the law through the deployment of sexuality" and "the economy of pleasure through the regime of alliance"—or kinship. The stories in *Pecunia* caricature the pathologies he describes as being the outcome of this interchange: nervous woman, frigid wife, precocious child, and perverse adult. The latter is especially important because, in terms of object choice, it cuts across the heterosexual assumption—something I felt wasn't clear enough in *Corpus.* So, in response to the famous or infamous Lacanian question, "What does woman want?" *Pecunia* might be asking its own question: Are there as many forms of identification as there are demands? But the problem for women—and the one that emerges as the crisis when maternal identity is lost or threatened—is the fragility of the primary identification ... not with the mother, but the father. Kristeva has suggested that it's the remaking of this imaginary father of the pre-Oedipal phase—being able to take his place within language—that's the basis of "sublimational possibility." The last narrative in the "Filia" sequence signifies exactly that failure to identify with the paternal figure in the woman's symptomatic ambivalence about her economic independence.

HF: In *Corpus* and *Pecunia,* there are more references to the signs of class than in *Post-Partum Document* (though they are certainly there, too). Is this taken further in *Historia* and *Potestas*?

MK: Yes, I think so. *Historia,* for example, is concerned with social and political, rather than personal, identity. I mean, there are personal accounts of the historical phases of feminism, but the privileged term of enunciation in these narratives is *we.* I wanted to find out how this collective form of address is constituted, how "we" represent "our" histories. This collectivity isn‘t the seamless entity invoked in slogans like, "Women of the world unite!" The work cuts across this utopian formulation—perhaps a bit too cynically in the slapstick conversations of the "Continued on the Next Page" series—but I think this is a necessary counterpoint to the "reality effect" of the documentary histories and the "nostalgia" of the quotation sequence. One of the consequences of this juxtaposition, which takes the form of a montage of typefaces, is that it problematizes the unity of feminism as an ideology. Even when the point of intersection in the women's stories—there are four, one in each book—is the discourse of psychoanalysis, the meaning of this discourse takes on a specific character depending on the conjuncture in which it emerges for them as a relevant or determining element in their political practice.

HF: Are questions of ethnicity, of whiteness, also addressed? Or are they of secondary importance in the different historical conjunctures which *Interim* works through?

MK: For me, the question of political identity necessarily entails the problem of ethnicity, but that isn't addressed in my work as tokenism; it's taken up around the trajectories of difference—not only sexual difference, but the way white women erase difference in the field of the social or ethnic "other," and, at the same time, vigilantly insist on it when it comes to the other's "Other" … I mean white men. But let's go back a minute to the interest in collective identity of the early women's movement. It was founded on the notion that "woman" is radically "other"; excluded from language, barred access to pleasure: Lacan summed it up: "She does not exist." So, to come into being … to exist, as it were … seemed to require a transcendent form of identification: "We are all alike." Within the arena of political organization, the effect was to deny conflict, to disavow hierarchy. One of the quotations in *Historia* describes the ecstasy of a collective writing project. Seized by the discourse of the other—the woman who writes well—they claim it as their own. In another quotation, the "social other," the abject, is projected and then internalized when, in a description of working-class women at a union meeting, someone begins, "They looked indescribably tired, in a way anonymous, perhaps middle-aged or appeared to be even if they weren't." That is, not like us. Then, she refers to the music in the background, "the chora," which allows her to transform this feeling into its opposite. The piece ends, "And like us, she loved to dance." There is also a quotation about Vietnamese women which revolves at first around terms like "cold," or "without expression," which signify distance, incomprehension, and difference. It's only when the Vietnamese women talk about their own experience of the war that the white women can identify with their suffering; they're constructed as victims and, I think, for us there is a kind of vicarious overidentification here, which obliterates the political imperative to allow specificity and difference without objectification or hierarchy. Frankly, I don't know how that's done, but perhaps this is a beginning.

HF: *Interim* concerns the desires and fantasies of feminine subjects. How do you regard masculine viewers of your work? How are they positioned by this work? I mentioned to you once that, particularly in front of *Corpus,* I felt like an eavesdropper who was sometimes caught, in a flush of shame—like the voyeur, described by Sartre, who is suddenly seen. You mentioned, in reply, "the fourth look." What did you mean?

MK: Women, I mean the psychic consequence of the historical existence of a women's movement, the word of the "other" internalized in the place of the Law and the father. She sees you seeing.

HF: What do you think about the recent investigations of masculinity? What are the problems of "men in feminism," of "me-too-ism," from your point of view? You mentioned once a problem that fascinates me: the reluctance of women to allow the men they love to give up the phallus. What are the feminist investments in "this Other of the other"?

MK: I think it's strategically important to say that men can be, are, and have been, feminists. The critique of masculinity—and by this I don't mean exposés of male fantasies about women, but explorations of the power relations between and among men—is comparable to the issue of ethnicity, that is, the taken-for-grantedness of "whiteness." We can't really progress without the "other" side of both of these coins. Now, as for the second part of your question, I can't really answer it, though perhaps I can clarify or complicate it, as the case may be. When I was ruminating over why there was no outcome to the Oedipus complex for the girl, which wasn't ipso facto neurotic, I began to think that perhaps the boy's resolution of this Oedipal drama wasn't so easy, either. I wondered if it would be possible to take Millot's distinctions regarding the masculinity complex for women, and relate them to men. For example, does the woman who fantasizes the possession of the penis parallel the man who acts out its absence in transvestism? Or, is the woman who masquerades as the feminine type—who disguises the lack of a lack but really makes no demands on her sexual partner—is she comparable to the man who "does what he's got to do"? I mean, what Lacan calls the "male display"; he seems to sense it's a fraud but, in fact, he has no sexual desire for the woman. And, I suppose, you could also take up the woman's desire for the child-as-phallus, and ask what the man's stake is in giving her this "gift"? It seems to me all of this suggests that, for both men and women, demand constructs a rather tentative relation to being or having this phallic term. Of course, no one has it, but I wondered why women seemed resistant to, as you said, letting men relinquish it. It has a parallel in theory, too, because I feel that when we suggest that women have a privileged relation to the mother's body, we are doing more than explaining a different relation to castration, I think we are asserting our difference from men. This assertion seems to point to a certain fear, a fear that's linked, on the one hand, to the desire to be like "them" and, on the other, to the fear of being the same.

HF: I am intrigued by a comment of Lynne Tillman's (related by Laura Mulvey in your 1986 *Interim* catalog) that in the narrative of the mother-child relationship in *Post-Partum Document,* theory occupies the position of the father in the Oedipal triangle—the "term" that the mother both refers the child to and struggles against. Is there any truth in this for you? If so, has the position of theory changed in *Interim*? How so?

MK: That's interesting. There's a sense in which I did think of *Post-Partum Document* as a kind of secondary revision, in psychoanalytic terms—that is, a rationalization or working through of a difficult experience. You could say this: that theory, like the "third term" of the Oedipal triangle, was the distancing device that made separation from the child possible, but this is simply an analogy. In another sense, though, you could say that psychoanalysis itself became the "third term" in the feminist debate, and provoked a separation from the mother's body—that is, the utopian community of all women—by providing a vantage from which to look at the tentative, constructed nature of femininity and sexuality. The Lacanian diagrams visually represent this "struggle" with theory, which was specific to that historical moment. Now, the terms of the debate have shifted. They're no longer presented as a confrontation between feminism and psychoanalysis, but as a struggle over definitions of feminism and postmodernism. So, the position of theory in *Interim* has changed; it has been assimilated and integrated into an accessible form in the narratives of each section. The question as I saw it when I started this work was how and to what extent had psychoanalysis become another orthodoxy. It now seems evident to me that the political complications of theorizing sexual difference go way beyond this, but I didn't have a position in advance. It's something I worked through, both visually and theoretically, in the making of *Interim.*

HF: How do you see this "struggle over definitions of feminism and postmodernism"? What are its positions, stakes, and strategies?

MK: I'll give you three disparate but, I hope, related examples. *Historia* repeats the image of an unknown suffragette, part cliché, part memento mori, and invokes, in place of the hysterics in Charcot's theater, the spectacle of women in the political "theater" of the early 1900s. Dora's mother again … but the implications, I think, are not simply that Freud dismissed his patient's "real" mother … yet another gap. He certainly knew of the existence of the women's movement—you can tell by the tone of his address to women in his paper on femininity, and there's his association with Bertha Pappenheim, who was herself an activist—yet there is a refusal to contaminate the new science of psychoanalysis with the issue of feminism. Jacqueline Rose has written a provocative piece about a similar reticence on the part of theorists of postmodernism in our time—[Fredric] Jameson or [Jürgen] Habermas, for instance—to acknowledge a certain debt to feminism. Psychoanalytic concepts are applied to questions of sexuality and representation as if the discourse was always there. No reference is made to a specific political formation or to the women writers who initially disrupted the complacency of the structuralist paradigm. Perhaps, like Freud, they've never made their "acquaintance." In the art world, especially, even in postmodern practices of resistance, there has been a tendency in some cases to "mediate" the issues into collectible artifacts. Even among women artists, there seems to be an attempt to obliterate, or at least disguise, any trace of feminist commitment. Politics, not sex, has become the pornographic referent in the field of vision. I'm not saying that art should espouse a particular ideology, but I feel it would be relevant … no necessary … in the present context, to try to make work that recaptured the historical dimension and the public ambition of the premodern era. I mean this in terms of extended audiences, and not just larger work. I always think of [Théodore] Géricault working on *The Raft of Medusa,* although that might seem like a strange example.

HF: No, it's a good one. We might see it now as official art, another of the great nineteenth-century canvases in the Louvre, but, in fact, *The Raft* was "historical" and "public" precisely because it was contestatory; it was a new kind of history painting which criticized the deadly duplicities of the institutions (political, military, and artistic) of the Restoration regime. The question is, where does one locate analogous critiques today? Granted the restrictive artificiality of terms such as "conceptual" and "feminist" art, one could argue that the contemporary critique of art institutions was initiated by the first and transformed by the second. In what way is a critique of such institutions—specifically the commodity form of the art object, its exhibition value—articulated in your work, particularly in *Interim*?

MK: I don't believe there can be feminist art, only art informed by different feminisms. The difference lies in how these filter through the work, which is essentially the difference between an appropriation, or colonization, and a "deappropriation," or decolonization, of images of the "other." In my view, decolonization depends on a specific contextualization of the discursive space that surrounds these *objets d'autres*. For example, *Interim* is not simply concerned with imaging the problem of feminine sexuality, but with the historicization of the debates that formed that question in the first place. For me, this approach seems to demand, almost intrinsically, a rupture in the paradigm of single, rather seamless, artifacts. Since the early 1970s, I've worked almost exclusively in the format of extended projects. Each work is divided into sections (*Interim* has four, *Post-Partum Document*, six) and develops over a number of years. Each section in *Interim* engages with a particular institutional discourse: fiction, fashion, and medicine in *Corpus*; the family in *Pecunia*; the media in *Historia*; and social science in *Potestas*. These all interact in specific ways within the institutions of art, the museum especially, which are fundamentally split between the demands of education, on the one hand, and those of entertainment, on the other. So, it seems to me that the way to critique the commodity status of the art object may not necessarily be to reproduce it in, what's assumed to be, the critical space of the installation—perhaps this is what's wrong with "the Levine effect"—but to question the very assumption of a spectator who is "supposed to know," meaning also, supposed to buy. I don't think the diversity of positionalities, of spectatorship, can be addressed by a neo-self-referential art of simulation.

HF: Since its beginnings in Vasari, art history has been discursively bound up with biography. Your work complicates the notion of biography, of the artist-as-subject, radically. Moreover, your projects—with their conversations, notes, graphs, and the like—involve extensive forays into the social, and you have mentioned to me the model of the artist-as-ethnographer. What are the ramifications of this model in general, and in your practice?

MK I suppose in a way my method of working resembles fieldwork—the participant observer keeping notes, writing up the results—but I was thinking more of the "new ethnography" when I said that. It's characterized by two things: an emphasis on the constraints of institutional power, and an interest in forms of experimental writing. This writing,

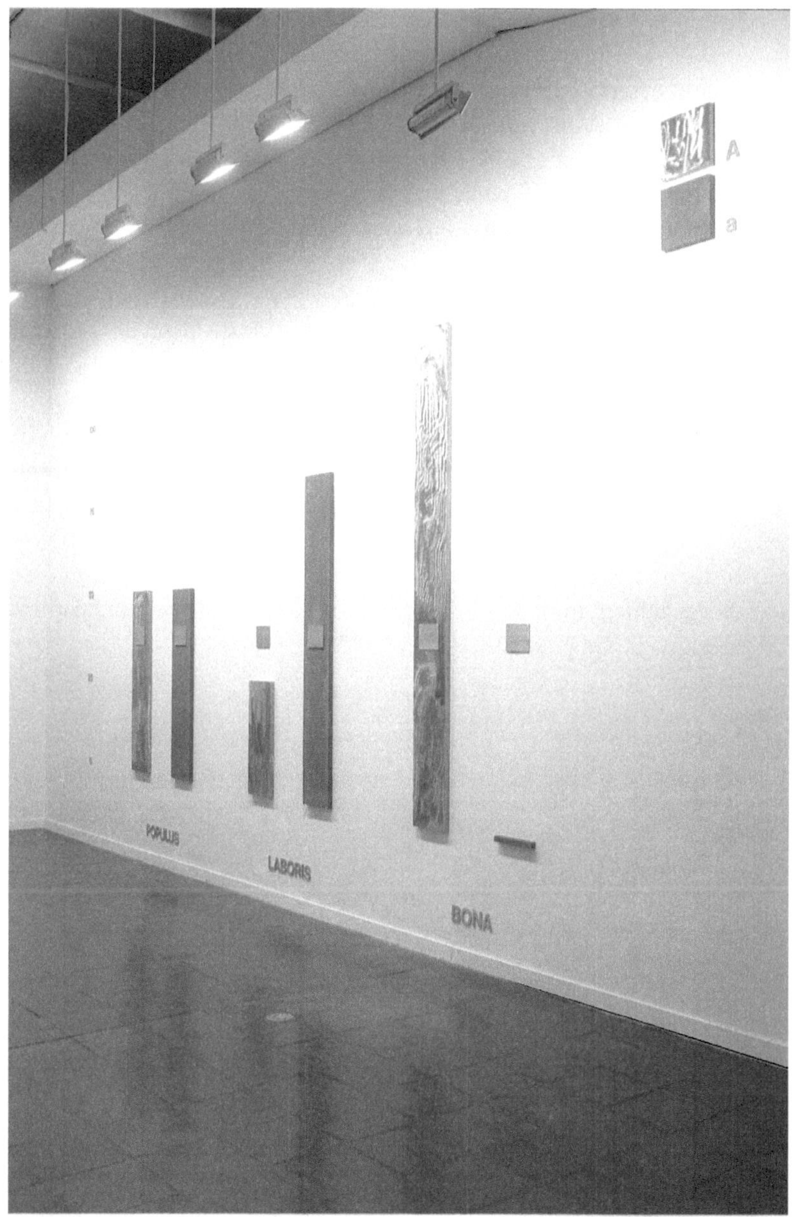

Mary Kelly, *Interim, Part IV: Potestas,* 1989. Etching, brass and mild steel, 14 units; 100 × 114 × 2 in. (overall). Installation view, New Museum of Contemporary Art, New York, 1990. Collection of New Museum of Contemporary Art, New York/Helsinki City Art Museum. Courtesy New Museum, New York. Photo by Fred Scruton.

James Clifford says, acknowledges that "identity is conjunctural not essential." So, if I am the indigenous ethnographer of a particular group of women, observing, as it were, the "rituals" of maternity or aging, I'm also, as Clifford points out, "caught between cultures, inauthentic." In the *Document*, as well as in *Interim*, it's the insistent polyvocality in the writing and in the use of media that somehow expresses this. I can think of other artists who use what I would call an ethnographic strategy—Broodthaers, Baumgarten ... maybe Rollins, Rosler, or Kolbowski—but I am thinking mainly of someone like Hans Haacke. His projects involve extensive research and deploy diverse visual materials in often brilliant institutional critiques. But I've always been troubled by the univocity, by the assumed authority of an artistic or ethnographic presence outside the text. Here I'm not advocating autobiography, but a kind of dialogistic, textual production, in which the historical inscription of the subject describes more than sexual positioning, it questions a particular relation of power. The significance of this attitude, or "model," as you call it, for me is that it leads to work that solicits a certain degree of active engagement in the critique of subjectivity. As for the ramifications in general, well, they're endless.

Note

1. Mary Kelly, "Re-Presenting the Body," in *Imaging Desire* (Cambridge, MA: MIT Press, 1996), p. 135. This text is adapted from a paper Kelly presented at the Institute of Contemporary Art, London, in 1987.

The Art of Analysis: Mary Kelly's *Interim* and the Discourse of the Analyst

Parveen Adams

Mary Kelly makes an exhibition of us. Though who we are I have less and less idea. The New Museum was showing Mary Kelly's *Interim,* which I want to try to think about through psychoanalysis and through the question of love and identity—that is, through the category of transference.[1] Now Mary Kelly's work has always displayed the question of psychoanalysis. There it is, in *Post-Partum Document,* in question and algorithm, making theoretical production and the infant's productions different moments of a representation.[2] In *Interim*, the psychoanalytic glosses are minimal. But my argument is that the fundamental situation of *Interim*—that of the series, the spectator, the artwork, and the fantasy of whatever goes under the name of Mary Kelly—finds its analogue in the analytic situation. I am suggesting that going to the exhibition is like going to analysis. Of course one is not a substitute for the other; I am not suggesting that you choose between going to analysis and going to see *Interim*. But I do think that the relation of transference helps to clarify what is going on in *Interim,* especially where the exhibition confronts that most delicate of issues, that of ways of going on.

Let me start with the famous question "What do women want?" As will become clear, I have nothing to add by way of an answer. I am not concerned with the answer but the question, the question which itself needs to be questioned. Indeed, what is a question? Who questions? Who answers? What kind of answer is demanded by what type of question? What does the question want with us? Who does the question

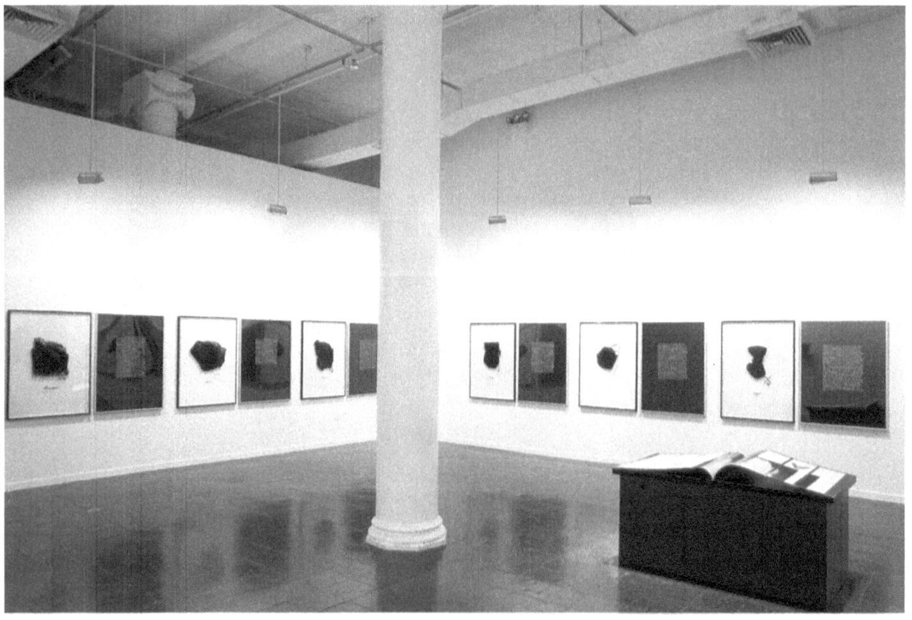

Mary Kelly, *Interim*, 1984–1989. Installation view, New Museum of Contemporary Art, New York, 1990. Courtesy New Museum, New York. Photo by Fred Scruton.

want us to be? How does the question want us to answer? What relation to truth does the question demand of us? For we can imagine the question "What do women want?" to be involved in radically different situations. There isn't one world in which the question is posed. We cannot even think about the question and its meaning until we think about the scene in which the question is posed.

I feel helped here by Lacan's notion of discourses as a way of thinking how even the same question can mean and imply such fundamentally different situations.[3] For discourses describe the structures of different social bonds. Discourse is a fundamental apparatus which is prior to and which determines the whole relation of subjects to subjects and subjects to objects as they appear within that apparatus. Lacan develops this conviction by constructing four different discursive apparatuses to demonstrate how much hangs upon the situation of a discourse and how little on the semantics of a situation. They are the discourses of the master, the university, the hysteric, and the analyst. Each of these is a possible apparatus that has entirely different effects upon the subject. When you are inserted into the apparatus in these different scenes, you are a person quite differently in each. For example, to be within the discourse of the master is to be within a fundamental structure. You can get a new master; you can change him for a mistress. It might be better, but you remain within the same structure. A change of sex doesn't undermine the place of the master, for that place is prior to gender. A structured change only occurs at the level of the discourse. Later I will suggest that what was on show at the New Museum was not the setting for the discourse of the master, or the university, or the hysteric. I will suggest that it was the setting for the discourse of the analyst, a discourse that structures the conditions under which questions and answers circulate.

But first we must follow Lacan's position in more detail. For him there are a number of elements that define a discourse, that is, the apparatus. There is the point from which speech is enunciated, the space of the *agent*. There is the point to which the speech is addressed, the *other*. When the agent acts upon the other, it sets up a third, the space of *production*. Lastly, any discourse has a dimension of *truth*. This space is necessitated by the psychoanalytic discovery that one does not know what one is saying. For a discourse to function in its own particular way, there is always something at the place of truth that remains masked. What counts as truth for the discourse itself is another matter. The four elements define the discursive machine in which the product is always separated from truth.

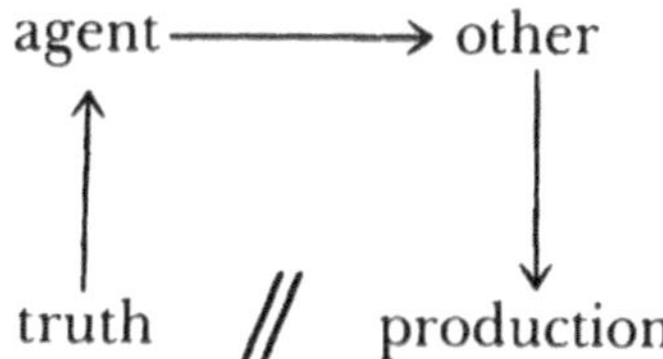

The person who speaks has to be fitted into this machine, and there is more than one way this can be done. We cannot talk of the person who speaks as a unity; we have to disengage three terms that mark the person who speaks—$\$$, S_1, and *a*. Let us start with a full subject S, and see how speech produces the subject as barred, for the subject is barred inasmuch as he speaks. Now, what is the Lacanian subject? It is a signifier. A signifier is a subject for another signifier. Let us call the first signifier S_1 and the second S_2. Although the signifier only exists through difference, S_1 is a single signifier. It is a signifier without signification; it is outside the chain of signifiers. This is the master signifier in the name of which the agent speaks. (Some of you will know Jean Laplanche and Serge Leclaire's paper on the unconscious, in which they locate the originary signifier, the S_1, in the signifier *licorne*, the bit of unconscious non-sense to which the analysand Philippe is subjected.) Now if the originary signifier is the subject for another signifier, it is the second signifier that engages the signifying chain. This is S_2, the signifying other. It is the place from where one speaks and it is also the place of knowledge. S_2 is the knowledge that S_1 activates. The subject, then, is represented in the relation of S_1 and S_2.

What has happened to the full subject S we started with? What has happened to the living body? In Lacanian theory, language deprives the body of jouissance, which finds refuge only in the limited zones of the body that Freud called the erotogenic zones. The entry into language produces the barred subject by depriving the body of jouissance. It is thus the origin of the Lacanian *manque-à-être*, the lack-in-being. Now what comes to take the place of this lack is the object, which Lacan designates object small *a*. In place of the original full subject we now have $\$$ and object small *a*, the complement of being of the subject. We have the order of the signifier and another which is heterogeneous to it. Which is to say that there is no signifier of object small *a*, the leftover of jouissance. There is a hole in the signifying network. Analysis is of course the talking cure. Yet this object without a signifier has a key role in analysis. And I will show that it has a key role in *Interim*.

The four terms—$\$$, S_1, S_2, and *a*—which I have just described fit the four places the apparatus provides to give us the discourse of the master, where S_1 is at the place of the agent, S_2 in the place of the other, and *a* is in the place of production. You can think of $\$$ as the repressed term in the place of truth.

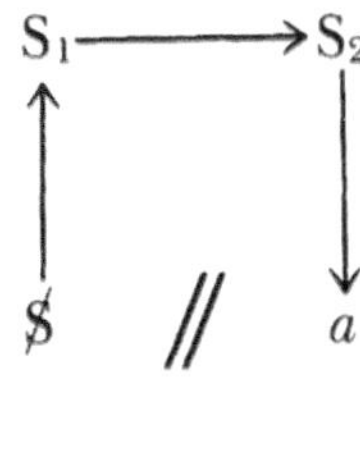

discourse
of the master

Now in the discourse of the master, the relation of speech introduces the social bond as mastery. But a great deal depends on how you distribute the terms across the four places which remain constant. If you rotate the terms counterclockwise through the four places, you get in succession what Lacan calls the discourse of the university, the discourse of the analyst, and the discourse of the hysteric. And being located in one discourse rather than another has radical consequences for speaking and being.

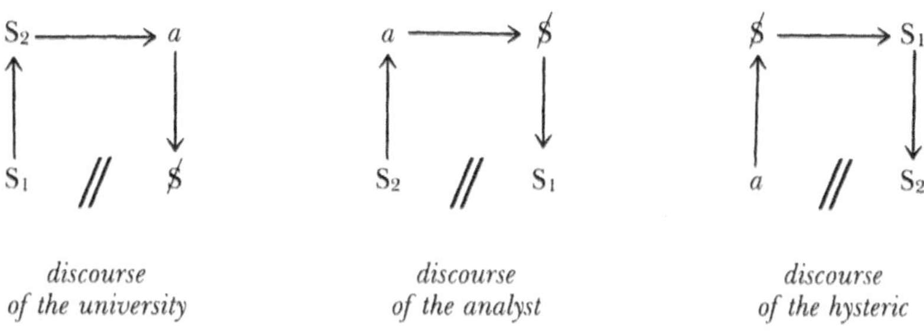

discourse
of the university

discourse
of the analyst

discourse
of the hysteric

Let us see how these diagrams might be read. Take the discourse of the hysteric. In the hysteric, the gap between subject and object is most visible, and she raises the question of the object that resists interpellation in demanding to know what her desire is. She addresses this demand to the man; typically, in the nineteenth century, to the medical man. You can see from the fact that the S_1 is in the place of the other that she addresses her demand to the master. The result is S_2, a knowledge about the hysteric. But the barrier between production and truth is here precisely the barrier between knowledge and object small *a*. The medical man can never succeed in telling her who she is; the hysteric forever taunts him and forever remains unmastered.

Now take the discourse of the analyst. Lacan often says that the discourse of the analyst hystericizes the analysand. The two discourses are only a quarter turn away from each other. You can see that where the hysteric was the barred subject at the place of the agent, the analysand is the barred subject at the place of the other. If we start with $\$$, the terms follow in the same order, but it makes a great difference that they have changed their place. Although the subject of analysis is hystericized, the impasse between medical man and hysteric is not repeated. Moreover, if the medical man was master, the analyst is not; notice that he appears in the form of object small *a*. Finally, what does it mean that S_1 appears in the place of production? That analysis brings to light the originary signifier of the subject is clear; the question whether this is a new kind of master signifier remains open.

Let me finish this brief account of the four discourses by performing an experiment. Let us take a sentence and run the same sentence through each of the discourses as a way of demonstrating the power of the structure of the discourses to determine the situations we find ourselves in. Let us take a famous sentence, "I am that I am," and let it be the sentence enunciated by the agent in each of the discourses. To begin at the beginning with the master, for that is where he always begins. God says, "I am that I am." Well, where does that leave us? He is announcing that he is the prime mover, not just as a fact but as a structure; or rather, the fact includes the fact that we are his subjects. He is the Way and therefore He is the Truth. Now let us move to the university. The professor lectures us with the example "I am that I am." The professor is teaching us the logic that if p then not q. He is teaching us about propositions and their relation to Truth. Logic obeys the Truth as *knowledge*; although the situation does not avoid the S_1 of the master stalking the lecture hall. In the discourse of the analyst, the situation is much stickier. Actually the analyst doesn't say, "I am that I am," but this doesn't prevent the patient from hearing it. And what the patient has heard finds an echo in his longing. "If only I could say that," muses the patient. Yet this is not what actually comes to pass, for the patient may come to hear something different at the end of the analysis; may, if he is lucky, hear the analyst's version of "I am that I am" as "I am only what I am." He realizes that the analyst does not have what he wanted and at last he can make his lack his own. In the discourse of the hysteric, "I am that I am" is of course a question—"Who am I?"—a question put in a thousand exasperating ways that unman the master who is supposed to tell her.

Our experiment demonstrates that the sentence "I am that I am" can run all the way from revelation to question. We see that what comes to the place of the agent need be no master at all, and what is more, that elsewhere the master does not always have mastery. But we have not finished with our sentence. What happens if we shift the emphasis from the "I" of "I am that I am" to the "am"? "I" is about speaking; "am" is about being. What about the object in all this? In the discourse of the master, object small *a* is the remainder, the leftover of meaning; in the discourse of the university, the object is acted upon and yields to meaning—the discourse produces the barred subject; in the discourse of the hysteric, the object resists meaning—you cannot succeed in telling her who she is; only in the discourse of the analyst is the object asserted at the same time as meaning.

It is important to my argument that the analyst is not the master. What enables him to abdicate that position is this fact that the object is asserted at the same time as meaning. In the discourse of the analyst, object small *a* and the barred subject occupy the places of agent and other. By virtue of this, the relation of the subject to the object can be worked on directly and modified, because there, between agent and other, is where the action is. What appears at these two places is crucial in the organization of a discourse, and if the discourse of *Interim* is like that of the analyst, we should be able to locate the spectator as barred subject and the artist as object in those places.

But first we must ask about what goes on in analysis to make the analyst appear as object small *a* and the analysand appear as the barred subject. I will call what goes on in analysis the textuality of the analyst, on the one hand, and the silence of the analyst, on the other. By speaking of the textuality of the analyst, I refer to the fact that he interprets, and that interpretation works on the analysand as the subject of the signifier. To the extent that it does, this interpretation does not, of course, produce the analyst as object small *a*. If interpretation were his only job, the analyst would remain the master, the subject supposed to know that the analysand takes him to be at the start. Interpretation per se does not make the subject any less subject to the signifier, and this is why the subject would be no less subject to the analyst who embodies the Other of language.[4] The analyst's interpretation draws out the signifiers of the subject's past history and puts them in a dominant place in the discourse. What was repressed yields to signification. So when the analyst detaches the subject's signifiers in this way, he reinforces their symbolic weight. In or out of the analytic situation the signifier offers shelter to humans. Signifiers supplied by social apparatuses yield humans the relief of an identity. The signifiers detached by the analyst are no exception.

The textuality of the analyst cannot be the whole picture. So let us look at a phenomenon of analysis that cannot be interpreted but that is crucial to the analytic relation, the phenomenon that brings the object into play: transference love. The analyst does not interpret transference love. But neither does he respond in the role of love object. Instead, he takes the form of object small *a* by responding with the silence of the analyst.

Let us start with the relation between subject and object that is found in transference love. We know from Freud that in love, the overestimation of the love object is the same thing as narcissism. The loved object yields the subject a narcissistic satisfaction. Now to say that the loved object is overestimated is to say that it is put in the place of the ego ideal, that place where the subject is mapped in an ideal signifier. This ego ideal is necessarily involved in narcissism because the ego ideal is the point from which the subject feels himself to be satisfactory and loved. In other words, a symbolic identification with the place of the ego ideal precedes narcissistic identification. Lacan explains this when he speaks of

> the sight in the mirror of the ego ideal, of that being that he first saw appearing in the form of the parent holding him up before the mirror. By clinging to the reference point of him who looks at him in the mirror, the subject sees appearing, not his ego ideal, but his ideal ego, that point at which he desires to gratify himself in himself.

The story that follows puts the point very simply: "Not so long ago, a little girl said to me sweetly that it was about time somebody began to look after her so that she might seem lovable to herself."[5]

In transference love, it is the analyst who is put at the place of the ego ideal; it is the analyst who is called to embody the capital I of identification of the ego ideal. It is from the place of the analyst that the analysand wants to see himself as satisfactory and loved. What this does is to make the analyst the master and analysis suggestion. It is what Jacques-Alain Miller mentions as the problem of clones—all the analysands who end up looking like each other by virtue of sharing an analyst.

How could that change? Put simply, the object has to be detached from the ego ideal. Because the object doesn't belong there. Let me explain why. We know that the analysand as barred subject lacks the object. What we have just seen is that he fills out this lack with the object that the Other, the analyst, is supposed to have. But this is to confuse the I of identification and object small *a*, cause of desire. You will remember that the lost object *qua* breast founds the Freudian wish. Lacan's formulation of this is that the lost object causes desire—object small *a*, cause of desire. The object comes *before* desire. Desire, which is always the desire of the Other, misrecognizes the object because when it pursues the object, it fails to recognize that the object is not in front of desire but before it.

Desire is in the field of the Other, and transference love merely increases the subject's alienation in the Other. Something has to happen to break the grip of the signifier. This something is what Lacan calls separation. The difference in the two operations of alienation and separation is given very precisely in Miller's diagrams.[6]

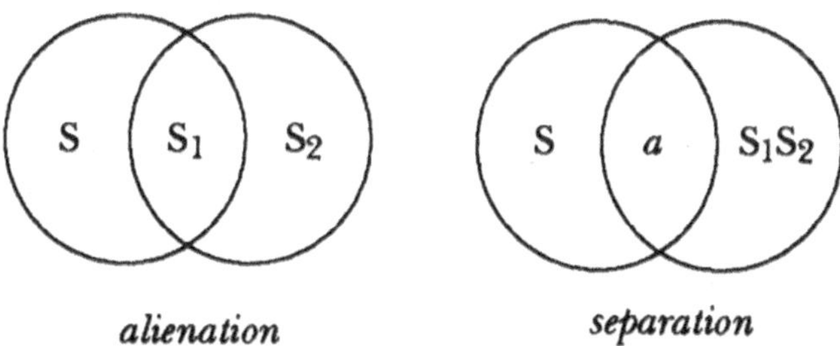

alienation　　*separation*

The diagram for alienation concerns the barred subject and the field of signification; object small *a* does not figure in it. In the diagram for separation the *a* appears in the intersection of the fields of the subject and the Other. But note that the *a* is quite outside the S_1 and the S_2 that constitute signification. What this diagram shows is that the Other is also lacking, that the object is separated from the Other, that the Other does not have a final answer. Here is the opening for the analysand: by identifying his own lack with the lack in the Other he can avoid total alienation in the signifier.

But for this to happen the analyst must fall from idealization and become the support of object small *a*; the analyst must embody the function of lack. It is notoriously difficult to pin down what Lacan meant by the desire of the analyst, but it is certainly something of this order—that the analyst be seen as desiring in the sense that the analyst also lacks. The analyst doesn't have it.

But how does the analyst show that he doesn't have it? By his silence. I borrow this answer from Michel Silvestre's paper on the transference where he describes this silence. I quote:

> Certainly not conventional silence, for it is indeed necessary to be silent in order to hear the other who speaks, but the refusal to respond there where the analyst would have something to say, but the leaden silence which comes to redouble that of the analysand, but again the mute question, anguished echo of the limit of the Other's knowledge. The being of the analyst is silent, through which he makes himself massive and enigmatic presence.[7]

It is only when the analysand realizes that the analyst doesn't have the object that he can live a life in which he is no longer completely locked into the desire of the Other but has a little bit of leeway.

My argument about *Interim* is that there also something of textuality and something of silence engage the spectator so that the relation to the signifier and the relation to the object are both in play. And that there also the place of the master is left vacant.

I linked the textuality of the analyst with the activity of interpretation that he engages in. But you mustn't think that interpretations work on some unorganized raw material. They work on a textuality of the analysand that is itself a texture of interpretations. You can see this in the dream that the analysand takes to the analyst. Even when it seems nonsensical, his very telling of it already involves what Freud called secondary revision. It is in this sense that textuality and interpretation are inextricably bound. There is no recounting of a dream that is not also an interpretation; there is no interpretation that doesn't represent a text. Even if we wish to retain the separation of text and interpretation as different functions, in practice they always come together.

Now pictures are certainly texts, and they come impregnated with interpretation, as if the truth of the painting is also there in the painting, the truth which is stated by the artist supposed to know. We all know the errors of referring to the meaning of the picture as contained within the authorial intention to mean. But what interests me is that knowing this argument doesn't stop our fantasies about the artist, not so much as a person but as a function, the vanishing point at which the picture and its truth would intersect as the source of the picture's correct interpretation. We may call this fantasy of the artist the ego ideal of the spectator, the place from which the spectator's interpretations may be felt to be validated. At this point, when it works, we do indeed think we are looking at a masterpiece. For the spectator, then, pictures are certainly texts that come impregnated with interpretation.

Before I speak of interpretation and transference love in *Interim*, I would like you to think of Aeneas. Perhaps you have forgotten that in one of the episodes of Virgil's *Aeneid*, Aeneas is a spectator before a picture, for he finds before him, on the walls of a temple in Dido's Carthage, scenes from the Trojan War. He is a special kind of spectator, one whose own past is laid out before him. The picture has an effect; Aeneas weeps. Does the picture just stir sad memories? Or is it that his story is being told? Is being told by one who knows, who exhibits the order of signifiers of arms and the man? In front of the picture Aeneas says, "Great valour has due honour; they weep here / For how the world goes, and our life that passes / Touches their hearts." His story is understood; he sees it as it is seen. Aeneas as subject of the signifier finds his past before him. There is a subject supposed to know, and there is interpretation. Aeneas says, "Throw off your fear. This fame insures some kind of refuge." Is it too far-fetched to say that this ordering of signifiers brings a certain peace of mind? Is it too far-fetched to say that this is the trust in the subject supposed to know that Lacan speaks of? Finally, is it too far-fetched to say that it is Dido, queen of Carthage, who is the point on which these effects converge?

For where there is a subject supposed to know, there is transference and transference love. Of course in Virgil we are told at length about how Dido's passion for Aeneas is kindled by the boy god of love.

Aeneas's passion for Dido is left unexplained. It is ascribed neither to her powerful position nor to her beauty. There is room to suggest that Aeneas's love is transference love. Transference love, we know, is real.

If there is an analogy here with the signifying side of analysis, it is clear that the ingredients on the side of the object, so important for an analysis, are missing. Dido is no analyst. Far from letting Aeneas liquidate the transference, she tries her utmost to keep him trapped in it. Dido demands love. So for Aeneas the object continues to coincide with the ego ideal and he tears himself away from Dido only when Jove himself intervenes to ensure that Aeneas sails away to fulfill his destiny in Italy.

Remember, we have been talking about the effects of a picture.

Now Aeneas is in trouble when he arrives in Carthage. Many of his ships and his men have been lost in a storm at sea, and he wants to know what he can expect in this strange land. The picture gives him his answer. And when you go to an analyst you also want to be told what things mean. Isn't there something of this when you go to see a picture in an exhibition? Of course the interpretation has to engage you before you set up a subject supposed to know and before there can be anything that can be called transference love. But then you do expect to be told about yourself.

This is what happens in *Interim*. I will speak of the inscribed stories of the *Corpus* section, stories which have been worked up from hours of conversation with feminist friends. The spectator can identify with the point of view from which these conversations have occurred. The spectator watches, if not her own history, then a history from which she can identify herself. The elements come from something like her history, from something in respect of which she has a history. The stories are not so much quotations as a selection of signifiers, where selection is always an interpretation. But the selection is not a collusion or a simple sharing. For an interpretation always involves discomfort, the recognition that something else is at stake, something other than what we thought we said. Indeed, sometimes the most devastating interpretation *can* take the form of quotation. Indeed, how can we more efficiently persecute others than by reminding them of what they have said? Not that *Interim* persecutes us; but we probably don't feel comfortable. I am saying that the spectator recognizes as her own the reference to worry—a worry over

Mary Kelly, detail of *Interim, Part I: Corpus (Supplication)*, 1984–1985. Laminated photo positive, silkscreen, acrylic on Plexiglas; 48 × 36 × 2 in. Courtesy the artist and Pippy Houldsworth Gallery, London.

fat legs, unflattering lighting, and so on. She may not like it, but she recognizes her subjection to these signifiers.

Now the grimace and the grin testify not just to the reference to getting older but also to something that lies behind this; what the signifiers represent is not just the wrinkles in reality but something absent behind the wrinkles. The signifiers hollow our spaces and intensify absences. The spectator realizes that signifiers are wanting; there is something that is not yet signified. In this sense *Interim* points to the absence behind identity.

Perhaps you go to analysis for a fresh identity; perhaps you go to a feminist exhibition to find positive images. Perhaps you go knowing that your identity is fictional and hoping for a new one. You make the same point as the philosophical critique of the fiction of identity, where fiction means error. But the psychoanalytic critique of the fiction of identity makes a different point. Psychoanalysis does not tell you that while your present identity is not really you, matters can be rectified by clothing you in more fitting attire. You pay your couturier for that original number that will express your identity, to run up something that is absolutely *you*. You don't pay the analyst for that. You pay the analyst for the dubious pleasure of the knowledge of the conditions under which that special outfit that we long to make our own has become the object of our desire. And that has to do with producing the place of the object as empty.

After all, what would happen if we demanded positive images? What is a positive image? It would be as if some images are in deficit of what we want to identify with as adequate representations. If that were so, we would want to escape from an order of signifiers that we could call a male order; we would want to free ourselves from imaginary capture by this order and construct, in accordance with a demand that might be called feminist, a feminine order of signifiers. This strategy would be to place on *Interim* the demand that we be captured by a feminine imaginary, the demand for a feminine gaze in which we might bask. Perhaps indeed, what *Interim* does is to whet your appetite for a feminine ego ideal, for a point of view from which we can feel satisfactory and loved.

But if I am right in drawing together the discourse of the analyst and the space of production of *Interim,* then this promise won't be made good. Certainly the analyst talks, and this artist makes images. And at the limit of the analyst's speech there is silence, while at the limit of this artist's images there is emptiness. They both function to refuse the imaginary capture by a positive world in which identity is *prét à porter.* They both seek to undo the confusion between the object and the ego ideal.

We have gone beyond interpretation and transference love. If interpretation were the goal of analysis, the analyst would simply be the master, and I wouldn't be trying to argue that the art practice of Mary Kelly is like the discourse of the analyst. But the analyst vacates the place of the master and becomes the support of the separating *a*. Where is the object small *a* in *Interim*? How can a picture interrogate the object of desire and interrupt the movement of desire in its misrecognition of the object? How does *Interim* move from the signifier to something that is radically heterogeneous to it?

Well, there are pictures that give us images as the objects of desire, and there are pictures that work at the limit of the image. *Interim* gives us the place of the object small *a* at the limit of the image. Which is to say, at the limit of the symbolic. You might well ask how you are to think of this limit, and I will answer by saying that you think the limit through the notion of an apparition. An apparition is both sublime and horrible; an apparition is silent, being outside signification. I think Lacan draws a picture of an apparition in speaking about the "*toi*" that comes to our lips in an attempt to find the signifier of the remainder, that which cannot be signified. The "*toi*" is a reference to the Other of jouissance, a primal Other, a presymbolic Other—a very different Other than the Other of language referred to throughout this essay. Now this Other of jouissance is precisely a reference to object small *a*, the lack in the Other of language, the object that must figure in *Interim*. The picture Lacan draws might serve as a model for us.

> How can we represent the utterance, the articulation, the surging forth out of our self of this "*toi*" which can come to our lips in a moment of disarray, distress, of surprise in the presence of something that I will not too hastily call death but certainly another singling us out, around whom our major preoccupations turn and who troubles us nonetheless? I do not think that this "*toi*" is simple. I think that in it there is the temptation to win over the Other, the prehistoric Other, the unforgettable Other who ventures to surprise

> us all of a sudden, and to throw us from the heights of his appearing. "*Toi*" contains I know not what defense and I will say that at the moment when it is pronounced it is entirely in this "*toi*" and not elsewhere that that which I have presented to you in *Das Ding* resides.[8]

I think this pictures an apparition. The Other of jouissance is awesome, silent, and threatening. He troubles us from "the heights of his appearing." His silence is the silence of the presymbolic, the silence of the Thing in itself.

Now let me tell you that when Slavoj Žižek, the Slovenian Lacanian, saw one of the leather jacket frames of *Corpus* in my house, he let out a yell of terror. Did I expect him calmly to inhabit a room with that Thing in it? It takes an apparition to perturb loyal subjects of the signifier.

How then does *Corpus* produce its effect? Take the images of the leather jacket folded in three different ways. This section called the Body hasn't a body in sight. The body of fashion, the body of medicine, the body of romantic fiction are all absent. Not a fashion model, not a dissected organ, no pair of ethereal lovers. If these images of the leather jacket, these looming presences, yield a body, it is the real body, the awesome, silent jouissance of the body. I am saying that the images of *Corpus* take the form of the apparition. When *Corpus* was first exhibited in England, the catalog carried an image from *Gray's Anatomy* that shows the throat in sections. Next to it was the second folding of the dress. The juxtaposition is startling. There is a decided resemblance between the folds of the dress and the muscles of the neck, but this play between the two is disturbing. The dress is not something that might clothe the neck. Nor is the dress a representation of the throat, for all the similarity of lines and wrinkles. When we look at the image of the dress we see neither a wrinkled dress nor a wrinkled throat. What we see are folds, wrinkles, hollowings, marks on the Plexiglas that take on a life of their own, a silent life, precisely outside any signifying network. This is the apparition at the limit of the symbolic. The field of the signifier is penetrated by something other.

Marks without meaning. We find them again in *Pecunia*. What is going on when we see a word like *Soror* punctuating the space of the gallery wall? From *Sister* to *Soror* to the string of letters S O R O R.

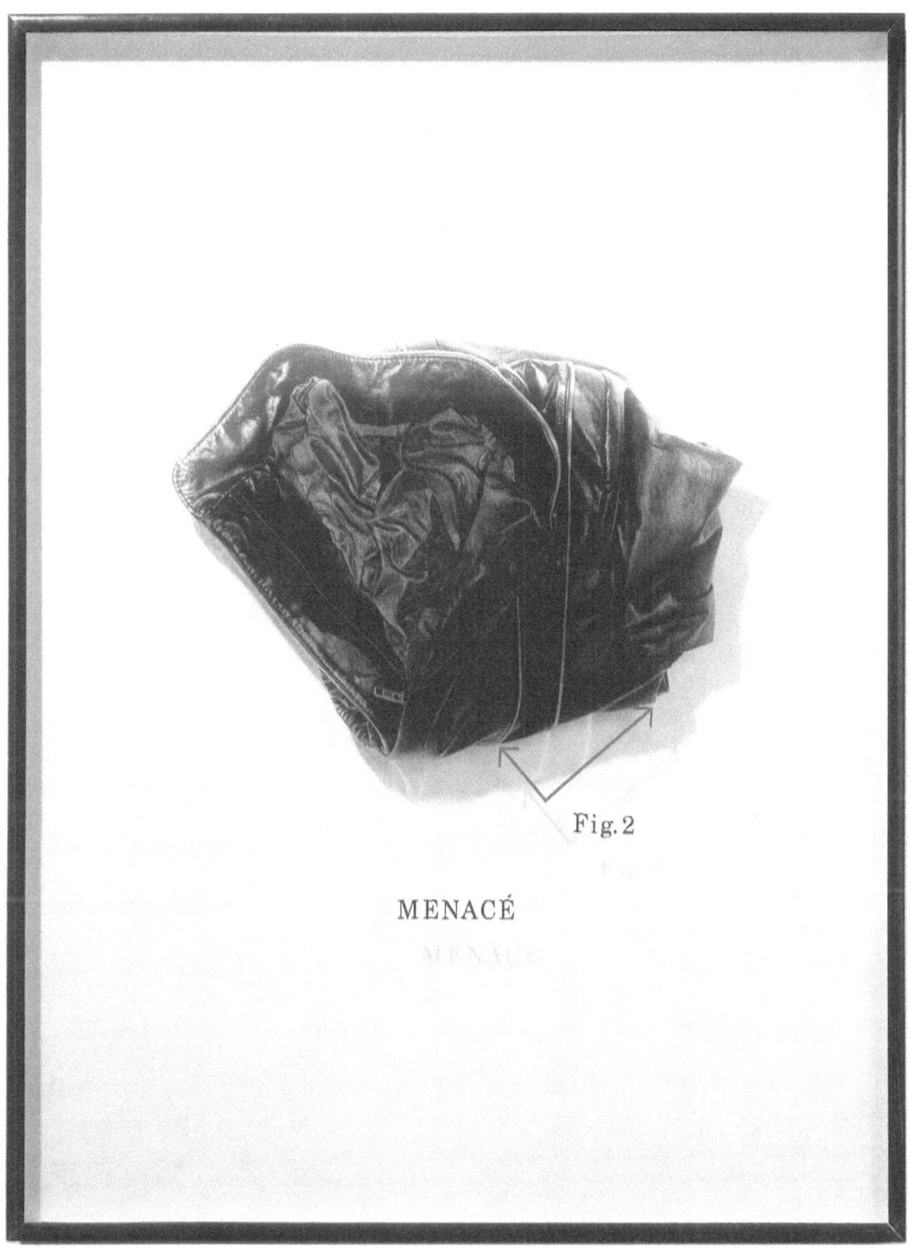

Mary Kelly, detail of *Interim, Part I: Corpus (Menacé)*, 1984–1985. Laminated photo positive, silkscreen, acrylic on Plexiglas; 48 × 36 × 2 in. Courtesy the artist and Pippy Houldsworth Gallery, London.

From meaning to the letter. From meaning to the dimension of the lost object. For the letter is a signifier emptied of signification; it is the signifier as a mark. We have here a signifier that is not articulated to a system but has the value of a distinguishing mark, a badge. You can also call it a signature, an X. It is like a hieroglyph. It is at the origin of the signifier, though it is outside signification; but on its other side it is the mark of the loss of jouissance, the mark the subject makes to mark the loss of the object.

Since I have mentioned the signature, I cannot resist the temptation to comment on the *mk* that is found under each of the images of the third set of foldings in *Corpus*, those which make reference to the discourse of romantic fiction. I found this most puzzling. Does the artist's signature endorse something about romantic fiction? Do the knots of the images tell us that Mary has it all sewn up? The *mk* troubled me—as perhaps it did you. Now I am clearer: the signature has the

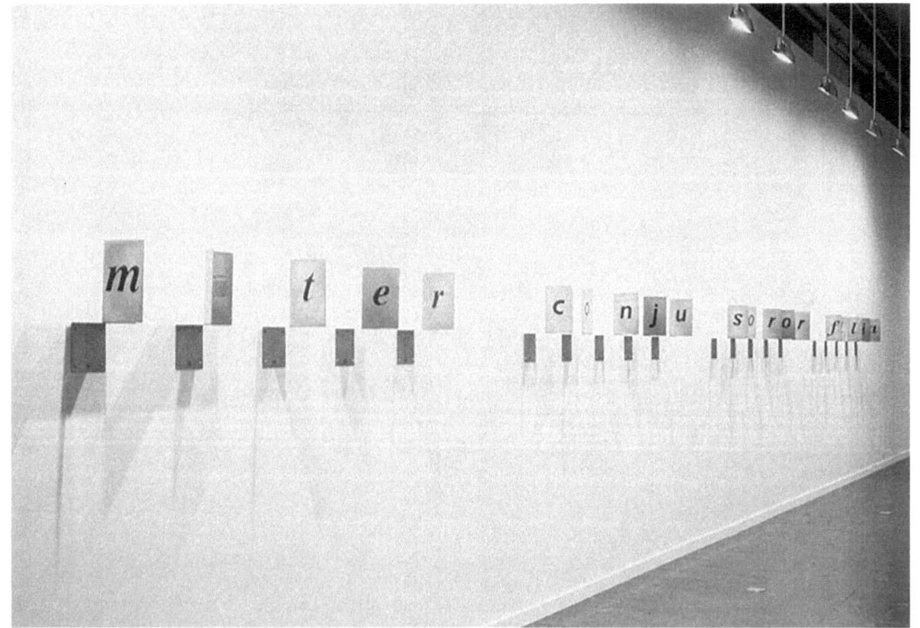

Mary Kelly, *Interim, Part II: Pecunia (Soror)*, 1989. Silkscreen on galvanized steel, 20 units; each 16 × 6.5 × 11.5 in. Collection of Vancouver Art Gallery. Courtesy New Museum, New York. Photo by Fred Scruton.

function of the letter that marks the loss of the object. But nonetheless, why do the letters happen to be *mk*? And why does the signature *mk* appear in *Corpus* at the point where there is a reference to masochism? For in the set of third foldings there is always a tying—the arms of the jacket tied around itself, the laces of the boots tying one to the other, the sash of the dress knotted around its waist, and so on. I do not think these motifs of masochism lend the images a masochistic appeal. This is *not* a positive image waiting to confound my argument. Masochism can be no more or less of an answer to the question "What does a woman want?" than any other answer. In masochism, the marks of flagellation do have an affinity with the jouissance of the body. But the masochist offers himself as an object of jouissance for the Other; he seeks to complete the Other. The knottings and tyings in these images from *Corpus* do not function in this way; they have the quality of the apparition that puts the image at the limit of signification. These images draw out the inconsistency between the object and the Other by emptying out the place of the object. Mary Kelly's signature endorses the apparition and the lack of the object in the artist herself: the *mk* in the subject supposed to image.

The artist does not have the object any more than the analyst has it. *Interim* does not provide a perspective from which the spectator can see herself as satisfactory and lovable. Without that perspective, what do we see in the mirror? In *Corpus,* the nearest thing to a mirror is the reflecting plane of Plexiglas on which are the laminated photo positives, screen prints, and painting. Of course you may see yourself shadowed in the Plexiglas; but what is vivid is the image in which you cannot see yourself reflected, the image pushed to its limit, and the empty place of the object given at that limit. The mirror no longer adequately reflects; it produces as apparition the object that cannot be reflected in the mirror. A moment of blindness—the artist's analogue to the moment of the analyst's silence in the talking cure.

These moments allow desire to emerge in the subject. The empty place of the object will come to be occupied by new things among which may be the work of art itself.

Notes

1. *Interim* was on show at the New Museum in New York during February–March 1990. *Interim* is made up of four major sections: *Corpus*, *Pecunia*, *Historia*, and *Potestas*. I make reference to the first two: *Corpus* consists of photographs of five articles of clothing laminated onto Perspex; each article is presented in three different foldings and each is accompanied by a framed text. *Pecunia* consists of four subsections, *Mater*, *Conju*, *Soror*, and *Filia*, each consisting of five galvanized steel plates with silkscreened texts.

2. This has appeared in book form as Mary Kelly, *Post-Partum Document* (London: Routledge and Kegan Paul, 1983).

3. The relevant seminar has been published recently: Jacques Lacan, *L'Envers de la Psychanalyse 1969–70, Le Seminaire XVII* (Paris: Editions du Seuil, 1991).

4. It should be noted that interpretation can also be conceived as a cut that produces the analysand as subject of desire. Through the equivocation of the analyst's signifiers, the weight of the presence of the object of desire emerges in the gaps between signifiers. So interpretation itself is one of the ways in which the full silence of the analyst is made present. In this essay, mainly for purposes of exposition, I contrast interpretation and silence.

5. Jacques Lacan, *The Four Fundamental Concepts of Psychoanalysis* (1964), trans. Alan Sheridan (London: Hogarth Press and Institute of Psychoanalysis, 1977), p. 257.

6. I am grateful to Mladen Dolar for this point, which Miller first made in an informal seminar in Paris.

7. Michel Silvestre, "Le Transfert," in *Demain la Psychanalyse* (Paris: Navarin, 1987), p. 76.

8. This passage is from Jacques Lacan, *L'Ethique de la Psychanalyse 1959–60, Seminaire Livre VII* (Paris: Editions du Seuil, 1986), p. 69.

Fetishism and Visual Seduction in Mary Kelly's *Interim*

Emily Apter

"How is a radical, critical and pleasurable positioning of the woman as spectator to be accomplished?"[1] This question, posed by Mary Kelly in an essay in 1984 and echoed by Griselda Pollock in her *Vision and Difference* of 1988, remains as vexing as ever in the 1990s. As before, the theorization of female spectatorship hinges on the old binaries: male subject, female object; masculine observer, feminine representation; active, sadistic look versus passive, masochistic stare; and so on. Seeking to circumvent these monotonous dyads, Pollock and others have looked for a reconfigured gaze in the work of paintings by and of women. Commenting on Mary Cassatt's *Woman Bathing* of 1891, Pollock wrote:

> The maid's simple washing stand allows a space in which women outside the bourgeoisie can be represented both intimately and as working women without forcing them into the sexualized category of the fallen woman. The body of woman can be pictured as classed but not subject to sexual commodification.[2]

Implicit in Pollock's sympathetic reading of Cassatt is the premise that the body of a woman that *has* been subject to sexual commodification is a body necessarily mediated by a male gaze. The fetishized, feminine Imago, conforming to a commercialized ideal of what seduces the eye, is thus barred to the female spectator. In this picture, there are no female fetishists.

Of course there are many reasons why feminist theorists have been inclined to distrust the seductive power of the image, particularly when that image historically attracts and pleasures the gaze by catering to a masculine viewer. The scopophilic look that fetishizes the female body through cutting, decortication, and hyperfocalization (all in an effort to thwart castration anxiety by placing in view a displaceable prosthesis intended to stand in for the missing female phallus) inevitably impersonalizes its object, rendering subjectivity expendable. Feminism has sought to constitute a theoretical ontology of the feminine subject just as it has sought to challenge the poststructuralist "death of the subject."

More recently, however, psychoanalytic feminism has pursued a slightly different course: rather than use the notion of fetishism to rehash the evidence of visual exploitation of women by men, it has sought to revise the androcentric bias within the perversions themselves.

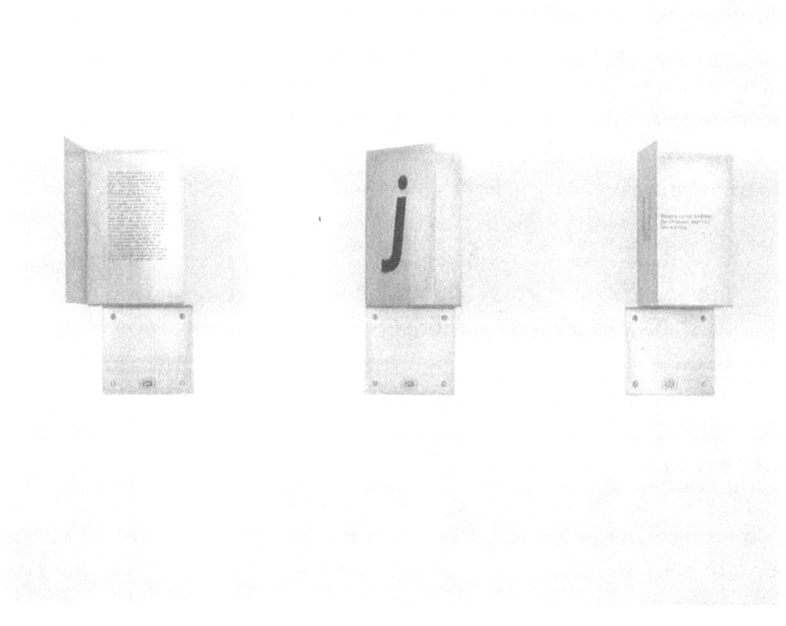

Mary Kelly, detail of *Interim, Part II: Pecunia*, 1989. Silkscreen on galvanized steel, 20 units; each 16 × 6.5 × 11.5 in. Collection of Vancouver Art Gallery. Courtesy the artist and Pippy Houldsworth Gallery, London.

Fetishism, with its implicit valorization of phallic potency, has, in this sense, been altered from within, but the politics of gendered looking, scopic seduction, and commodity fetishism remain far from being resolved.

Mary Kelly figures strongly among the critics (Naomi Schor, Elizabeth Grosz, Teresa de Lauretis) who have challenged the status of the male fetishist gaze by attempting to posit a female fetishism where none existed within classical psychoanalysis. Often their more experimental formulations have led away from simplistic equations between fetishism and visual fixation, and toward more nuanced understandings of what fetishism might come to mean in art and feminist theory. Certainly art, in its depiction of the female body, comes off historically as an essentially fetishistic enterprise, for it freezes into a prosthetic sham the so-called natural body of its subjects (particularly when this subject is female and nude). Against this, and explicitly antifetishistic in its rejection of painterly artifice, Mary Kelly's *Post-Partum Document* (1973–1979)—a museal gathering of intimate artifacts—nonetheless supplies a female fetishism that challenges Freudian psychoanalysis in its critical rereading of maternal cathexis.[3] Unlike many of her contemporaries who had used fetishism against itself (Ana Godel and Alexis Hunter, for example, deployed images of women's feet in high-heeled shoes to emphasize the dependency of male arousal on the shackling and bondage of, as Jean Fisher put it, "that part of a woman's body furthest removed from the head and therefore the personality"), Kelly's subversive move consisted in undermining and converting patriarchal psychoanalytical dogmas.[4] In Kelly's later installation titled *Interim* (1985–1989), female fetishism was returned in the assemblage of monumentalized greeting cards (*Pecunia*), bar charts of statistics on career women (*Potestas*), and plates commemorating historic turning points in the women's movement (*Historia*).

At the same time, the woman as consumer—a continuing motor of the commodity fetishism of late capitalism—was also placed in view. Meal plans, beauty secrets, shopping lists, and materialist fantasies formed a narrative counterpoint to *Corpus*'s striking series of photographed garments. In *Corpus,* sartorial ghosts were captured in Plexiglas boxes, their moody, feminine silhouettes—shoes in bondage, nighties and jackets anxiously tied up in knots—offering a chilling, masochistic beauty. *Corpus*'s riveting icons of femininity without face, of female bodies

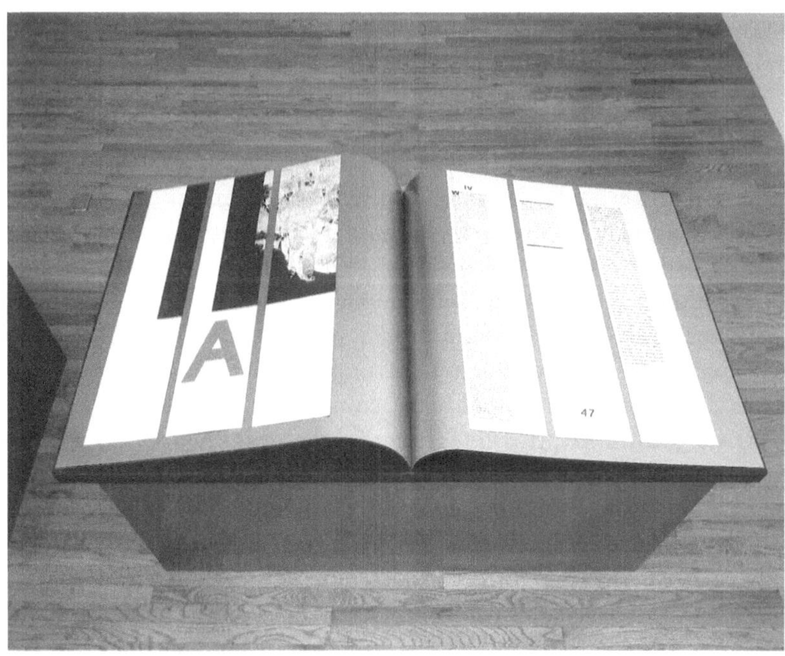

Mary Kelly, detail of *Interim, Part III: Historia,* 1989. Oxidized steel, silkscreen, stainless steel on wood base, 4 units; each 61 × 36 × 29 in. Installation view, New Museum of Contemporary Art, New York, 1990. Collection of Mackenzie Art Gallery, Regina. Courtesy New Museum, New York. Photo by Fred Scruton.

without breath, had the effect of bringing the allegorical representation of feminine seduction to crisis, to, as Parveen Adams noted, "the brink of visuality."[5] By absenting the lifelike female subject from the subject of femininity (just as she had occluded the photographic image of the child in the maternal reliquary of *Post-Partum Document*), Kelly made all the more visible the reifying regime of scopic masculinism.

Insofar as the "feminine" has been identified in Western painting with sartorial objectification, nonheroic or nonepic historical attitude, period costume, ornamental or domestic detailism, and so on, *Corpus*'s apparitional vestments constitute a hermeneutical perplex, for in refusing the female figure they retain that extraordinary power of image historically ascribed to the female body in painting. The lone, dumpy handbag, fixed in its case like an entomological specimen, in no way forfeits its plaintive call to the eye. Commenting on the spellbinding effect of these dressed-up fetishes, Laura Mulvey noted that Kelly "seems to have transcended the seventies paranoia about visual pleasure." This work, she wrote when *Corpus* was first exhibited in Britain in 1986, is "unashamedly beautiful and satisfying to the spectator."[6]

Yet has this "seventies paranoia" been truly eroded? The debates currently surrounding the reception of work by Mary Kelly raise this question directly, along with other more tangled theoretical issues arising from the relationship between what I am calling feminist antifetishism (a kind of puritanism of the eye translatable as *photophobia*, Karl Abraham's nomenclature for "avoidance of light" or the excessive "love of veiling" in a female patient) and visual seduction.[7] What I want to do is to move this debate away from certain rehearsed assumptions—namely, that visual seduction, in its complicity with male fetishism, necessarily makes for bad feminism—and to consider the problem in terms of the more complex relations between feminist politics and the aesthetics of femininity. I want to argue that there exists an optical sexuality deployed in certain works of art that unmasks masculinist ways of looking while keeping visual seduction alive and well. I want to argue for a recuperation of the seductive image (often flush with the image of female seduction) that escapes the brutalities of a commodifying fetishism, that successfully recirculates feminine glamour and desirability for the female viewer, and that "plays up" to the scopophilic hunger of the gaze without necessarily compromising female subjectivity.[8]

Interim catalyzes these dilemmas by asking the question, Can one seduce through an abstracted visual femininity while derealizing the female body in art? Many remain skeptical; indeed, at the crux of feminist antifetishism is the fear of what happens when the female corpus is left out. Reviewing Kelly's show, for example, Mira Schor faulted the work for its misguided response to the "traps of visuality." By criticizing ageism without actually showing aged female bodies, by "refusing to present the viewer with a seductive self-image" yet at the same time sustaining elegance of manufacture in the objects themselves, *Interim*, Schor claims, becomes mired in "inherent contradictions."[9] I think it safe to say, in response, that these contradictions are there for a reason. Kelly does indeed want to avoid any culturally fixated construction of feminine "self-image" (just as she would want to avoid what many feminists ask for, namely a "role model"). The seduction of image is left intact, but the seductiveness of feminine "self-image" (ironized through

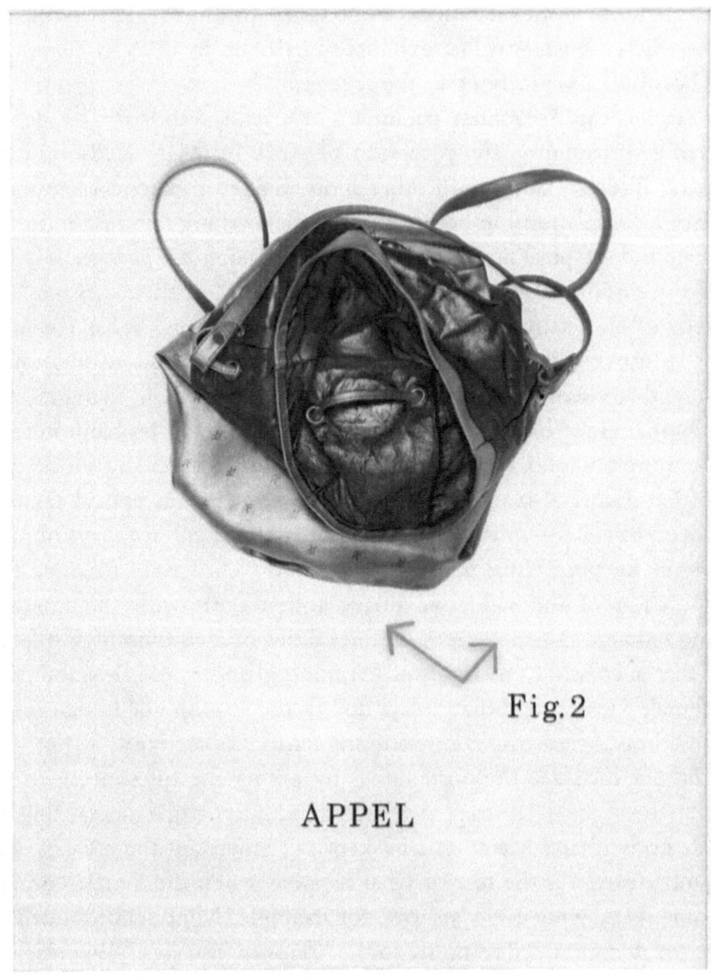

Mary Kelly, detail of *Interim, Part I: Corpus (Appel)*, Preliminary Artwork, 1984. Photograph, paper, acetate, pencil, ink, collage; 23 × 18½ in. Purchased by Centre Pompidou Foundation for Centre Pompidou, Paris. Courtesy of the artist and Pippy Houldsworth Gallery, London.

frozen poses and memorialized clothing) is subversively put into question. Placing "self" and "image" out of sync while keeping femininity and scopophilia in step seems to be one of the more interesting ways in which Kelly destabilizes a social gaze conditioned by essentialist codifications of gender, race, class, and age.[10]

It is in this context that one might situate Mary Kelly's presentation of object *a*. The algorithms, anamorphoses, and elliptical rhetorical conceits by which Lacan himself pictured the "cause of desire" or object small *a* are paradoxically corporealized in *Interim*. In *Potestas,* the letters of the Other, big *A* and small *a*, are raised up; they are embossed on the wall above the vertical bars of the career woman's narrative. The latter, alternately qualified as a "lack-in-being" (*manque à être*) or deficit of desire, is, strictly speaking, unrepresentable. By placing small *a* transparently on the wall, Mary Kelly has, in a sense, made an object out of a pure sign. Small *a* "*fait signe*," or "shows itself," but, of course, in principle it is never supposed to do this quite so visibly. Small *a* usually passes unnoticed, is "misrecognized," or is caught out in the barest flash "at the limit of the image," as Adams has observed—that is, in a tear, rift, crinkle, *Spaltung*, or bar. "I am in the picture. … I see myself seeing myself," says the subject. But it is precisely this narcissistic illusion of an ego ideal that Lacanian theory punctures on the screen through the punctiforms or little "nos" of object *a*. A figure of "radical subjective destitution," according to Slavoj Žižek, small *a* functions as a reminder that the subject will always be subject to primordial demand and doomed to perpetual separation from the object: whether breast, feces, phallus, or ego ideal.[11]

Corpus stages the uncanny "apparition" of this nonpresentified object *a* again and again in the creases of leather bags, in the striations of jackets in bondage, in the oleaginous lipstick traces of missed erotic encounters. Both *Corpus* and *Potestas* deal with the representation of object *a*. But where *Corpus*, in its erasure of the female body and scotomization of the commodified visual signs of desire, represents small *a* true to Lacanian form (that is, on the sly), *Potestas* in some sense breaks the rules by placing it too clearly in view.

Both *Potestas* and *Pecunia* put object *a* into play in a way that allows gender and the masculine pleasure of the image to be put into question. Drawing on an arsenal of psychoanalytic works by women, from Joan Riviere's pivotal 1929 essay "Womanliness as a Masquerade" to Catherine Millot's "The Feminine Superego," Kelly in a sense re-genders the Lacanian model of desire without returning to the body.[12] True to her disavowal of "woman's art" but critically feminist nonetheless, Kelly makes an art that doubles as Lacanian revisionism by unmasking the masquerade of femininity. For Lacan, as Jacqueline Rose has argued, "Masquerade is the very definition of 'femininity' precisely because it is constructed with reference to a male sign."[13] *Interim* rigorously records and dissects the genuflecting of feminine subject-positions to the invisible force fields of a male gaze, but the scenarios are injected with a politicizing irony that undercuts implicit phallocentrism. And in the hushed exchange of confidences from woman to woman, desire is diversified: feminine speech acts are eroticized, encouraged to be polymorphously perverse, sprung loose from heterosexualist *doxa*.

Orality and visuality converge and ghost each other throughout *Interim*. Kelly's use of language is visual in itself: her cursive script registers the ghostly tracery of the author much like the shadows falling beneath the empty clothes mime, nostalgically, the contours of a lost East Village fashion plate. She also uses foreign languages mimetically to distance the viewer from immediate verbal meaning. Refusing to translate J. M. Charcot's terms for the passional attitudes of hysteria, she activates the memory of early psychoanalysis, grounded, as she reminds us, in the French visual method of pointing to hystericized body parts. Plaster casts of the *pied tors* and the *pied bot*—indicative malformations of the hysteric's anatomical extremities fashioned by Charcot's assistant Paul Richer—were typically complemented in the 1880s and 1890s by scholarly treatises on the "hysterical breast" or the contracted "*pli fessier*" ("buttock fold"). The visual sign and its attendant verbal etiquette functioned, each for the other, as didactic pendants to the scopic regime of scientific method; and the hysteric's body, scrutinized in the textbook or on the amphitheater floor, took the *talion* punishment meted out by the male gaze in retribution for her overactive "masculinity complex."

Menacé, *Appel*, *Supplication*, *Erotisme*, *Extase*, these frozen signifiers also emerge as so many tropes, figures of speech that act out their lexical origins in Greek. Many tropes derive etymologically from roots designating specific physical attitudes; moments within the chorus, histrionic moves on stage. Insofar as these tropes refer to the gesticulations of female performers, we can read this hysterical talking *Corpus* as a model lexicon, replying to the demand of French feminists such as Luce Irigaray or Monique Wittig for a utopian, foundational, gynocentric language of her own.

The Latin inscriptions of *Pecunia* and *Potestas*—*Pecunia olet* (money smells) or *Populis, Laboris, Bona* (Population, Labor, Wealth)—also return us to the patriarchal language of Roman law: like institutional facades inscribed with hortatory sententiae or classical maxims, Kelly's gallery walls approximate a frieze of dead paternal letters. Coming from a feminist artist, the effect is countermonumental, a spoof on the name of the Father, a joke on Moses's tablets.

Finally, Mary Kelly uses the verbal medium to literalize allegories of feminine "interiority" and what Julia Kristeva has termed "women's time." When one of the speakers in *Corpus* says "the image grates," the trope is literalized in the little red grid or grating that surfaces on the shoulder of the leather jacket. As another female voice laments over (what bourgeois society sees as) the unsightliness of pregnancy in middle age with the phrase "It's not becoming to come," the image of woman trying "to be come," that is, "to be" jouissance ("awesome, silent, and apparitional" as Adams says), flashes referentially before our eyes. When we see the word *Soror*, it reads like a homonym of "sorrow" or a rebus in which the signifying "S" of the fragile feminine subject hovers over a figure of undecidability: "or ... or"—like the French "*ni ni*" of denegated repression and the Kierkegaardian "either/or" of ironical self-doubt. Even the signature *mk* subliminally sounds out the dominant consonants of the word "*m*aso*ch*ism"—that perversion which is not a perversion in women, according to classic psychoanalysis, but a symptom of woman's generically "passive nature."

The visual pun is particularly prevalent in *Potestas*, where it contains, I think, a specific reference to theories of the masquerade. At the top right of the installation, Lacan's big *A* and small *a* appear as a key coded to the vertical "bars" in rusted or polished steel below. The polished panels corresponding to big *A* sport brass plaques featuring narratives of women identified with masculine superegos: a female world leader, "a darling of third world democracy" (Benazir Bhutto? Corazon Aquino?), contemplates the spectacle of her presidency "thrust upon her." A faculty wife at high table wonders whether she should "spit out the olive pit or swallow it?" Big *A*, blessed with the appanages and insignia of power, seems to "be" the phallus, or at least to pass as a credible facsimile once she is armed with the dildolike accoutrements of power and money. She resembles Riviere's female masquerader defensively compensating for being phallic by impersonating a masculine ideal of the feminine ("she regards herself as a man who passes for a woman," according to Millot). Projecting her "femininity" as a camouflage, flirting with her male audience when she speaks at conferences, big *A* lives in fear of retaliation for impersonating a feminine superego, if such a thing were to exist (she apes nothing, but as we all know, "nothing" is "something").

In another plaque coded to *A*, the career woman avows that she is unsure of her license to play the role of the father. She says: "The proof was her receipt, but did she have a Driver's License?" Here, even the artist's poetic license is not enough; the female speaker can't seem to make good on the paternalist loan, even though she has repaid in full. And when she "presses her lips into a narrow line," this narrow line, visually reiterated in the brass bar below, doubles as a rebus of the "barred" feminine superego. The same *narratrice* also makes a revealing slip of the tongue. As she describes how she "looked at them as if they were … she was … her father had … her friends or someone would … tell them who was who," we hear not only the profoundly subjunctive tense of the female subject-position but also the classically repressed utterance of the female masquerader: "She was … her father …"

Here big *A*'s story interlocks with that of small *a*. The texts on the rust-colored panels suggest that *a* has a regressive tendency to return to an Imago of the pre-Oedipal mother. As Millot has argued:

> Identification with the father has as a corollary the fact that the paternal Other is reduced, precisely by that identification, to the status of a little other, while the mother is restored to the place of the big Other. Henceforth, the girl, identified with her father, will replay with her partners and with her own real mother, the history of her pre-Oedipal relations.[14]

We can see *a* enacting this desire to regress in *Pecunia,* where, as Mary Kelly has said, the woman's "archaizing of the drives," her coprophilic attraction to objects that smell, render her insensitive to the attractions of odorless capital.

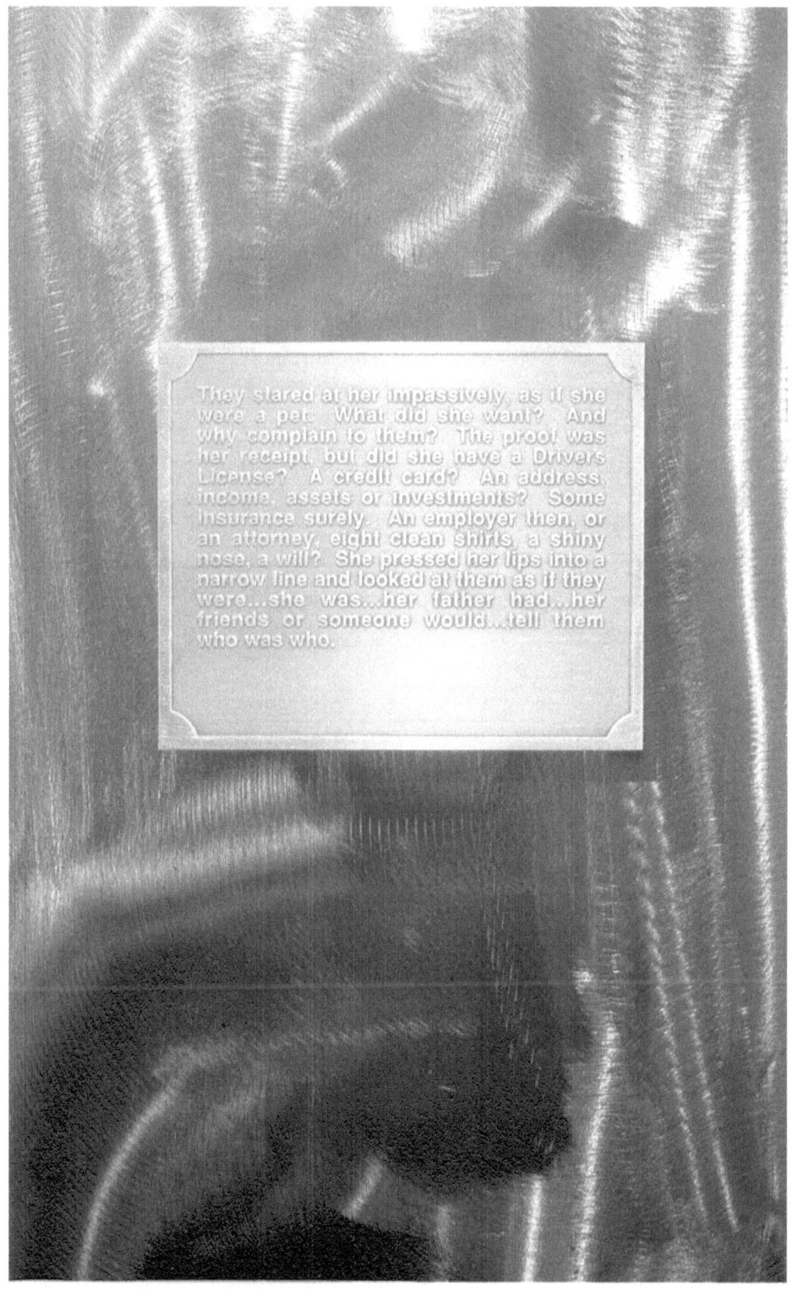

Mary Kelly, detail of *Interim, Part IV: Potestas*, 1989. Etching, brass and mild steel, 14 units; 100 × 114 × 2 in. (overall). Installation view, New Museum of Contemporary Art, New York, 1990. Collection of New Museum of Contemporary Art, New York/Helsinki City Art Museum. Courtesy New Museum, New York. Photo by Fred Scruton.

In *Potestas*, small *a*'s struggle against maternal identification through "virile display" similarly breaks down. An academic lecturer attempts to strap on a phallic image—"How do you get your curriculum vitae, vitalis, vitabilis to look that long?" The woman at a board meeting, failing to insist when her male colleagues dismiss her attempt to enforce affirmative action, "remembers Guatemalan money: on the bills, the women were bare-breasted." It is as if the stain of mother's milk has left its compromising blot on the "clean" medium of exchange represented by the banknote. In this image of the culturally displaced bare breast, we have a particularly apparent instance of Kelly's revisionist approach to Lacanianism: the gender-neutral figuration of object *a*—that "stand-in" for desire's value—is soldered to a critique of female disempowerment in the global financial market. Capitalist speculation and the specular inflation of masculinity within femininity are thus thematically fused in *Potestas*.

Mary Kelly's unmasking of the masquerader mirrors, furthermore, her own refusal to adopt the "mistress" position of the "woman artist." Her invisible female subject denies the spectator a "positive image" or "feminine ego ideal." This abdication of the mistress position may be interpreted positively insofar as it foils the construction of facile feminism. Kelly's "thick descriptions" of loss, like her histories of feminism's lost illusions, are difficult, but this difficulty is part of the analytic process, part of the work's layered hermeneutic.

Loss and lack commingle in *Interim*'s mysterious materialization of object *a*. The effect is one of what Lacan calls "retroversion"—a turning back to go forward. Adams describes this effect when she speaks of how "desire, which is always desire of the Other, misrecognizes the object because when it pursues the object, it fails to recognize that the object is not in front of desire, but *before* it."[15] One could say, perhaps, that *Interim* gives us retroversion as "retrovision"—a revisionist looking backward, a proleptic retroactivity ultimately leading up to death. In a late novel by Guy de Maupassant, *Fort comme la mort*, an aging mother experiences terror at having her face compared by her lover to its younger replica on the body of her daughter. *Corpus*'s sartorial ghosts may be seen as metonymies of just such a face; the creases in the empty clothes record the fault lines into which the youthful visage has disappeared. These wrinkles are shorthand for the death of youth and a prediction of the grand death to come. They spell out a "little death"—*la petite mort*, that

Mary Kelly, detail of *Interim, Part IV: Potestas*, 1989. Etching, brass and mild steel, 14 units; 100 × 114 × 2 in. (overall). Installation view, New Museum of Contemporary Art, New York, 1990. Collection of New Museum of Contemporary Art, New York/Helsinki City Art Museum. Courtesy New Museum, New York. Photo by Fred Scruton.

male postcoital melancholia which, when gender transposed, refers, as Adams has intimated, to the loss of jouissance. *Interim*'s object small *a* thus foretells *objet petite mort,* what Mary Kelly has designated, quite frighteningly, by the letter X.

In focusing our attention on the status of Lacanianism in the work of art, Kelly's *Interim* raises larger issues pertaining to the merging of psychoanalysis, feminism, and art practice. How do women as artists and spectators provide a critique of the historic gender bias of psychoanalytic theory without resorting to the essentializing frames of "femininity" or "women's art"? How does one dislodge the scopic domination of women in the clinic or on the couch through an archive of images themselves placed "under the gaze"? How does one perform gender or "send up" masculinity and femininity so as to unfix, ironically, the reified codes of sexual identity while at the same time preserving the pathos and sorrow of a "different" female body growing older? How does one seduce visually without fetishizing the female body?

As if in response to such questions, *Interim* undermines feminism's more paranoid reading of the masculine supergaze (if it is everywhere, then, by implication, *we* are *it*) by replacing the figuration of the female body with a scopic target which attracts; showing itself through history as "being seen," a figuration that opens onto the strictly nonfigural. Red lozenges, red circles, red grids, red check marks, red arrows, and red Xs direct the scopic drive to fixed points on *Corpus*'s numbed but eloquent sartorial subjects. These points—images of *béance,* vertiginous disclosures of that gaping chasm opening onto "what you want and cannot have"—remind me of the power to arouse ascribed by René Laforgue (Sigmund Freud's French disciple and rival) to *scotomization* (from the Greek *skotos,* a "darkness" linked by Freud and Laforgue to visual castration). Unlike fetishism, which expresses desire through the verbal disavowal of lack, scotomization proposes a *reticulated* affirmation of lack, an image that manifests sex appeal by calling out to the sex in the gaze. By this means, lack no longer need be read as synonymous with deficiency.

Kelly's red markers, launched by the image and lobbed at the retina, may be read as so many techniques of seductive affirmation set out to rhyme with the unconscious visual after-echo of red words. Reappropriating scotomization (from male psychoanalysis) for feminist purposes, transforming the visual cut into an eye-catching visual object, Kelly produces an alternative to those traditional aesthetics of the feminine subject that depend on the "photophobic," veil-enveloped masquerade. No longer do we find "woman" presented as a shadowy afterimage of the masked Lacanian phallus; in these photopositive Plexiglas panels slashed in red, female fetishism or scotomization is actively employed as a "cutting-edge" probe of critical vision rather than passively inscribed as a masochistic ploy. Kelly's speaking sartorial fetishes work through psychoanalytic conundrums that scopically ensnare while challenging the commodity fetishism of figural female bodies. In its shattering beauty, *Interim* constructs a nonrepresentational picture of the optical sexuality of women. And though the object of visual desire adopts no fixed or permanent guise, its strategies of visual seduction figure, in absentia, the glamour of a feminine subject.

Notes

1. Mary Kelly, "Desiring Images/Imaging Desire," *Wedge* 6 (1984): 9.

2. Griselda Pollock, *Vision and Difference: Femininity, Feminism, and the Histories of Art* (London: Routledge, 1988), pp. 88–89.

3. Mary Kelly, *Post-Partum Document* (London: Routledge and Kegan Paul, 1983).

4. Jean Fisher, "Object of Fetishism," in *Framing Feminism: Art and the Women's Movement, 1970–1985*, ed. Rozsika Parker and Griselda Pollock (London: Pandora Press, 1987), p. 323.

5. Parveen Adams, "The Art of Analysis: Mary Kelly's *Interim* and the Discourse of the Analyst," *October* 58 (Fall 1991); reprinted in this volume.

6. Laura Mulvey, "Impending Time: Mary Kelly's *Corpus*," in *Visual and Other Pleasures* (Bloomington: Indiana University Press, 1989), p. 149; reprinted in this volume.

7. Karl Abraham, "Restrictions and Transformations of Scopophilia in Psycho-Neurotics; with Remarks on Analogous Phenomena in Folk-Psychology" (1913), in *Selected Papers of Karl Abraham*, trans. Douglas Bryan and Alix Strachey (London: H. Karnac, 1979), pp. 169–233.

8. Jane Gaines seems to be making a similar argument in her "Introduction: Fabricating the Female Body," in *Fabrications: Costume and the Female Body*, ed. Jane Gaines and Charlotte Herzog (New York: Routledge, 1990), pp. 1–27.

9. Mira Schor, "Troubleshooter," *Artforum* 28 (Summer 1990): 17–18.

10. That *Interim* succeeds in destabilizing this social gaze for the male viewer is attested to by Norman Bryson, who in his catalog essay for *Interim* characterized as "diffraction" Kelly's refusal of a neat fit between vision and gender. See Norman Bryson, "Interim and Identification," in *Interim* (New York: New Museum of Contemporary Art, 1990), p. 26.

11. Slavoj Žižek, *The Sublime Object of Ideology* (London: Verso, 1989), p. 116.

12. See Joan Riviere, "Womanliness as a Masquerade" (1929), in *Formations of Fantasy*, ed. Victor Burgin, James Donald, and Cora Kaplan (London: Methuen, 1986), pp. 35–44; Catherine Millot, "Le Surmoi féminin," *Ornicar?* 29 (Summer 1984), translated by Ben Brewster as "The Feminine Superego," in *The Woman in Question*, ed. Parveen Adams and Elizabeth Cowie (Cambridge, MA: MIT Press, 1990), pp. 294–314.

13. Jacqueline Rose, *Sexuality in the Field of Vision* (London: Verso, 1986), p. 67.

14. See Millot, "The Feminine Superego," p. 304.

15. See Adams, "The Art of Analysis" [emphasis added].

Mary Kelly in Conversation with Margaret Iversen

Margaret Iversen and Mary Kelly

MARGARET IVERSEN: Recalling that historic exhibition in 1976 here at the Institute of Contemporary Art (ICA), when you showed the first three sections of the *Post-Partum Document*—in what was then the male-dominated arena of conceptual art—alongside works by Dan Graham and others, I wonder how you relate to Conceptualism now, if you still consider yourself in that tradition or are critical of it?

MARY KELLY: I don't think what I say here is the last word on the work. I usually insist that I am just another reader of it, but when I look at that historical moment, and especially 1976 when the work was here at the ICA—in a series of programs that Barry Barker organized, including artists like Lawrence Wiener, Dan Graham, Art and Language, Victor Burgin—it seems significant to me now that I used a visual strategy similar to theirs, but tried to turn it around so that it did not refer specifically to the institution of art itself, but elsewhere. That is, questions, debates from outside, were brought in to challenge it. I suppose this is where the confrontation between feminism and Conceptualism arose, and marked a turning point in the art movement, too, where it became something else.

MI: You are often referred to as a conceptual artist and also as feminist artist. Is that something that you subscribe to?

MK: I think the important way to describe it is to say I am an artist whose work is informed by feminism. The way that many people—not so much now, but in the 1970s particularly—tried to define feminist art forms, I think simply reinforces a rather prescriptive ideology. It is more interesting to think that there are many different tendencies, and that a work comes out of a specific history and addresses the questions in a way that is not at all universalizing.

MI: How did you come to the concept of your most recent work *Gloria Patri*? Did it grow out of *Interim* or was it prompted by the Persian Gulf War? What was the specific occasion for that work?

MK: Both. It was definitely the experience of the Gulf War that motivated me to complete it, but I had been thinking about it for some time before. Maybe I should say something about the organic quality, the project nature of the work, which takes up certain aspects of the earlier questions about conceptual art. First of all, I wasn't interested in producing a discrete object but in realizing a project over an extended period of time. It's a very familiar antiformalist strategy to think of all the ways of getting around the problem of composition, such as series, or system, or chance. But to place emphasis on the "idea" means that there is a real shift in the way that you visualize the piece. What I am aiming at in the installation is to get something which is not about style and not about a gestalt of form but an accumulated sense of these different visual events that really hits you later, a kind of delayed reaction. I think this also comes from film and my interest in what I call the "narrativization of space." It's not just that I use narrative in the work; I am also interested in the way the spectator can be drawn into the space and involved in the experience of real time. Only secondly am I concerned about the way a conventional narrative can operate in that space. For example, it is not just a literal reading of the text, as there are a lot of other things happening in your peripheral vision, especially in this installation; trophies, for instance, which are slightly out of your eye line when you're reading the shield; and also, way above you, there are other kinds of slogans that you are taking in at the same time. I don't think this is at all like reading something which is in a book. It's only in the context of reading in the installation that the writing has its full effect. For me, there is such an organic relation between visualizing and theorizing that I have a hard time saying what comes first. It's certainly not a matter of defining the theoretical issues in advance and then, say, simply illustrating them. It is more a matter of discovering, in the process of doing the work, what these issues are. So in *Post-Partum Document*, in looking at the question of the mother's desire, the mother's relation to the child, I focused on the construction of femininity as maternal. But it was obvious to me, when I was making this work, that there is so much that is left out: all the other moments in a woman's life, and the question of postreproductive women in particular. This made me look at how a woman would configure her desire—her narcissistic pleasure or whatever—outside of that maternal relation. By raising a whole range of questions to do with money and power and history, this investigation seemed to have excavated a psychic disposition which was deeply troubled by the idea of being like a man: the hysteric's dilemma could, in fact, be posed, "Am I a woman or am I a man?" The next step logically would be to examine the construction of masculinity. So in *Gloria Patri*, this is what I was concerned with: to look, not at the construction of femininity, but at how masculinity functions for the woman.

MI: You seem to be saying that you started with the story that comes last in the series: the woman's story. The exercise scene described in the *Gloria Patri* text illustrates the masculine ideal that the woman adopts. It became evident, then, that this was going to be a question while you were working on *Interim*.

MK: Yes, you have just reminded me that there is a certain reversal, not only in this work, but in the whole trajectory of my work, that I hadn't really thought about before, in that I started with what is, in a sense, less visible in Western culture. Certainly, representations of the mother have been absent since the nineteenth century in any explicit way. What I've ended with is an exploration of what is most visible in terms of, I suppose, a quality of masculine display or a certain form of masculine ideal that this work represents. It's very present, very consuming. But at the same time, it suggests a kind of underside: a repression of the feminine that had been the topic of the works before.

MI: There is a documentary aspect to your works: you research them, in an ethnographic way. For *Interim*, you interviewed many women and studied women's magazines. Was there any similar empirical research which was important in the making of *Gloria Patri*?

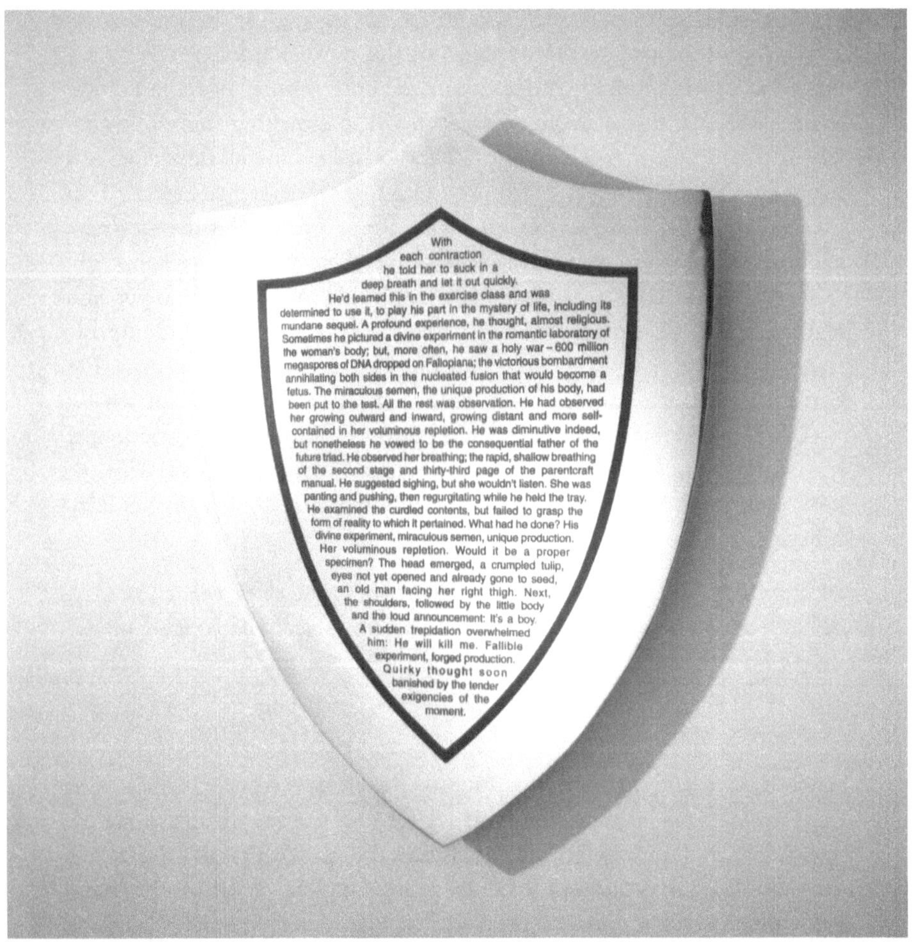

Mary Kelly, detail of *Gloria Patri* (shield 1 of 5), 1992. Etched and polished aluminum; 29 × 24 × 2.25 in. Photo by Kelly Barrie. Courtesy the artist and Pippy Houldsworth Gallery, London.

MK: What I refer to as the "ethnographic" part of this appears in the etched plaques which have quotation marks on the trophies. It was during the Gulf War that I heard soldiers, both men and women, making their comments on the war, and I was very struck with the range, from something incredibly inane like "Gosh, not enough Gees and Gollies to describe this," to something very sinister—"Well, we have to cut it off and kill it." So this constitutes the backdrop—for observation, so to speak.

MI: What about previous works of art? I know you have mentioned a painting by Géricault as being pivotal in your thinking about the precariousness of masculinity.

MK: Yes, I was thinking specifically of Géricault's *Charging Chasseur.* But this takes me back to some more involved thoughts on the Gulf War: how it was presented as a spectacle on television and the foregrounding of the technology involved. I will get back to Géricault in a minute. I was interested, first of all, to present masculinity as something that becomes pathological predominantly in the historical and cultural context of war: something to which Adorno referred, between the two world wars, when he said there is a certain gesture of virility which should be regarded with suspicion. A more recent writer, Klaus Theweleit, in *Male Fantasies*, describes the protofascist organizations of the thirties and says there is a certain construction of this totality, which he calls the troop machine, made up of soldiers, men who lose their individuality in the process of becoming a kind of hard exoskeleton, poised to confront the other. He also suggests that as a means of expression, this totality presents itself as straight lines and hardened geometric shapes. As I was thinking about how the work would represent this materiality, well, it had to be polished aluminum. When I saw the prototype for the shield, I knew it was right, because the surface practically made me sick it was so severe. Theweleit goes on to say that the troop machine actually sets the stage for other types of totalities, like the nation. And of course, the national crisis facing the United States as a military force immediately paralleled for me what Géricault saw in the crisis of the Napoleonic Empire at the time he painted the awkwardly mounted soldiers. Writing about the Gulf War, Noam Chomsky said that the United States no longer had a diplomatic role in the world. It had entered an era of alienation, especially in the Middle East, where it couldn't really use diplomacy in the same way. There was also the problem of its economic position, which was certainly by no means what you could call dominant, although this is a more complex question. So all it had was military force. Now this meant, I thought, that you had a really ironic situation: where the United States was producing this war hysteria filtered through a facade of efficacious militarism, and at the same time, the world in general was entering a period of demilitarization at the end of the Cold War.

So I wanted something that would communicate this facade: everything two inches off the wall—you know, even the trophies had to be "faux"—they couldn't be "in the round." It was very much like the surface of the thing that you see on television: the spectacle that the media presented. It just seemed incredible that all the protest about the war suddenly faded away when they took the vote in the House and in the Senate, then everyone brought out the yellow ribbons and decided they had to back it. You had this instant production of nationality and with it a certain masculine ideal which had already shown itself to be problematic. So if you take that historical stage and you pose against it what I was saying about the soldiers' comments, here they are supposed to be managing this incredibly complex technological machine and all they can say is "Not enough Gees and Gollies to describe it." Then you can see how vulnerable and how human they are. It is nothing like the fascists of the 1930s; it has become a parody. And then you have to add to that another dimension, which is that here we had women for the first time in the military, and they were demanding the right to go to the front, to have the right to kill, and at the same time, gay men were protesting their exclusion from ROTC. But once you have women, or gay men and lesbian women, in the military, it can no longer really function in the homogeneous or hegemonic way it once did, because it has already become more heterodox: it's ruined, it's absolutely ruined as an ideological tool in some sense, and this is what really interested me.

To get back to Géricault, I was hoping that when you went into the installation, at first there would be a fascination with this facade of militarism. But then, when you came closer and read the stories, it would be like the soldier falling off his horse, because each story sets up a scene of mastery only to completely undo it. The plot doesn't work, and the spectator's relation to the installation is a bit like that, too, because you don't expect the stories to be so sympathetic when everything else about the work is a bit forbidding.

MI: Also, the stories aren't about war itself.

MK: No, they're everyday situations which invoke different kinds of vulnerability, showing the impossibility for the man of living out, as it were, that mode of the masculine.

MI: Could we talk a little more about the visual form of the work? You mentioned earlier that you didn't want to be locked into a particular style or to approach the work in those terms, and that you start out with a certain set of ideas and perhaps some metaphoric connotations that are associated with certain kinds of films and materials.

MK: The visual references in *Post-Partum Document* are very personal, because I was dealing with a notion of fetishism for the woman; but with *Interim*, I was interested in a certain form of narcissism and an engagement with images from popular culture. So in *Interim* the materials change—for example, deciding to use photo laminates instead of the found objects. To place them in a way that was much more evocative of public space, in scale and in relation to the body, was important. But there are ironic references to certain forms of minimal sculpture, too, in *Interim*, such as the David Smith or Richard Serra "effect" in the *Potestas* section, or in *Historia*, when I used the rolled-steel pages of the book, I often thought about [Anselm] Kiefer's piece called *Women of the Revolution*. I was determined to write a different sort of history—one that wasn't closed or heroic but rather could be seen as a continuing process, and which was concerned specifically with the history of the women's movement. Even though I draw from popular culture, I think what distinguishes not just my work but that of many British artists who have used images from popular culture is that I never directly appropriate without using what Stephen Heath calls the "strategy of depropriation," something that suggests a decolonization of the image.

In *Gloria Patri*, when I made the montages for the discs which appear in the upper register of the gallery, I had such a great time because I found these pristine military logos and then I got to cut them up. I decided it was going to be restricted to cutting two in half, the minimal slice as I call it, and then exchanging them. I didn't let myself get involved in composing; there is just a simple juxtaposition, but enough to make an ironic comment, I hope.

MI: I thought it had the effect of obfuscating the symbols, so that you had to struggle slightly to decipher them, as you would with a Cubist painting. Also, because some of the military logos incorporated, say, an eagle or a lion, when collaged in this way they form peculiar hybrid creatures. I thought there might be a reference to them, or back to them, in one of the stories about the distorted reflection.

MK: I don't mind if that happens; that makes it productive from the point of view of the spectator. But it certainly is not my intention to make some complex, extremely metaphoric setup there but to make this intervention evident, and to use the placement of the logos (which is very high up in the gallery space) something to suggest the force of those institutional references. It worked very well at Cornell, because the ceilings were thirty feet high, and also because the university itself had so many emblems and logos of a similar type. In the ICA space, it is slightly more domesticated in terms of the architecture that surrounds it.

MI: You don't usually include iconic figures, but there are these trophy men who are carrying the letters of the Gloria, which reminded me of that marvelous figure in the Rockefeller Center, of Atlas bearing a globe.

MK: That's right, they don't make those figures anymore; they come from the 1950s, and I liked them because they were as anachronistic as the whole military project of the United States at that time. Having them carry the letter of Gloria, you could say, "What price glory?"

MI: What about the lighting? I found that very striking as well. Is it intended to evoke some kind of military scenario?

MK: I think it does indirectly, because it contributes to that facadelike spectacle, but when it is projected onto the trophies, the effect is one of casting the letters into a three-dimensional space. Ever since *Post-Partum Document,* when I stopped using the found object, I felt I had to find some way to bring back the quality of the index. It is interesting that you brought up the problem of images, representational images, because I'm often thought of as someone who never uses any. In *Post-Partum Document,* I placed a lot of emphasis on the indexical sign, but in *Historia*

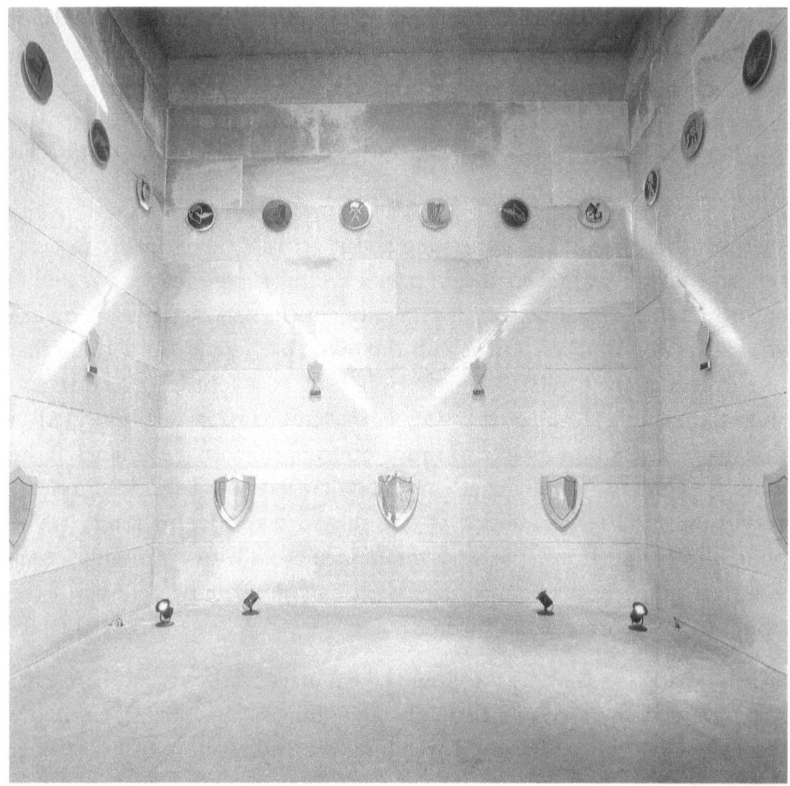

Mary Kelly, *Gloria Patri*, 1992. Etched and polished aluminum, 5 shields, 6 trophies, 20 discs; 5 shields: each 29 × 24 × 2.25 in. / 6 trophies: each 26 × 8 × 2 in. / 20 discs: each 17 in. (diameter). Installation view, Ezra and Cecile Zilkha Gallery, Wesleyan University, Middletown, Connecticut, 1992. Courtesy the artist and Pippy Houldsworth Gallery, London.

and in *Corpus,* there are in fact quite a few references to iconic images. What I like to insist on, though, is that it's important not to reduce the image to the iconic sign but to see it as a heterogeneous system of symbol, or icon and index. Obviously, in *Gloria Patri* you do have minimal iconic properties—the trophies, for instance, which are the closest you get to some figurative element. But in the logos you have a diagrammatic representation—a hybrid kind of symbol—so against that, against the hardness of that form of visual experience, the indexical quality of the light seemed important to me. Just as it did in *Corpus*—something that was contingent on the particular installation. The way the spectators get caught in the light when they go up to the shields, or the kind of reflections that you get from the lighting and from your own reflection in the piece, means that the work can be negotiated in different ways. I think I referred to that earlier: I am not just interested in what you read but in the affective force of what you are experiencing while you are reading it.

MI: I just thought I'd say something about actually being in the installation and how I was taken aback; it was a similar experience, but different, to having seen one's own reflection in the *Corpus* series. You see your reflection through and against the text. But here it's something that one immediately wants to resist, so at least as a female spectator you almost want to get out of the way so that your image isn't reflected in that shape. I would now like to move on from the visual elements of the work to your use of language and verbal metaphor. I think you are a very interesting writer, and that one should take care to listen to the puns, the connections, the way the stories are all very carefully composed. If you feel it's appropriate, perhaps you would read one of the stories to us before we talk further.

MK: "Ignoring the trail, he'd followed a tributary to the river. Sharp currents gouged their course through ferruginous clay, spalling iron ore from the bank where he stood watching the endless flow of water over the rocks: like a tap left on, he thought. That was ideal. It would trap the insects, flushing them down into still pools. There, the trout would be waiting, and he would be too, with bated breath, a snelled hook number four, and a wet fly. No weights or clips. He'd present the bait naturally, that way it would be carried with the current under the stones to the enemy's intimate entrenchment. They spooked easily and he stalked them with a delicate belligerence. Wading upstream, he stirred the sediment and his expectation swelled. He knew they were there. Sometimes he would catch a glimpse of them: scarlet gills, dark fingermarks on the silver side and a white underbelly. He longed to touch one, to feel it, wet and slippery, struggling, its life in his hands. He could do whatever he wanted: cut it up and eat it, or throw it back. When he pulled a hook through the tender flesh, it felt like the point of a sharp phrase that turned an argument in his favor, or the butt of a joke about big cocks and virgins. Lively but short-lived; a brook trout was fragile and delicious. Still, he would probably release it. Just to touch it, that would be enough. He would be satisfied. When a man touches a fish, he reflected, he touches something far away, something *real*. Nearby something gray and white and beaky watched him or his tackle, which one, he wasn't sure. Four feet high, black plumes behind the eye; a heron, possibly a Great Blue, waited to purloin his catch. Its canny presence moved him to observe the wilderness more keenly. The tangle of berries, the dank air, the soft earth, the scent of pine needles freshly crushed. It was life-sustaining, but at the same time threatening. Instinct poised, he prepared to meet the challenge before him, or after him as the case might be. His crested rival, moving closer, eyed the tuftless dibbler who, looking at himself in a watery reflection, saw the body of a beast and the head of a man at the mercy of his own imagination: then it shuddered and let out a raucous 'grak.'"

MI: I read this story as having two parts: the first part is a fantasy of mastery over nature, and of an imagined natural hierarchy of the fly, the trout, and then the man. You anticipate what is going to happen when you say he has "bated breath": he is caught in some kind of lure or fascination with an image of the great white fisherman. The mood completely changes when the bird is introduced and the man becomes objectified as a "tuftless dibbler." He then looks at his reflection in the river, which is all fragmented. There is also the issue of sadism. Was that part of your idea?

MK: Yes, there's an implicit heterosexual sadism being played out metaphorically. Each story has a different function in terms of the fantasy of mastery it explores. In contrast to this one, there is another story where the man is witnessing the birth of the child, so it's asking a question about his stake in paternity. Or in the baseball story, it's much more about the man's homoerotic relation to other men, also his loss of control, about his age and his body. But it is overdetermined by his class position, and by what he represents as an unemployed man in a specific social context. Then, probably surprising, the fourth one is about an adolescent boy who listens to Nine Inch Nails (industrial/techno), which locates him in a way as dissatisfied, white, and working class, but his idea of mastery is primarily one that's associated with transgressing his mother's desire. This is interesting when you think about the bad boy/bad girl image in art, too. You know how it's just the other side of the authoritarian coin, because it is only when you're positioned within that ideal—which is constitutive of a certain masculine identity—that you compose yourself either as the law or as breaking it. In a certain sense, the feminine term falls outside of it, not literally, but in terms of this negotiation: it's hard to be bad if you have no position from which to make the transgression. The way the characters, in the third and fourth stories, view women makes it logical that in the last story, you will think there is every reason why a woman would not want to be a woman: that she would actually try to distance herself from that image of abjection and embrace this notion of mastery, rather sadomasochistically, against herself.

MI: We have been circling around some psychoanalytic concepts: we have just raised the issue of abjection. One of the reasons why I wanted the story in front of us is because I think you can get so much out of the stories in themselves, without a whole backlog of psychoanalytic theory. I know because I teach some of your work to undergraduates who don't know anything about psychoanalysis. But it might be interesting to rehearse quickly some of the important psychoanalytic concepts which are in the background of your work, although they are not stated on the surface or even necessary for a comprehension.

First, there is the issue of ego formation and the mirror stage. It's unfortunate that the English term "stage" has the theatrical resonance but doesn't convey the sense of a stadium with the connotation of a competitive arena. I think most of us think of the mirror stage as the necessary illusion of a coherent body image in anticipation of a future coordination. But we tend to forget about the unpleasant aspect of this experience: the way it's linked with an original infantile distress, the fear of the fragmented body, so that in very close proximity there is this shockproof image and this total fear of fragmentation. There is also the way in which narcissistic identification with another, who is perceived as superior, unleashes fraternal rivalry and aggression. Clearly, notions of aggressivity are very important in the context of this work.

But I wanted to suggest to you that perhaps one way of looking at your work as an intervention—I mean, you have never been supine in relation to psychoanalytic theory—is that you might be suggesting that Lacan's formulation, the notion of the ego, is in fact a description of a certain masculine pathology of the ego. I brought along what I think is proof positive that this is the case: a passage right at the end of a 1953 article, "Some Reflections on the Ego," which was first published in English, where Lacan talks about *Homo Psychologicus,* and the relation between him and the machines he uses. He says that they are very striking, especially in the case of the motorcar: "We get the impression that his relationship to this machine is so very intimate that it is almost as if the two were actually conjoined: its mechanical defects and breakdowns often parallel his neurotic symptoms. Its emotional significance for him comes from the fact that it exteriorizes the protective shell of his ego, as well as the failure of his virility." So masculinity and the structure of the ego are very closely linked.

MK: That is exactly what I was interested in: what you could describe as this defensive structure of the ego. But I'm very fascinated by what Lacan *didn't* say, and how you work through the gaps. For example, the quote that you just gave reminded me of another statement on the notion of display which comes from the *Four Fundamental Concepts,* where he says that the "male" animal in this play of combat throws off something like a skin to cover the frame of a shield. Why is it the "male" animal? So much time has been spent thinking about the construction of femininity: using the concept of masquerade to describe a psychic structure for the woman that was aligned to a certain notion of passivity and silence. It was assumed that in making her visible, precisely in being looked at, that she played out this part as "lacking." That is, she disguised the lack of a lack, created desire through that kind of veiling. But isn't it absolutely true that this is the case for men, too? If you look at something like bodybuilding, it is not the penis but the body itself that is phallicized, made into something to be looked at rather than "listened to." And you could say that this discussion of masquerade shouldn't be restricted to the discussion of sexual difference, in that explicit sense, because it also has implications with regard to race and class. I remember thinking about that in the 1970s when the punk movement produced a certain form of subcultural visibility that was about marking the body with a sign of lack, and in terms of "ethnic" identity: Who is it that wears the native costume? I recall how on Guatemalan money, the women are bare breasted, but the men are in modern dress. Acting out the phantasm of what the other wants you to be—Homi Bhabha talks about this and of course, [Frantz] Fanon, in *Black Skin, White Masks.* Although I would align masquerade with the visualization of that position of otherness, I don't think of difference as symmetrical in the sense of self and other. What you have is the heterogeneous nature of difference posed against what is the same or homogeneous. So if we go back to the quote from Lacan and think about another psychic structure, one which involves the notion of display, it seems to suggest at least three things.

The first, you could say, has to do with playing out the part of having the phallus, or the fraud of the phallus, that is, a certain definition of display that concerns the sexual aim. But there's another use of it, which is not implicated in this "sexual travesty," as Lacan calls it, but comes out of his discussion of mimicry. That is the notion of camouflage, which, for me, in relation to the military, is irresistible. When someone puts on a uniform, what happens? He loses any visible distinction from the others except as he's positioned in that particular organization. He obliterates difference in order to install himself in this hierarchy, and in fact loses the body totally in order to have a speaking presence, to have authority. It's not just the man in his military uniform, but the businessman in his suit, or the artist in his leather jacket; it is all about what will give you a place from which to speak, at the cost of having a kind of bodily presence. In the installation it is important to me how, at one level, the body seems to have been erased, with this hard, shiny metal surface, but then as you negotiate that space, the body reappears and dramatizes that whole relation of absence and presence. Third, there is what Lacan describes as intimidation: not the lure, which is what is effective in devising the masquerade, but this thing that he calls the shield of thrown-off skin that defends us against the vulnerability of visibility and body.

Although this is a little controversial perhaps, I would say that it is impossible to think about that defensive structure of the ego without also thinking about the problem of identification. I know this is an extremely schematic suggestion, but if it's the object of desire and not the object of love that is feminine, then there is something about constituting the subject in terms of this object of desire that is taking place in the whole phantasmatic scene of masquerade. And there is something else taking place on the side of what I have been calling the display that concerns how you set up an ideal. It's what you love—what you want to be, not what you want to have. When you talked about the mirror stage, you alluded to the fact that there are two end points: the first is aligned to that aggressive moment of identification, but the later point involves an internalization of the image and the setting up of an ideal. I think it is culturally overdetermined that the ideal will be (for want of a better term) masculine. And my project, in short, is to see what that means for women. Perhaps we have unconsciously incorporated a form of masculinity that is equally problematic, and this crisis of women in the military is just a symptom.

Mary Kelly's *Ballad of Kastriot Rexhepi*: Virtual Trauma and Indexical Witness in the Age of Mediatic Spectacle

Griselda Pollock

On December 11, 2001, the Santa Monica Museum of Art opened an exhibition that included a chamber orchestra and singer. The American artist Mary Kelly created the dual event under the title *The Ballad of Kastriot Rexhepi*.[1] Kelly's artwork was snaked, about head height, around the vast chamber of this cavernous gallery in an almost continuous movement of 206 feet of black-edged, Perspex-framed, gray lint. The lint—the fluff that comes off clothes and is caught in a filter in a domestic tumble dryer whose simple industrial shape became the formal unit for this work—was mounted in alternating curvilinear sections. This pattern of repetition and inversion evokes both a visual register of sound waves and images of pulse and flow as well as recalling the structure of biological life, the helix. These associations work to generate in the viewer, at the level of already abstracted systems of representation, a sense of sound and movement while none is directly part of the work's effect. A running thread of black text—what one critic called her "rhythmic prose"—holds a constant line either just below or just above the median point of the curved sections created by the exact shape of a large domestic tumble dryer in which, by the washing and drying of four thousand pounds of specially selected black-and-white clothing, Kelly created the material that is the evocative medium for this work: compressed lint, the blown residual tissue, or the waste and relic of daily domestic rituals, whose complex imbrication with social and psychic life have been the substance of her whole career's faithful investigation.[2]

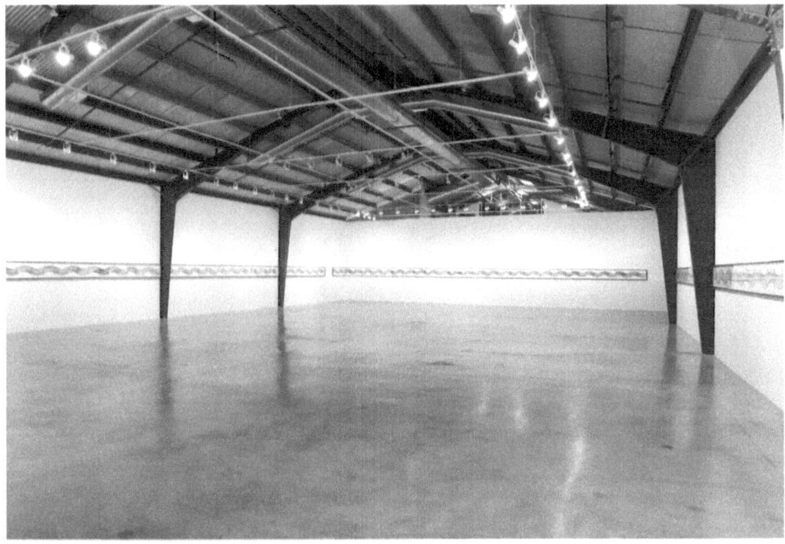

Mary Kelly, *The Ballad of Kastriot Rexhepi*, 2001. Compressed lint, 49 framed panels; each 17 × 48 × 2 in. Installation view, Santa Monica Museum of Art. Courtesy the artist and Pippy Houldsworth Gallery, London.

Thus between the given or readymadeness of the conceptualist's favored choice of industrial form—the filter's shape and screen, and the registering from domestic labor of a fragile substance that has a tenuous link with the human body which these textile fibers once touched, and yet is colorless, shapeless, and discarded—Mary Kelly has created a material as medium that is both virtual and indexical, both matter and nothing, onto which to impress in painstaking manufacture with a simple printing process the blown words of historical tragedy that she wants to embed in the moving track of cultural memory and personal affect. Finally, lint's curious variations of tone with its prevailing grayness gives a photographic effect from a distance—the photograph being both substitute for direct witness and index, as Roland Barthes declared, of trauma in photography:

> Truly traumatic photographs are rare, for in photography the trauma is wholly dependent on the certainty that the scene "really" happened: the *photographer had to be there*. ... Assuming this (which, in fact, is already a connotation), the traumatic photograph (... all

> captured from "life as lived") is the photograph about which there is nothing to say; the shock photograph is by structure insignificant: no value, no knowledge, at the limit no verbal categorization can have a hold on instituting the signification. One could imagine a kind of law: the more direct the trauma, the more difficult is the connotation; or again, the "mythological" effect of a photograph is inversely proportional to its traumatic effect.[3]

By this same token, the photograph's impossible relation to the trauma that founds it becomes virtualized in transmission, becomes for everyone else a kind of spectacle, since that guarantee of the indexical witness—the photographer was there—cannot be repeated and raised to the level of signification. Thus Mary Kelly's production of a substance that in its minimal materiality evokes the photographic visual effect while yet bearing no image, and staging no sight, again performs a constant Kelly move: to stage in a created artwork a commentary on the modes of seeing and knowledge typical of our cultures and media, one face of our creation through the interface with these signifying systems as social subjects. From the aniconic materiality freighted so economically with the traverse of public and private, labor and spectacle, the work once again probes who we are when we look, hear, and see our world.

A small orchestra briefly occupied the center of the large exhibition space at the opening event, performing a score specially created for this work by Michael Nyman. Words that were intaglio-printed onto the waveforms of domestic lint which circled the musical ensemble were sung by Sarah Leonard, whose earlier performance of Nyman's composition for Peter Greenaway's *Prospero's Books* (1991) with Nyman's setting of the poetry of Paul Celan, *Six Celan Songs for Low Female Voice,* had led Mary Kelly to invite the composer to participate with her on this new project "by writing a score for an exhibition, rather like music for a silent movie."[4]

In his 2002 review of this installation/event, Ernest Larsen astutely suggests that all Kelly's major artistic projects "in one way or another investigate the processes by which the subject intersects with a wider history."[5] Maurice Berger's essay in the 2001 catalog phrases this slightly differently. "*The Ballad* … is the latest installment in her thirty-year aesthetic inquiry into the question of subjectivity and historical memory."[6]

This work, however, takes on the current understanding of the subject's encounter with history as "traumatic." Through the distilled economy of a still profoundly reasoned conceptual aesthetic (if this is not a contradiction in terms) that secretes the depth of its theoretical insight that *trauma is a transmitted effect* in its minimal gesture, Kelly's work catches us in unexpected encounter not with the real but with an ethical art making and viewing that reframes us as witnesses. Art here reworks the current theorizing of trauma, delay and belated witness, shaping it through an aesthetic economy that is simultaneously a site of art-thought: *theoria.*

Since her arrival in London in the early 1970s after several years of teaching in Beirut during a particularly intense period of Middle Eastern history in the later 1960s, Mary Kelly has made major cycles of artwork that have consistently pushed at the limits of Lacanian accounts of the subject to accommodate both feminist and Marxist concepts of sociality and history. At the point of intersection between the social determinations of the subject within terms of class, gender, or race, there is what psychoanalysis uniquely introduces into cultural theory:

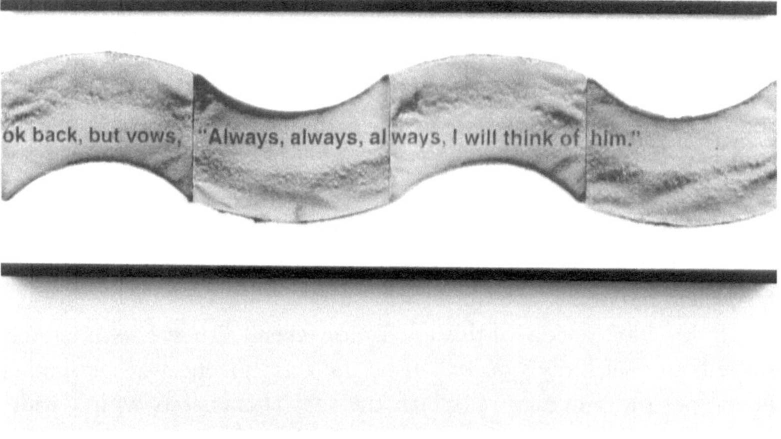

Mary Kelly, detail of *The Ballad of Kastriot Rexhepi*, 2001. Compressed lint, 49 framed panels; each 17 × 48 × 2 in. Courtesy the artist and Pippy Houldsworth Gallery, London.

both a theory of the mechanisms and processes of subjectivity itself, and a theorization of the recalcitrance of what is, psychically, irreducible to social determination of the subject, precisely because there could be no subjective impact of social determination without the mechanisms and processes of subjectivity that are partially autonomous of and excessive to the social.[7]

The subject is logically always-already historical, situated, generationally, and geographically located, and overdetermined, predisposed as it were through its arrival in the cultural framings that anticipate its becoming and accessing to a symbolic order. Yet elements of subjectivity are always in excess of these socioeconomic and linguistic dispositions by virtue of what has to be incited in the human person to become a subject: lack, fantasy, desire, sexuality, the unconscious, and what remains from these processes, death drive, abjection, affect, melancholia, and so forth. As Jacqueline Rose wrote many years ago:

> Like Marxism, psychoanalysis sees the mechanisms which produce those transformations [of ideological processes into human actions and beliefs] as determinant, but also as leaving something in excess. If psychoanalysis is to give an account of how women experience their path to femininity, it also insists, through the concept of the unconscious, that femininity is neither simply achieved nor is it ever complete. The political case for psychoanalysis rests on these two insights together—otherwise it would be indistinguishable from a functionalist account of the internalization of norms. … The difficulty is to pull psychoanalysis in the direction of both insights—towards a recognition of the fully social constitution of identity and norms, and then back again to that point of tension between ego and unconscious where they are endlessly remodeled and endlessly break.[8]

What is of interest in *The Ballad,* however, is not the processes of subjectivization "as usual." It is those moments of exceptional encounter not between the subject and its histories but between the subject and history that mark the current intellectual interest in trauma which has formed the focus of Mary Kelly's work since *Mea Culpa* (1999), which itself followed on from work on masculinity and war during the first Gulf War, *Gloria Patri* (1992).

The event that triggered the making of the large work, *The Ballad*, was an article and photograph in the *Los Angeles Times* on July 31, 1999. Under the banner headline "War Orphan Regains Name—and Family," the article reported the reuniting with his parents of a twenty-two-month-old Albanian child, who, at eighteen months, had been left for dead when his parents escaped a Serbian attack during the Kosovo war of 1999.[9] Kelly's oral/textual *Ballad* begins:

Unnatural spring;
Metal seedpods germinating bloody flora,
Anticipating the "expulsions"
Men in uniforms of blue and green
Faces masked,

And having described the terrors of hiding, starving, watching their child grow weak, stop breathing, lie still, it continues:

She lays his body on the disbelieving ground;
Does not scream, does not look back, but vows
"Always, always I will think of him."
His downy crop, his coral mien

Found on the battlefield and given a Serbian name, Zoran, the child was again abandoned as the Serbians retreated. Kelly's version goes:

Kastriot is found sitting in a field,
Battle in full thrall, a body sprawled nearby,
Severed head at its side.
He speaks not a word.

Reclaimed by Albanians, he was renamed Lirim, before he was finally reunited with his grieving parents for whom he was their lost son "Kastriot." The report of this extraordinary story with its "happy (?) ending" amid the traumatic devastation of "a nation razor-wired to loss" (Kelly) was accompanied by a staged photograph of the tiny blonde child being kissed on both cheeks simultaneously by his parents—"*pater, mater, familia*"—whose large adult heads create a dark frame around his smiling but bemused face in one of those classic images that in capturing the

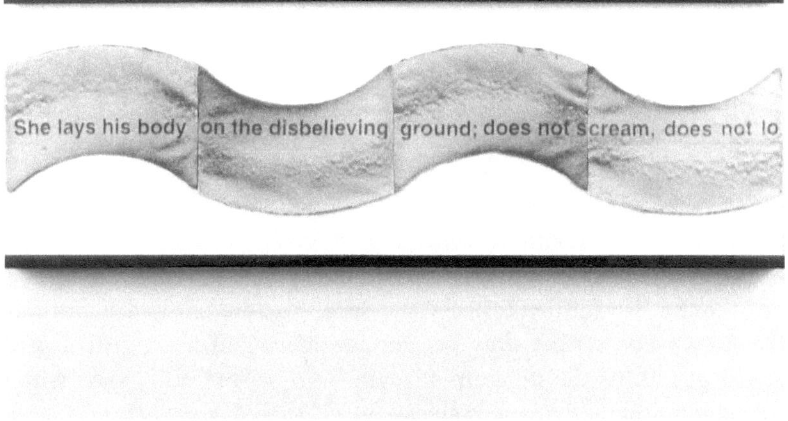

Mary Kelly, detail of *The Ballad of Kastriot Rexhepi*, 2001. Compressed lint, 49 framed panels; each 17 × 48 × 2 in. Courtesy the artist and Pippy Houldsworth Gallery, London.

most banal of new photographers' clichés, unwittingly stages/images the clamp of the symbolic that this child had almost missed: his first and Kelly's work's final word is "Bab"/Dad.[10]

Kastriot Rexhepi endured a trauma to which perhaps he will never be able to give testimony. The event of almost-death, resurrection, claiming and naming, loss and abandonment, reclaiming and renaming, and finally "coming home" as another reinsertion into name and family marked by the first word he spoke, "Bab"—Albanian for "Dad"—all these highly significant and decisive moments occurred between eighteen and twenty-two months. The artist who had made *Post-Partum Document* (1973–1979) as a study of the mutual subjectivization/socialization of the maternal and infant pair could not but notice the psychosymbolic significance of this timescale which raises the child's story from within the events of the Kosovo war and the scourge of ethnic cleansing to a mythic status without losing its historically specific clothing. It is the artist's work to hold the double frame of psychosymbolic and historical time before us, the space of the social subject and the psychic space of the subject:

> I looked at the story closely: Kastriot was only eighteen months old when he was left for dead, then found and renamed by the Serbs. So he was literally learning to speak at that moment, entering into the order of language and culture, you could say, taking on a sexual identity, and in this case, a very confused ethnic identity. When he was reunited with his Albanian parents, Kastriot was twenty-two months old, usually the age when a child can put words together in an elementary syntax, and, psychologically, can project an image of himself as "I." Significantly the first word Kastriot said, according to the reporter anyway, was "Dad."[11]

It was Kelly's politically acute and theoretically informed "reading" of the everyday news report of fin de siècle near-catastrophe and good news in the Balkans that revealed the deep structure of myth at work in the story: "For me the story became less literal and more generic as I got into it. It has the structure of myth—can be told many ways without altering the underlying themes—and I wanted to reflect this in my writing."[12] Pared down to phrasings that poetically expose the mythic armature within this single story of political barbarism and genocidal atrocity, the work makes us hear the rhythm of, or register acoustically, the affect that is trauma in contemporary history which disseminates to other bodies and other homes via the immediacy and inscription of the media.

In one sense, the newspaper or news programs make us all witnesses to catastrophic events. The instantaneous beaming back of on-site footage and reportage brings the traumatic event directly into homes and countries far distant from the actual occurrence. Transmission occurs at several levels. Unlike the shock of discovery that attended the American and Allied troops as they entered concentration camps in 1945 and began to send home first verbal and then photographic reports that seared the viewers—remember Susan Sontag's powerful witness to the impact of seeing these images as dividing her life into a before and an after—we have no delay in the age of satellite and digital communications.[13] Embedded journalists at the center of war as it unfolds make every day's news bulletins as potentially traumatizing as that first time in 1945—yet the constant stream renders even outrageous atrocity just another news item. Sontag has long since argued that shock wears

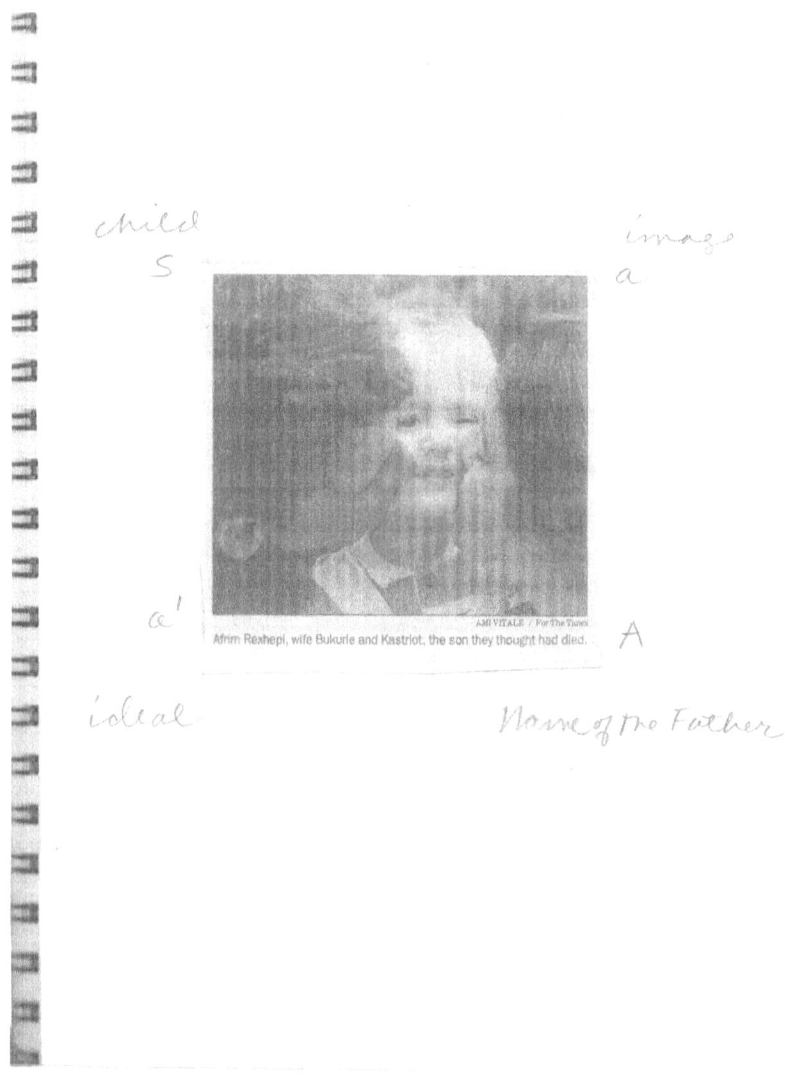

Untitled photograph from *Los Angeles Times*, July 31, 1999, with notes by Mary Kelly. Courtesy the artist and Pippy Houldsworth Gallery, London.

off, that "images anaesthetize," and "repeated exposure only makes the event less real."[14]

Even with these apparently unmediated, immediate floods of digitized information to which we have access, the mythic structuring of the material into narratives and stories that service deep, ideologically and culturally charged interests is inescapable. Thus the potential witness created by the image is subtly or grossly supplanted by a fabricated consumer patterned to receive the mythically familiar. The Barthesian analysis of myth as "depoliticized speech," as the naturalization of the historical through the process of an ideological reinhabiting of the borrowed and denuded signifiers of historical events, raises important questions for theories of witness which are addressed in significant ways by the theorization offered through artistic translation.[15] As with all Mary Kelly's work over the last thirty years, *The Ballad* triangulates the question of aesthetic form, the traumatic/subjectivizing event, and the mode of subjectivizing encounter that invokes the question of *theoria*. *Theoria*—to look at, to view, to travel to see, to be sent to visit an oracle, to judge one thing by another, to contemplate, consider, theorize—is a seer. Hence theory is itself a kind of witnessing, a mode of seeing, considering, and thinking that involves the real or metaphoric experience of sight/insight and, of course, its opposite, blindness.

In *The Ballad*, Mary Kelly seems to offer nothing to see—in the form of image or representation. What she offers is not the story but an architecture for the transmission of the affective residue of trauma precisely in order to create an order of theoretical seeing, insight, into that which we are called to witness, but which the mythic translation by our media and cultural apparatuses of daily exposure render so already known that it ceases to instigate reflection or affective response. The family under stress in the crisis of war is the very symbol of destruction, as Picasso suggested in his response to the sight of the first photographic images of the German death camps. His painting *The Charnel House* (1944–1945) deployed the artistic handwriting created for his visual scream, *Guernica* (1937)—monochrome Cubist faceting—to depict the father, mother, and child of a shattered family home, recuperatively centering the entire Nazi project to destroy all humanizing structures and particularly the affective bonds of family, precisely on its most sentimental antithesis. In the newspaper photograph that serves visually to anchor the sentimental resolution of the fairy tale of a lost child returned to its proper parents, country, name, and identity, Mary Kelly catches a more troubling ambivalence. She registers another resonance or tone that can be aesthetically explored, as she has so often done, by abandoning the iconic site of mythification—the mother/child (*Post-Partum Document*), the older woman (*Interim,* 1984–1989), and the hero (*Gloria Patri*) for the registers of sound and substance that work together between abstraction, formality, and Conceptualism to hold both affect and understanding.

The signifying economy created by the now embedded legacies of Minimalism and Conceptualism exceed the museal narratives of a succession of styles to register the battle with, and distance from, the dominant registers of visual representation and popular narrative that enclose us in the mediatic spectacle of global information and entertainment. These show us things before which we are made spectators—or worse, consumers—but never witnesses. To wrench the encounter—the traumatic event—into a relation of humanizing knowledge, what Bracha Ettinger might call coaffection, requires a calculated impoverishment at the level of spectacle, and a displacement of the mythic to other registers of acoustic and visual memory that can use affective response to generate understanding.

In a work of 1999 that initiated the use of printed pressed lint, *Mea Culpa,* Mary Kelly showed four works comprising sixteen to twenty units combined to form one panel assembled from four to five sections, 17 × 190 × 2 inches (four sections), and 17 × 235 × 2 inches (five sections). The process is printmaking (monotype) using the filter screen of a domestic dryer on which in low-relief intaglio print, a line of words is placed so as to be impressed onto the lint as its accumulates in a drying cycle. The four sections deal with four major traumatic events:

1. The Khmer Rouge massacres in Phnom Penh in 1975
2. The bombing of the refugee camps Shatila and Sabra in Beirut by the Israeli air force in 1982
3. The massacre of Muslim refugees in Sarajevo by Bosnian Serbs in 1996
4. The Truth and Reconciliation Commission in post-apartheid South Africa in 1997

Each historical trauma or event is marked by a cryptic line of words that runs just below center of repeating curved shapes created by the filter's readymade form. These are grouped in what the artist names a musical form of four-four time: "A beat which holds back on both the speed and lyricism of the piece. You might have noticed that a work always ends on four, even if the narrative stops before then. The rhythm determines how the spectator walks through it." To which the interviewer adds, "Four-four being a march time as well."[16]

Each of the narratives printed onto the compressed lint, apart from the confessional South African report, focalizes through the use of a third-person pronoun: "she." In each case, this "she" sees or hears something. In *Phnom Penh 1975*:

> She watched the soldiers in a rice paddy beat her daughter with the butts of their rifles until she was dead. Then she had headaches and trouble with her eyes. To distract herself, she worked at the bridge of her nose with a knife. When the pain subsided, she could no longer see.

Sarajewo 1992 reads:

> A few bathroom tiles and the smell of burning: nothing else left. Probing the ashes she retrieved a family photograph. Their faces scratched out with a drill bit. She rocked back and forth on her heels. What shall we do? Slit their throats said her four-year-old son.[17]

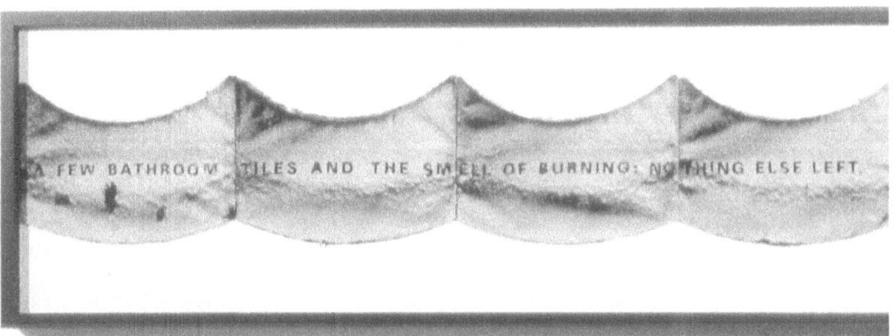

Mary Kelly, detail of *Sarajewo 1992*, 1999. Compressed lint, 4 panels; 17 × 190 × 2 in. (overall). Collection of Oak Brook Bank, Illinois. Courtesy the artist and Pippy Houldsworth Gallery, London.

These abbreviated narratives carry the mark of their origin in newspaper or television reports stripped of all sensationalism and sentimentalization with an analyst's understanding of the psychological import of casual utterance. Mary Kelly tells interviewer Juli Carson that her work often begins with a photographic and verbal archive, a kind of cultural ethnography in which she listens to what is said around her as an analyst might for the core elements, the trigger phrases, the deep psychic valences. But she is also "on the couch" responding to the noise of her archive with the selective attention that marks it with her own desire and psychic urgencies. In this case, Kelly collected material on war-related atrocities, which themselves lured the artist's personal rather than dispassionate interest, and activated her memory perhaps of time in Beirut and growing up through the Vietnam War, the first war that was so daily brought home to American televisions.[18] But her attention was also drawn to aspects of intense experience: fear of losing one's child.

The mutilated family photograph came this way from an accumulated archive, but the South African episode was prompted by a report from the Truth and Reconciliation Commission overheard on a television from another room. It is this relation of chance encounter—overhearing—with the trace of the traumatic events occurring somewhere else and to someone else, that marks the distance between the failure of witnessing that is reportage and the new creation of the conditions of witnessing that is the artwork in order to refute the current overemphasis on authenticity and testimony. Reflecting on the theoretical underpinnings of this position, Carson pointed out that Mary Kelly is not intending to present the "reality" of war atrocities and thus fall prey to the ethical dangers of representation. Mary Kelly tells her:

> I think there is a mistaken idea that trauma has to do with an immediate experience—when something happens to you. We usually attribute a certain authenticity to the account of survivors, although the "accident" is shaped in tandem with a person's particular sexual disposition or phantasy life. Following Freud's contention that it isn't the real event, but the psychic *effect* that produces trauma, I started to think about the impact that atrocities have even when they are received second hand through the media. The way they

> seem to induce different forms of identification with the victim, whether they are hysterical or megalomaniacal, I'm not sure, but I couldn't deny the traumatic effects of these representations and how they filter into the everyday.[19]

Mary Kelly describes how as part of the long gestation of the work *Mea Culpa,* she herself staged a photograph of her own body as if dead, shrouded in sheets: "I needed to act out this tendency to experience the unimaginable vicariously in order to get some distance from it." Carson glosses this:

> That's exactly how Lacan describes trauma, as a *missed* encounter with the Real. To actually have that encounter would, of course, be the death of the subject. What I mean is, to look beyond the spectacle of representation, of language, behind that screen upon which we project every one of our life-sustaining (traumatic) phantasies, is to encounter that, in fact, "nothing" is out there. Contrary to claims made in some recent cultural theorizations of the Lacanian Real, that's an "encounter" you don't walk away from as a subject.[20]

Mary Kelly speaks of the displacement from the body in the image, the identification with the image of the victim which renders death a mere performance rather than this brush with "nothing," the annihilation of the subject, and talks about wanting to find a means to "translate" the material onto which the issue is displaced into a process of making the noniconic image. I cannot stress enough the import of this attention to the relations between coming to terms with the process of making and its materiality, which forms a typical part of any engagement with conceptual post-Minimalist art practice, and the ethical dimension of her practice in its social and historical engagement. It is here that the possibility of an indexical relation to the historical real is transferred in potential at least to the most conceptual and depleted modalities that can still promise, but never guarantee, the necessary affectivity, or coaffectivity that marks the transmission of the traumatic effect sufficient to create a work of political witness.

Kelly's process produces something anamorphic—for the viewing subject in the exhibition hall cannot master or grasp the whole work from any single position but becomes a subject in and of the space, whose rhythmic prose "narrativizes" events for that decentered subject. The complex aesthetics of making use of a domestic industrial machine associated with cleansing to stage affective encounters with the atrocities of war and ethnic violence functions at yet another level of challenge to and interruption of the mediatic, which as I am suggesting, virtualizes the event. Mary Kelly says:

> I think human rights legislation—which was actually launched in 1948 by Eleanor Roosevelt—will become the major issue for democracies in the twenty-first century. More specifically, I'm interested in the way artists like Shirin Neshat and William Kentridge import cinematic devices into the gallery space without the aspect of spectacle.
>
> But I wanted to go in a very different direction—to explore the possibilities of material indexicality as a visual experience, as a pleasure really, compatible with the archaic nature of the gallery space—archaic in relation to the dominant cultural forms like film, television and technology-driven entertainment. That's why it seemed somehow appropriate to invent an outmoded medium—washers and dryers, after all, belong to the industrial rather than the information era. I find Walter Benjamin's suggestion that there is a redemptive aspect to the outmoded more and more meaningful. ... I do think it is important not to forget the kinds of social relations embedded in past events—simple ones like reading a book, as well as complex and traumatic ones, like war.[21]

Drawing on these terms, I propose that beyond the problematic of representation, which is so complexly virtual and virtualizing, the now archaic forms of modernist-made art, historically freighted with its own social relations and memories, perform the indexical relation not via the icon but the material as a transport medium capable of inciting a transsubjectivity that is not voyeuristic or identificatory. To bring this finally back to the theory of witness, I want to introduce one of founding thinkers of witness: Dori Laub. In his study of Holocaust testimony, "Bearing Witness" —which involves both the survivor giving testimony and the witness who was missing at the time of the event—Laub typifies the dangers of witnessing, as the receiver defends him- or herself from the invasion of the other's trauma. He notes a range of defensive responses: a sense of total paralysis or fear—fear of merger with atrocities being recounted; a sense of outrage or anger directed at the narrator; a sense of withdrawal and numbing; a flood of awe and fear leading to a fake sanctification of the victim; obsessive interest in facts to foreclose the affective charge; and hyperemotionality that looks like compassion but floods out the testifier with the listener's defensive affectivity.[22]

Held by the fineness of calculated aesthetic forms addressing the rhythms of seeing and hearing in narrativized space, inviting the viewer's work upon its materials and forms, Mary Kelly's work since 1999 brings a still deeply feminist perspective to bear on the question of history as trauma. Deeply feminist in its fidelity to the exploration of the complex hinge between subjectivity and the social and historical, this work swings round from the original refocusing of attention onto the domestic site of labor as one key locale of socialization and subjectivization within class and gender relations back to the public space of war and violence. Yet in its relay of current events to the intimacies of our homes, the media itself corrupts such distinctions, investing our homes and domestic spaces with the social and historical. When, as at the end of the last century, the fiftieth anniversary of the full exposure of the Nazi genocide found Europe riven once again by ethnic violence and atrocity, traumatic delay retriggered by traumatic repeat raised the theorization of history as trauma to the headline of theoretical research. The enormous volume of work on the Holocaust as the traumatic shadow-stain on twentieth-century Europe opens out to events which find traumatic resonance in almost every postwar society from Taiwan to Korea, almost all of Africa, throughout Latin America, and then the Balkans. Our relation to the scale and depth of human suffering must be one of the critical questions of our time, when the exhaustion of older frames of political formulation have been smashed, and globalization—the latest and most spectacular of the phases of capitalism—unravels most of our existing structures for the management of its terrifying forces of transformation.

The Ballad of Kastriot Rexhepi becomes an interesting theoretical event, creating a space in which to reflect upon who we are summoned to be in relation to another not in the age of mechanical reproduction but of digitized virtuality, which screens (in both senses of the word) the nature of brutal and violent physical reality for most of the world's populations, whom development, neocolonialism, and greed have reduced to levels of such atrocious and traumatic suffering that the whole of modernity's dream lies indicted. The arcane and esoteric exercise of conceptual art making in an advanced Western nation, whose conditions of existence involve galleries and orchestras and art magazines, seems utterly irrelevant to the scale of trauma that we now witness worldwide. But that is not so. For embedded in this archaic practice of made and viewed art is the complement to the necessity for synthetic, sociological knowledge of globalization and violence, namely, aesthetic knowledge, knowing for yourself, knowing in yourself, knowing at the level of human witness.

For many years, the focus of one area of my teaching and research has been the passage from trauma to cultural memory. In the timescale of that work (1990–), these terms have become major areas of investigation in cultural theory, acquiring an awesome bibliography that does some justice to the significance that each term, trauma and cultural memory, hold for a world repeatedly traumatized and increasingly seeking to hold onto/create meaning in events that traumatically knock it out. At the intersection with work that has largely focused on the trauma and cultural inscription of the memory of the Shoah/Holocaust, I have continued my other intellectual project as a feminist art historian and cultural analyst, working on interventions in art's histories from theoretically informed feminist analysis, the latter term invoking, hopefully, both a legacy of critical thought and psychoanalysis itself. Central to both projects has been the aesthetic: not as the beautiful or the best, but rather as a practice that articulates thought and affect through material and semiotic processes. I ask myself: What can art-historical work contribute to the philosophical, literary, and psychological/psychoanalytic literature on trauma and cultural memory? What is the role of art?

In introducing the course on trauma and cultural memory in relation to the Shoah, I ask my students: Who/what shall we be when we look back at this historical moment, which in the character of trauma, happened in historically determinable dates within which its effects are not confined, and thus returns with the force of the repressed out of time and out of place? I have written elsewhere of the danger of what I call the Orphic gaze, the second look that kills again.[23] The danger of voyeurism, abjecting the other, recoiling from their dehumanization in horror, and many other inappropriate but inevitable responses need to be considered before we even begin. So I propose the now well-known suggestion of Laub that we are called to become the belated witnesses eradicated from the genocidal process, which Laub characterizes as "an event-without-a witness."[24] Thus we restore to the testifying victim/survivor the human ear and subjective affirmation destroyed as part of the calculated violence of the planned destruction of entire peoples. But this is based on the model of testimonial exchange that forms its own new models of literature and historical writing.

It is a difficult proposition that bends time and place, and raises difficult questions. Laub's concept of the event without a witness has been taken up by Ettinger, and transformed into a general proposition about the belatedness inherent in trauma in which the impact of the traumatic effect may be deferred or even transmitted across generations and beyond the boundaries of the discrete subject. Ettinger also pushes this implicatedness to include the viewer of the artwork, who is, by definition, also a witness without an event. That is to say, the event, the experiential or other cause of the artwork and its making, is not the experience of the viewer. Yet the viewer is called upon to participate affectively in confirming the human significance of the trace of that now missing event: the making or even the maker, to raise the objective materials to the level of signification, communication, and subject-subject relay. We respond with our own emotions or thoughts to what is not ours while we are in turn transformed by the affect of the other within us. Thus witness ceases to be a mere legal or even a psychotherapeutic condition; it is an ethical relation to the suffering of what is no longer the other, but a coaffecting transsubjective dimension of subjectivity that is particularly operative in certain moments of engaged aesthetic practice. But Ettinger will take this one stage further, and expose that which had seemed at first—in the idea of witness—an ethical and affirming point of meeting, of mutual confirmation as something that still leaves a gap. Thus, to define the specific moments or elements of nonpsychotic transitivity that may be incited in the aesthetic experience (of making as well as of viewing), she alters the word *witness* visually to create "wit(h)nessing." Introducing the letter *h* from the word *with* breaches the dominant formulations of the conditions of subjectivity in which the subject only emerges when it ceases to be with an other, separates itself, defines its boundaried ego through a scarifying gap through which hole will whistle the subjective engine of desire. To be too much with, to overidentify, to fail to maintain clear boundaries between self and other, is to fall prey to a host of psychological problems verging ultimately on a psychotic disintegration of the self, an alienation so profound that intersubjective exchange becomes impossible. Thus the moment of balancing the varying potentials of subjectivity for its contact or collapse must be negotiated and staged. While there is a gulf of considerable theoretical significance between the Lacanian underpinnings of Mary Kelly's work and the post-Lacanian feminist matrixial theory formulated by Ettinger, it is possible to allow the latter to reflect upon the contribution to the relations of aesthetics, trauma, and witness because the work of Mary Kelly must itself be in excess at the affective level of its own self-understanding that generated the practice. The combination of the visuality of rhythm and the collaboration between Kelly's word poems and Nyman's music staged at the opening of each of the three venues for *The Ballad* suggested to me a third part to this exchange in the form of this theoretical statement:

> A rhythm of swerving in rapport of transmission and transference, conducting toward an unforeseen home while creating it, bypasses the on/off beat. This rhythm never arches total "on" or total "off." ... Co-in/habit(u)ation is primarily affective, not visual, and it destabilizes visuality by transgression of affect that causes infiltration of invisible trauma into appearance.[25]

Suspended between the inherent virtuality of subjective processes (fantasy and the unconscious), the indexical trauma that founds the subject who never knows it, and the virtuality of the socioeconomically conditioned media/information systems and the historical trauma they report but mythify, art making, and its specific aesthetic processes and practices (in a Kristevan not a Kantian sense), may create both witness and *wit(h)ness* that "cause infiltration of invisible trauma into appearance" and audibility, to create witness-subjects, which is not only an ethical but a deeply political effect.[26]

THE BALLAD OF KASTRIOT REXHEPI

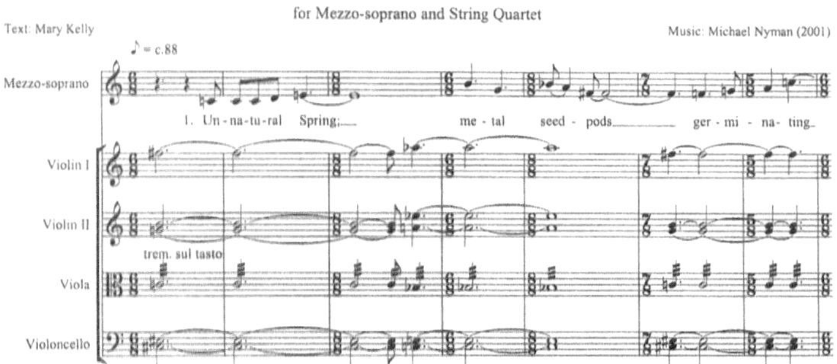

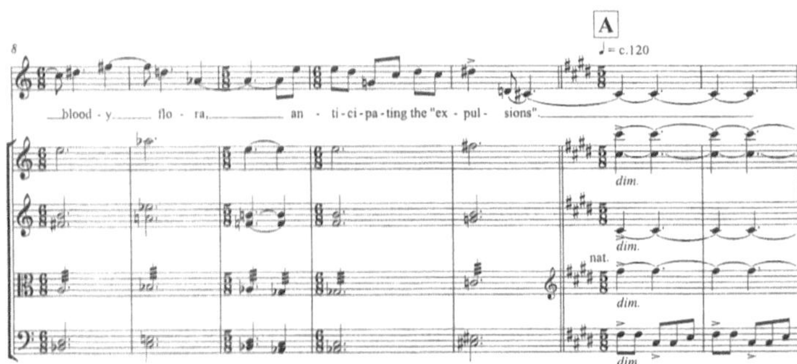

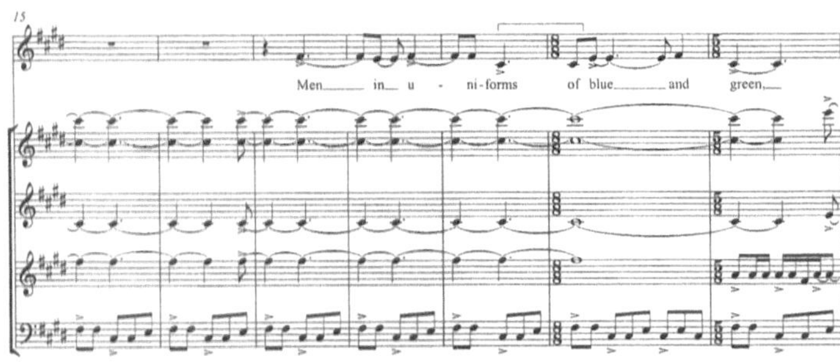

Score from *The Ballad of Kastriot Rexhepi*, 2001.

Notes

1. The work was subsequently exhibited at Cooper Union's Houghton Gallery, New York, November 21–December 21, 2002, and the Museo Universitario de Ciencias y Arte, Mexico City, October 18–December 12, 2003.

2. Ernest Larsen, "About a Boy," *Art in America* (December 2002): 99.

3. Roland Barthes, "The Photographic Message," in *Image-Music-Text*, ed. and trans. Stephen Heath (New York: Hill and Wang, 1977), p. 30–31.

4. Mary Kelly and Else Longhauser, "A Conversation with Mary Kelly and Elsa Longhauser," in *Mary Kelly: The Ballad of Kastriot Rexhepi* (Los Angeles: Santa Monica Museum of Art, 2001), p. 6.

5. Larsen, "About a Boy," p. 101.

6. Maurice Berger, "Mea Culpa: The Art of Mary Kelly," in *Mary Kelly: The Ballad of Kastriot Rexhepi*, p. 9.

7. This is the crucial point argued for by Jacqueline Rose in her response to a wave of feminist critique of the asocial character of psychoanalysis. See Jacqueline Rose, "Feminism and the Psychic," and "Femininity and Its Discontents," both in *Sexuality in the Field of Vision* (London: Verso, 1986), pp. 1–24, 83–103.

8. Rose, "Feminism and the Psychic," p. 7.

9. Scott Glover, "War Orphan Regains Name—and Family," *Los Angeles Times*, July 31, 1999.

10. Mary Kelly, *The Ballad of Kastriot Rexhepi*, canto 3, lines 20–21, reproduced in *Mary Kelly: The Ballad of Kastriot Rexhepi*, p. 18.

11. Kelly and Longhauser, "A Conversation," p. 7.

12. Ibid.

13. Susan Sontag, *On Photography* (London: Picador, 1977), p. 19–20: "For me it was the photographs of Bergen-Belsen and Dachau which I came across by chance in a bookstore in Santa Monica in July 1945. Nothing I have seen—in photographs or real life—ever cut me as sharply, deeply, as instantaneously. Indeed it seems plausible to divide my life into two parts, before I saw those photographs (I was twelve) and after." For an excellent historical analysis of the exact impact of the photographs versus the prose press reports, see Barbie Zelizer, *Remembering to Forget: Holocaust Memory through the Camera's Eye* (Chicago: University of Chicago Press, 1998).

14. Sontag, *On Photography*, p. 20.

15. Roland Barthes, "Myth Today," in *Mythologies*, ed. and trans. Annette Lavers (London: Paladin, 1972), pp. 109–158.

16. Juli Carson and Mary Kelly, "Mea Culpa: A Conversation with Mary Kelly," *Art Journal* 58, no. 4 (Winter 1999): 77.

17. In conversation about this discovered episode—the readymade of a war experience—Mary Kelly has remarked on the significance of these words of cold-blooded enmity emerging fully formed from the mouth of a child, already inducted into the terms of ethnic violence. The child repeats what he has heard as the normal response, his own imaginary already inhabited by the given terms of ethnic conflict.

18. Martha Rosler made a series of major photomontage works on this moment titled *House Beautiful (Bringing the War Home)*. See Catherine de Zegher, ed., *Martha Rosler: Positions in the Life World* (Cambridge, MA: MIT Press, 1999).

19. Carson and Kelly, "Mea Culpa," p. 75 (emphasis added).

20. Ibid., p. 76.

21. Ibid., p. 79.

22. Dori Laub, "Bearing Witness, or the Vicissitudes of Listening," in *Testimony: Crises of Witnessing in Literature, Psychoanalysis, and History*, ed. Shoshana Felman and Dori Laub (London: Routledge, 1992), pp. 72–73.

23. See Griselda Pollock, "Painting as a Backward Glance That Does Not Kill: Fascism and Aesthetics," *Renaissance and Modern Studies* 43 (2001): 116–144; Griselda Pollock, "Abandoned at the Mouth of Hell or a Second Look That Does Not Kill: The Uncanny Coming to Matrixical Memory," in *Looking Back to the Future: Essays on Art, Life, and Death* (Amsterdam: G+B Arts International, 2000), pp. 113–177.

24. Dori Laub, "An Event without a Witness: Truth, Testimony, and Survival,"' in *Testimony: Crises of Witnessing in Literature, Psychoanalysis, and History*, pp. 75–92.

25. Bracha Ettinger, "Traumatic Wit(h)ness-Thing and Matrixial Co/in-habit(u)ating," *parallax* 5, no. 1 (1999): 93.

26. I am thinking here of Julia Kristeva's definition of aesthetic practices as "signifiance"—that which transforms and renovates the unities of the symbolic order. See Julia Kristeva, "The Subject and the Signifying System," in *The Kristeva Reader*, ed. Toril Moi (Oxford: Blackwell, 1986), pp. 24–33.

Not-Forgetting: Mary Kelly's *Love Songs*

Rosalyn Deutsche

The age of protected democracy in which we live—when, as Giorgio Agamben writes, security is the normal technique of Western democratic governments—has had a serious impact on art that wants to play a role in deepening and extending the public sphere.[1] Among the most urgent consequences are state censorship—for example, New York governor George Pataki's recent cancellation of plans to make the Drawing Center part of the World Trade Center memorial complex—and criminal prosecution—the federal government's ongoing indictment of Steven Kurtz, member of the Critical Art Ensemble. A consequence of another kind, one that has captured less attention but that also limits art's participation in a richly agonistic public life, is a worsening of the left melancholy that surfaced in cultural discourse, including art discourse, in the 1970s.

"Left melancholia" was Walter Benjamin's derogatory term for a mood afflicting leftists who remain more attached to past political ideals—even, according to philosopher Wendy Brown, to the *failure* of a political ideal—than to possibilities of political change in the present.[2] Brown says that the left melancholic renders his political analysis thing-like and frozen, unamenable to transformation. Applying Benjamin's analysis to contemporary times, she argues that today's left melancholic adheres to a traditional leftist representation of the political—a representation that includes "notions of unified movements, social totalities, and class-based politics."[3] The melancholic therefore laments the challenges that have been posed over the last few decades to such unitary models of social change, scornfully calling them, among other names, "postmodern." The most basic challenge was the calling into question of the idea that society is totalized by a single, economic antagonism, which is the absolute foundation of all other social antagonisms and governs all emancipatory struggle. Against this questioning, the left melancholic tries to reground the political in the authority of an ontologically privileged foundation, insisting, as Stuart Hall observed in 1988, on the determinism of capital, and dismissing the political importance of postmodernism's concern with the subject and subjectivity.[4] A current example is the introduction to *Afflicted Powers: Capital and Spectacle in a New Age of War*, a book about the Iraq War that has attracted the interest of certain sectors of the art world. After wrongly claiming that academic leftists of the recent past dismissed the political significance of capitalism, the authors write, "It is 'the end of Grand Narratives' and 'the trap of totalization' and 'the radical irreducibility of the political' which now seem like period items."[5] The phrases they mock as outdated stand of course for various postmodern, poststructuralist, and feminist critiques of traditional leftist political analysis.

Brown suggests that left melancholy has a narcissistic dimension because the frozen analysis to which it clings once formed the basis of leftist self-love, giving "its adherents a clear and certain path toward the good, the right, the true."[6] Insofar as left melancholy rests on an image of society and social change that is centered on the presence of an element that guarantees wholeness, the analysis is also masculinist. Hardly surprising, then, is the left melancholic's rejection not only of postmodernism but also the feminist voice associated with postmodernism. For it was postmodern feminists, and in particular feminist artists, who explored the role played by totalizing images in producing and maintaining masculinist subjects. This exploration implied that subjective, psychic transformation, like material transformation, is an essential component, rather than mere epiphenomenon, of social change. Also predictable, then, is that critics and historians afflicted by left melancholia (including some who once theorized the meaning of postmodernism but now regard it as nothing more than "the cultural logic of late capitalism") would refuse to register the full impact of the feminist critique of the meaning of the political. Leftists may use the pressing nature of the current political situation to legitimate this refusal, but in the age of protected democracy, when the pursuit of mastery has become a self-evident virtue, the feminist critique seems more rather than less urgent.

The left melancholic's insistence on a pregiven ground of society and political struggle restricts the growth of democratic public spheres. For one thing, as Claude Lefort argues, the public sphere emerged precisely when the democratic revolutions withdrew the ground, making the meaning of society uncertain and, as a consequence, open to debate. For another, being in public means responding to the presence of others and therefore calls us out of our narcissism. Artists who want their work to be part of democratic public life are faced with the task not only of challenging protected democracy but resisting left melancholy. One way of doing so—suggested to me by Mary Kelly's exhibition *Love Songs*, held in 2005 at Postmasters Gallery in New York City—is through fidelity to the event of feminism.

"Fidelity to the event" is a concept formulated by the philosopher Alain Badiou. Like left melancholy, the phrase implies a relationship to the past, a type of history and memory of earlier radicalism. To distinguish fidelity from nostalgic forms of memory, Badiou describes the relationship as one of "not-forgetting." Fidelity to the event is also Badiou's name for a new conception of ethics, which he defines as a refusal of conservatism. The event for Badiou is something that happens in a situation, something that supplements, but does not complement, the order within which the event takes place, whether it is the political, personal, or artistic order. Examples are the political event of the French Revolution, the personal event of an amorous passion, and the artistic event of Arnold Schoenberg's invention of the twelve-tone scale. The event cannot be understood within the framework of already constituted knowledges. It "punches a hole" in such knowledge, releasing what Badiou calls a "truth-process."[7] The event is revolutionary, though not in the sense of something absolute that, as Julia Kristeva puts it in her criticism of revolution, will solve all problems.[8] Rather, the event presents hitherto unknown possibilities that put an end to consensus or dominant opinion in the order it disrupts; its course is uncertain, and importantly, it compels the subject to "decide a new way of being." The subject becomes the bearer of a fidelity to the event when she decides henceforth to relate to the situation from the perspective of the event. "To be really faithful to the event," Badiou writes, "I must completely rework my ordinary way of living my situation."[9] After

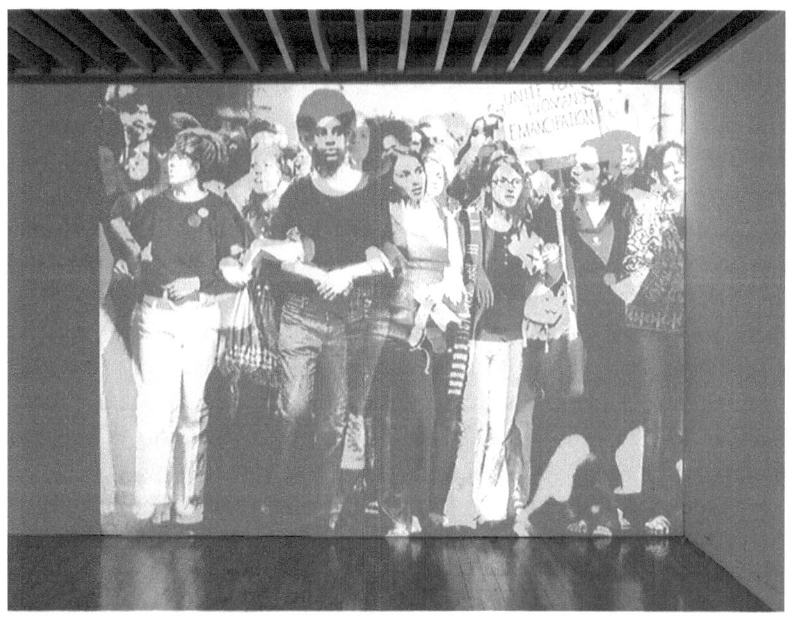

Mary Kelly, *WLM Demo Remix*, 2005. Black-and-white film loop, 90 sec. Installation view, Whitworth Art Gallery, Manchester, 2011. Courtesy the artist and Pippy Houldsworth Gallery, London.

Schoenberg, for instance, I do not go back to writing romantic music. I persevere in the interruption. I do not break with the break and return to continuity. But neither do I make the event absolute, giving it total power and turning it into a new dogmatism. For the event, cautions Badiou, does not reveal the substance of the situation in which it occurs. Rather, it names the void of the situation. For example, the void of the political order is the meaning of the political community.[10] If, as Lefort argues, the democratic revolutions constituted an event that did away with references to absolute sources of the meaning of the people and opened the political community to question, then to endow the people with a substantial identity, to name the unnameable, is to betray the democratic event and, of course, destroy the public sphere it invents.

For Badiou, the subject of a fidelity does not preexist the event. Rather, the subject is someone caught up in the event, "simultaneously himself and in excess of himself." The event and the unpredictable course of the process it unleashes "pass through" this someone, who thereby becomes engaged in the invention of a new subject—a subject she has chosen to be and that extends beyond herself. The question faced by the subject of a fidelity is, "How will I, as some-one, *continue* to exceed my own being ... via the effects of being seized by the not-known?"[11]

Kelly's *Love Songs* demonstrated fidelity to an event that Badiou does not mention: feminism, which, questioning masculinist conceptions of both the subject and the political, attempted to build more democratic forms of each.[12] As its title indicates, Kelly's exhibition treated the political event of feminism as also a personal one, an amorous passion, giving new meaning to the slogan of the women's liberation movement, "the personal is political." This slogan challenged both mainstream and traditional critical conceptions of the public sphere—conceptions that draw a rigid divide between public/political and private/nonpolitical space. Whereas the public-private division once forced women's issues into privacy, today the division is shored up by left melancholics who exclude feminist explorations of subjectivity from the public sphere. Against this exclusion, Kelly created a space—a kind of theater—dedicated to the history, memory, and postmemory of a feminism that mixes the personal and the political, a space in which the boundaries between the two could not be pinned down.

In her theater of not-forgetting, Kelly used a material that serves the philosopher as a metaphor for the event: light. The event, says Badiou, is "a kind of flashing supplement that happens to the situation"; it bursts forth as if into flame and gives off light, which disappears, leaving a "trace" in the situation, a kind of afterimage that refers back to the vanished event and guides the subject's fidelity.[13] *Love Songs* contains such traces: it took place in a darkened gallery; the only light emanated from the works in the show.

Running like a frieze around three walls of the gallery's front room was a work called *Sisterhood Is POW* ..., a title that transforms the early feminist slogan "sisterhood is powerful" into a phrase that registers the powerful impact—the POW—of feminism as an event. *Sisterhood Is POW* ... consisted of thirty-six black, cast-acrylic panels incised with laser-cut script. Supported on wooden shelves, the panels were lit from behind by strip lighting, which illuminated the words and turned them into literal "words of light," Benjamin's term for photography—a name

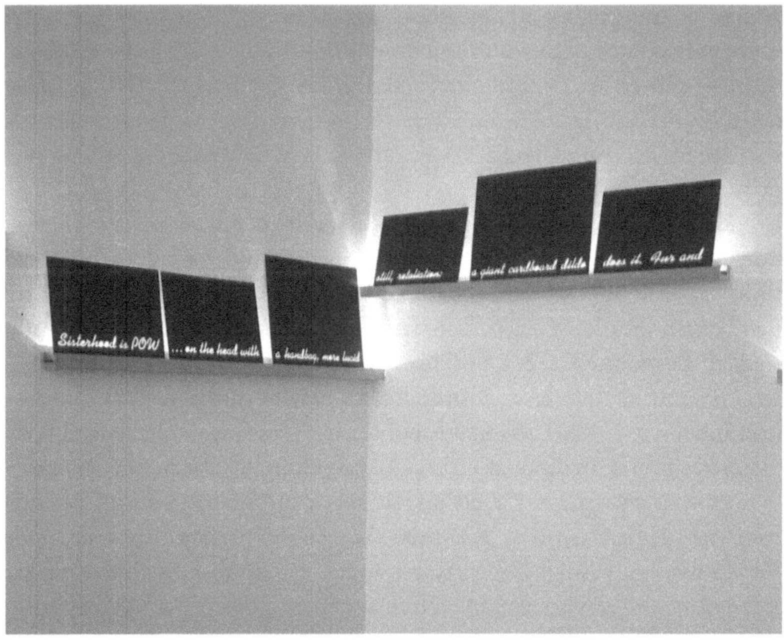

Mary Kelly, detail of *Sisterhood Is POW ...*, 2005. Laser-cut cast acrylic, linear strip lighting, wood support, 36 units; 24 units, each 15 × 20 in.; 12 units, each 24 × 20 in.; 72 ft. (overall). Installation view, Postmasters Gallery, New York, 2005.

that links photographs to language. Divided like lines of poetry, Kelly's text expresses her subjective not-forgetting of her participation in an episode of the British women's liberation movement, a demonstration against the Miss World Contest held at the Albert Hall in London in 1971. Undertaking a type of historical work that Drucilla Cornell calls "the recollective imagination," Kelly recalls what was taking place inside and outside the hall: inside, the Miss World contest, where "contestants flash / teeth and leg-length" as "judges tot up the / facts: figures, faces"; outside, a protest against this spectacle of patriarchal femininity in which "demonstrators, / arms locked, hands firm, fingers longer, / more lucid, flash / luminous nipples and / crotches at fans."[14] The group of panels bearing short phrases and placed at slightly varying heights resembled a cluster of picket signs contesting oppressive constructions of the feminine.

On the room's fourth wall hung another, related work, *Flashing Nipple Remix,* consisting of three light boxes containing large black-and-white photographic transparencies. The activities pictured in the photographs are based on a snapshot in Kelly's archive. The archival photo documents the street theater protest described in *Sisterhood Is POW* … and could be considered a trace of feminism as an event. Over their clothing, in the area of their breasts and genitals, protesters had placed bright lights, ironically mimicking the performance going on inside the Albert Hall. The first photo in *Flashing Nipple Remix* depicts a contemporary restaging of the protest by five young women. Representatives of a new generation of feminists, the women wore the same lights as the original protesters and set them in motion by shaking their bodies with increasing vigor. The women became radiant as their bodies dissolved into luminous streaks and patterns of light. A student of mine observed that the moving lights served as "a vehicle to problematize the definition

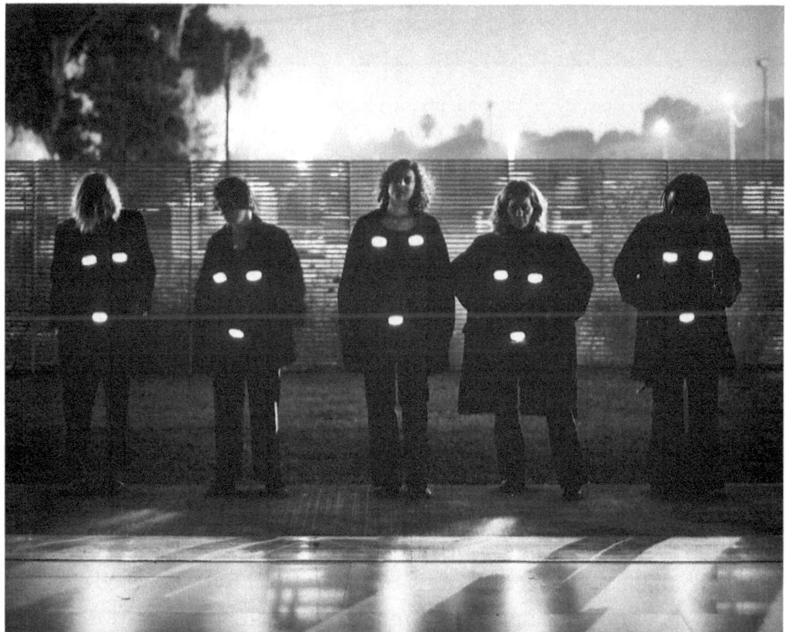

Mary Kelly, detail of *Flashing Nipple Remix,* 2005. Three black-and-white transparencies in light boxes; each 38 × 48 × 5 in. Collection of Whitworth Art Gallery, Manchester, UK. Courtesy the artist and Pippy Houldsworth Gallery, London.

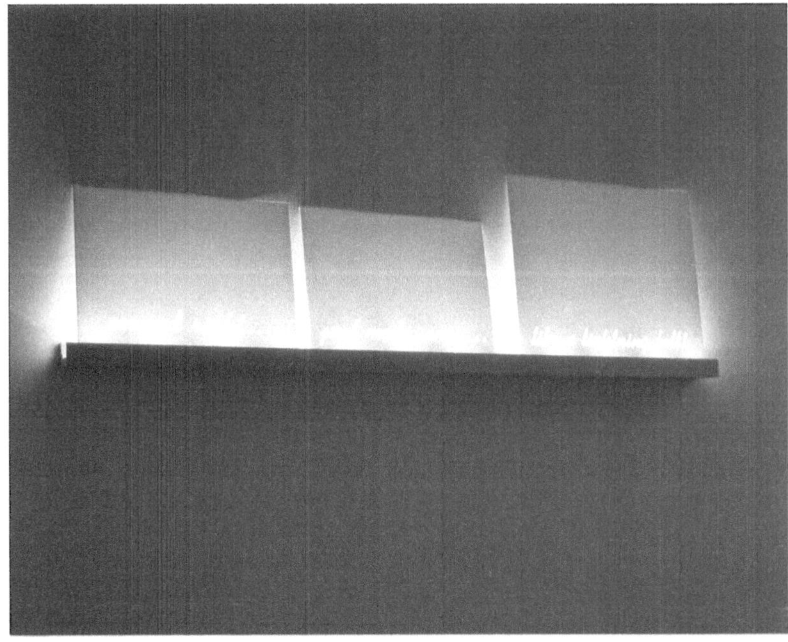

Mary Kelly, *Seemed Right*, 2005. Laser-cut cast acrylic, linear strip lighting, wood support, 3 units; 2 units, each 15 × 20 in.; 1 unit, 24 × 20 in.; 72 in. (overall). Courtesy the artist and Pippy Houldsworth Gallery, London.

of a woman by way of anatomical form. … Through their actions, the women become complex, ineffable figures of their own definition, defying the notion of a woman as an object presented for the enjoyment of the viewer."[15] The photos can also be read as somewhat humorous images of Badiou's subject of a fidelity, of, that is, women caught up in the flashing event of feminism, using a trace to guide them.

Love Songs continued in Postmasters' back room, which contained two works that echoed those in the front. *Seemed Right,* placed on the right-hand wall, repeated the form of *Sisterhood Is POW* …, only its acrylic panels were white, not black. As in *Sisterhood Is POW* …, the panels contained the recollections of older feminists, whom Kelly had asked to describe their initial responses to the women's liberation movement. The most common answers, once again written in light, a form that matched their thematic content, characterized feminism as an event: "seemed right," "just made sense," "like a lightning bolt!"

Across from *Seemed Right,* on the room's left-hand wall, Kelly projected a ninety-second film loop titled *WLM Demo Remix.* Like *Flashing Nipple Remix,* the film depicts both an early women's liberation movement street demonstration and its contemporary restaging. This work, however, uses an actual archival photo, a trace of the event, to represent the original demonstration, which took place in New York City in 1970, one of several demonstrations held across the United States to mark the fiftieth anniversary of the Nineteenth Amendment giving American women the right to vote. Like *Flashing Nipple Remix, WLM Demo Remix* portrays a transgenerational haunting. An image that carries the legacy of an earlier generation of feminists appears to the new generation. Likewise, the women in the later image inhabit those in the earlier one. Using a slow dissolve to combine past and present images, a technique that imitates the scene of the unconscious mind, the loop begins with the later image—the photo of the restaging—which gradually fades and disappears as the earlier image emerges and grows clearer. The image of the restaging never fades out completely, however, but remains visible behind the earlier one, which itself does not picture an originary event, because the 1970 demonstration, mounted by a second wave of feminists, was haunted by earlier street performances—late nineteenth- and early twentieth-century suffragist parades. The archival photo, then, also depicts a restaging. Literally and figuratively, Kelly's work is a visual remix: a recording produced by bringing together ingredients in a new formation that modifies their identities.

The phrase on the demonstrators' sign oscillates between "Unite for Women's Emancipation," which appears in the archival photograph, and in the restaged image, "From Stone to Cloud." A clear political exhortation to bring about emancipatory change, an exhortation recalling those of the suffragists, alternates with a far more cryptic word-image that describes a particular kind of change: a transformation from a thing-like thing, an entity—a stone—into something capable of remixing—a cloud. In the context of Kelly's exhibition, "from stone to cloud" can be read as a metaphor for at least two interrelated changes: mutations in the identity of feminism as a political movement, and mutations in the identity of the subject seized by feminism. Each moves away from a fixed state and grows into something defined by its ability to change, to be reborn, liberated. Feminism as an event and the subject of a fidelity to it leave behind a conception of politics grounded in solid foundations,

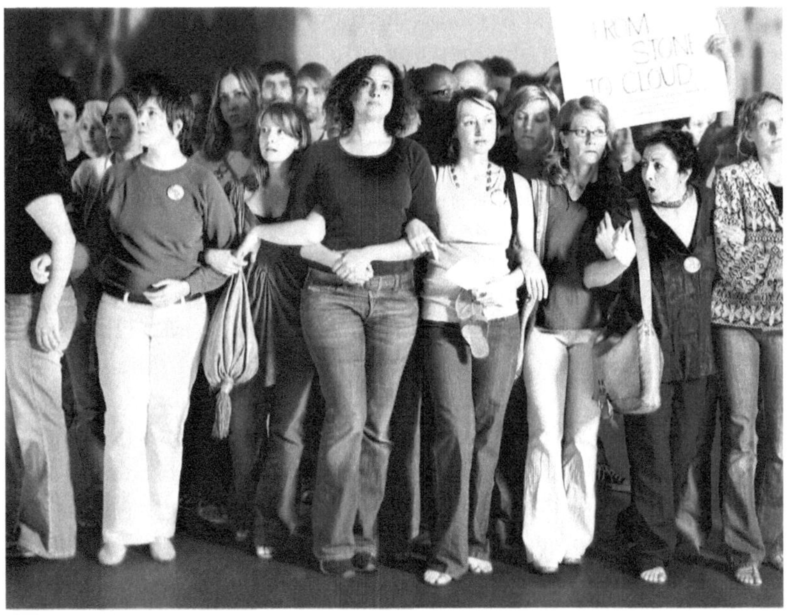

Mary Kelly, still from *WLM Demo Remix*, 2005. Black-and-white film loop, 90 sec. Courtesy the artist and Pippy Houldsworth Gallery, London.

and ascend to a more democratic one that exists in multiple incarnations and changes shape as it articulates with other political aims and objects—for example, human rights. Politics as a remix.

"From stone to cloud" is taken from a poem by Sylvia Plath titled *Love Letter*. Kelly's choice of *Love Songs* as the title of her exhibition bespeaks a debt: the show may be influenced by Badiou, but it operates, quite literally, under the sign of Plath, whose life and poetry have long haunted feminists, and whose poem begins

> Not easy to describe the change you made
> If I'm alive now, then I was dead,
> Though, like a stone, unbothered by it,
> Staying put according to habit.

Plath wrote the poem six months after giving birth to its addressee, a baby girl, who, as the poet describes it, also gave birth to her. Since the 1970s, when she made the *Post-Partum Document,* Kelly has been interested in the mother-child relationship. Following Badiou, she suggests that it might be considered a form of fidelity to the event of love.[16] More important, she compares the relationship to the intersubjectivity of a political project—in particular, to the kind of love that existed among feminists in the early women's movement. This love, she claims, characterized a feminist community that recognized difference and, as a result, attempted to forge nonhierarchical forms of political organization.[17] The implied "you" to whom Kelly writes her love songs is, I think, both new and older feminists, with their own irreconcilable difference, as well as feminism itself, which gave birth to a new subject and whose own birth the women quoted in *Seemed Right* also address, saying, as Plath does, "I knew you at once."

Jacqueline Rose, in her superb book *The Haunting of Sylvia Plath,* observes that in Plath, the boundary between personal, psychic history and political history is uncertain.[18] For this reason, Plath has been severely chastised by critics who want to separate the two. But she has also served as a site of contestation about the meaning of the feminist formulation that the personal is political. Rose points out that some feminists claim that Plath's late work reveals the emergence of the poet's authentic self.[19] Plath, they say, was emancipated into a resolute identity. Those who interpret Plath in this manner often render her personal journey political by turning it into an allegory of feminism understood as a movement whose goal is to enable the emergence of a transcendent female selfhood. *Love Letter* suggests otherwise. In this and other poems, the stone stands for separateness from other things. And it is precisely this hard separateness that characterizes the phallocentric self, the self understood as constituted outside of relationships, a private rather than a public being. Because Plath describes her liberating transformation as a move *away* from a stonelike state, the transformation cannot accurately serve as an image of a feminism that wants to move *toward* self-constituted female subjectivity—especially if we consider *Love Letter* in relation to *Magi,* a poem penned by Plath one day later. There, the narrator, fantasizing a group of transcendent beings hovering over a baby's crib, shrinks from their "loveless" abstractions and asks, "What girl ever flourished in such company?"[20] Kelly, like Rose, claims Plath for a different feminism, one grounded in the continual opening and remixing of feminist politics and the feminine, rather than in conclusive identities that disavow intersubjectivity and foreclose mutation. In *Love Songs,*

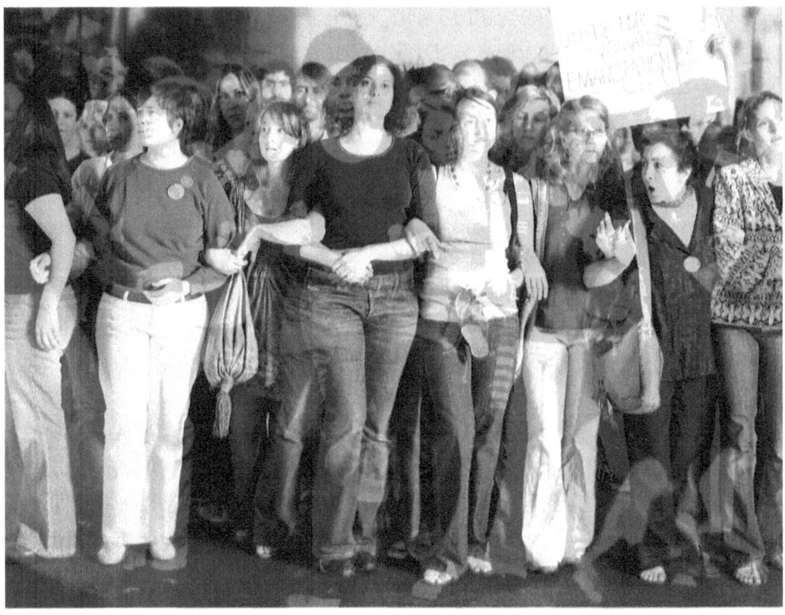

Mary Kelly, still from *WLM Demo Remix*, 2005. Black-and-white film loop, 90 sec. Courtesy the artist and Pippy Houldsworth Gallery, London.

"from stone to cloud" counters—protests against—the danger that feminism and the subject of feminism might, as Rose cautions, "find itself reproducing the form of phallocentrism at the very moment it claims to have detached itself most fully from patriarchal power."[21]

Both fidelity to the event and left melancholy remember the past and write history. But unlike triumphalist historical narratives, in which emancipation leads to resolution, Kelly's history is written in the tense of the future anterior, an order of time in which, as Cornell observes, reimagining never ends.[22] Theorizing the future anterior as the time of personal history, Jacques Lacan wrote, "What is realized in my history is not the past definite of what was, since it is no more, or even the present perfect of what has been in what I am, but the future anterior of what I shall have been for what I am in the process of becoming."[23] Lacan's description of personal history recalls Benjamin's philosophy of political history. The historian, as Benjamin famously wrote, does not reconstruct the past "as it really was" but bringing past and present into a constellation, "seize[s] hold of a memory as it flashes up at a moment of danger."[24] Kelly mixes Badiou and Benjamin—two philosophers of the flash and revolutionary not-forgetting. For in *Love Songs,* the women's liberation movement cannot be distinguished from the transformations it undergoes in the hands of a new generation and, perhaps most important, in both generations' fantasies. *WLM Demo Remix,* for example, literalizes the future anterior, never allowing the image of the 1970s' demonstration to appear in isolation. And while the image of the restaged demonstration does *technically* resolve, it, too, cannot be separated from its counterpart by virtue of its status as a theatrical reenactment, a repetition with difference, in which a group of women literally assume an image and in this way claim a relationship to an event in which they did not participate. Kelly's performers enact a mimetic identification that for Cornell forms the basis of feminist politics.[25] As a psychic narrative of repetitive time mixes with and reimagines a historical narrative of progressive time, Kelly writes feminism and herself as what they "will have been" for what they are in the process of becoming.

The principal way in which Kelly's fidelity to the event differs from left melancholy is in its refusal to "break with the break," to go back to prefeminist ideas of politics and history. In keeping with this fidelity, Kelly neither absolutizes the event nor takes up an authoritarian position in relation to a younger generation. Rejecting the paternal role, which would demand identification with a supposedly authentic feminism, Kelly foregrounds the category of fantasy, exploring her own and her young performers' imaginary investments in feminist history and politics. In this way, too, the subject of a fidelity diverges from the left melancholic, who must disavow his participation in fantasy, precisely in order to defend his fantasy of mastery.

Notes

1. Giorgio Agamben, *State of Exception,* trans. Kevin Attell (Chicago: University of Chicago Press, 2005), p. 14.

2. Wendy Brown, "Resisting Left Melancholia," in *Loss,* ed. David L. Eng and David Kazanjian (Berkeley: University of California Press, 2003), pp. 458–465.

3. Ibid., pp. 460, 462–463.

4. Ibid., pp. 461–462.

5. Retort (Ian Boal, T. J. Clark, Joseph Matthews, and Michael Watts), *Afflicted Powers: Capital and Spectacle in a New Age of War* (London: Verso, 2005), p. 9.

6. Brown, "Resisting Left Melancholia," p. 460.

7. Alain Badiou, *Ethics: An Essay on the Understanding of Evil* (London: Verso, 2001), pp. 41, 42–43.

8. Julia Kristeva, *Revolt, She Said*, trans. Brian O'Keeffe (New York: Semiotext(e), 2002), p. 104.

9. Badiou, *Ethics*, pp. 41–42.

10. Ibid., pp. 80–85.

11. Ibid., p. 50.

12. In Badiou's most recent book to be translated into English, feminism is absent from the philosopher's outline of the last forty years of French politics. Alain Badiou, *Metapolitics* (London: Verso, 2005), pp. xxxiv–xxxv.

13. Badiou, *Ethics*, p. 72.

14. Drucilla Cornell, "Rethinking the Time of Feminism," in *Feminist Contentions: A Philosophical Exchange*, by Seyla Benhabib, Judith Butler, Drucilla Cornell, and Nancy Fraser (New York: Routledge, 1994), p. 152.

15. Josh Tonsfeldt, "Mary Kelly, *Love Songs*" (unpublished paper, Barnard College, 2005).

16. Sasha Archibald, "Care and the Psyche: An Interview with Mary Kelly," in *At the Mercy of Others: The Politics of Care* (New York: Whitney Museum of American Art, 2005), p. 26. The exhibition was organized by the Helena Rubinstein Curatorial Fellows of the Whitney Museum of American Art Independent Study Program and ran May 18–June 25, 2005.

17. Ibid., p. 26.

18. Jacqueline Rose, *The Haunting of Sylvia Plath* (Cambridge, MA: Harvard University Press, 1992).

19. Ibid., p. 144.

20. On a BBC broadcast, Plath introduced this poem by saying, "Abstractions, by definition, are withdrawn from life and formulated in spite of life's minute and vital complexities. In this poem, 'Magi,' I imagine the great absolutes of the philosophers gathered around the crib of a newborn baby girl who is nothing but life." Sylvia Plath, *The Collected Poems* (New York: Harper and Row, 1981), pp. 289–290, n.130.

21. Rose, *The Haunting of Sylvia Plath*, p. 149.

22. Cornell, "Rethinking the Time of Feminism," p. 152.

23. Jacques Lacan, "The Function and Field of Speech and Language in Psychoanalysis," in *Ecrits: A Selection*, trans. Alan Sheridan (New York: W. W. Norton, 1977), p. 86.

24. Walter Benjamin, "Theses on the Philosophy of History," in *Illuminations*, ed. Hannah Arendt, trans. Harry Zohn (New York: Schocken, 1969), p. 255.

25. Cornell, "Rethinking the Time of Feminism," p. 155.

Mary Kelly's *Mimus*: Feminism's Waves

Mignon Nixon

Waves

Feminism, it is said, comes in waves. A wave rushes in, carrying with it some token of the past. A wave runs out, erasing its own tracks. The waves of feminism are mnemonic and amnesiac at once.

The waves of feminism, in Mary Kelly's evocation, mirror the diurnal, repetitive rhythms of domestic labors performed mostly by women. In *Post-Partum Document* (1973–1979), Kelly's foundational work, feeding, diapering, and play articulate the physical and emotional bonds between parent and child, while also symbolizing stages of separation and loss. It is through the intimacies of care, this work suggests, that our fantasies are formed, and that as children and later caregivers ourselves, we internalize our social roles. Feminist politics, as represented in Kelly's body of work, is grounded in the dynamics of care. In this context, care signifies not only labor—women's work, women's lot—but also a mode of feminist politics.[1]

Around the time that Kelly was bringing *Post-Partum Document* to an end, Julia Kristeva published "Women's Time." In feminist discourse, Kristeva observed, "The word 'generation' implies less a chronology than a *signifying space,* a both corporeal and desiring mental space."[2] Reflecting on the aftermath of the women's liberation movement—which was also the subject of Kelly's next project, *Interim* (1984–1989)—Kristeva proposed an alternative to chronological or recursive modes of history. Rather than imagining the next wave of feminism as embodied in "a new group of young women" or "another 'mass feminist movement' taking the torch passed on from the second generation," Kristeva envisaged a "third attitude," which would not, however, exclude "the *parallel* existence of all three in the same historical time."[3] This is, in effect, Kelly's proposition in *Interim,* in which suffragettes of turn-of-the-century Britain and hysterics of the Salpêtrière Hospital in Paris rub elbows with Kelly's own contemporaries, veterans of the women's liberation movement, now poised on the threshold of middle age.

In *Love Songs* (2005–2007), Kelly revisits the question of feminism's generations. *WLM Demo Remix* (2005), a part of *Love Songs,* is a short film loop projected with a slow dissolve. Summoning the iconic generation of 1968 through images of their younger selves, the piece bridges past and present through an oscillating image, as these avatars of 1968 appear to walk arm in arm with their sister-daughters, Kelly's students. The event that *WLM Demo Remix* reimagines is not one march, era, or wave, Kelly has suggested: "Not a moment of ecstatic communal identification, but the recognition of irreconcilable difference."[4] By overlapping episodes in feminist history, *Love Songs* meditates on the process by which "the event of feminism" takes on the psychic significance and volatility of personal memory, even for those who missed the women's liberation movement through the accident of belated birth.[5]

Feminist time, observes Rosalyn Deutsche, "is an order of time in which … reimagining never ends," enabling each generation to "claim a relationship to an event in which [it] did not participate."[6] Such reimagining is a process of "not-forgetting," she elaborates, invoking a phrase of philosopher Alain Badiou: a vigilant but vital, creative, open-ended mnemonics of "fidelity to the event" of feminism that counters melancholic modes of commemoration, which idealize and fix the past.[7] Through the luminous illusion of the slow dissolve, *WLM Demo Remix* also suggests that the event of feminism can beckon as a mirage, a tantalizing fiction, and that an order of time in which reenvisioning never ends, while hospitable to fantasy and psychic investment in the past, might sometimes be conducive to myth. "Mimetic identification" with past feminisms stimulates but might also constrain political imagination.[8] Or as Kelly has observed in a different context, "There's a certain tyranny in fantasy, too. It works over the hackneyed themes, if you like."[9]

Inscribed in the oscillating structure of *WLM Demo Remix* is this double dynamic. The intergenerational politics of feminism is "personal" in the specific sense that it conceives history as a personal order of time.[10] Feminism lays claim to its own vulnerable history—a history that History recurrently disappears—by registering it in the tense of personal experience, allowing each participant imaginatively to "own" the movement. Yet, Kelly concedes, this subjective investment in feminism is also ambivalent. Younger feminists of today, she reflects, may identify with their predecessors while at the same time reproaching them for their failures.[11] Perceiving that the past is not fixed but mutates over time, feminist politics anticipates that future generations will differentiate themselves, even radically, from earlier feminists and earlier feminisms. Fidelity to the event of feminism therefore entails acceptance of "irreconcilable difference" in the present and with the past.

To care for feminism is to conceive it as separate from, never identical with, one's own history. For Kelly, it is to recollect traces of the past in which one did and did not participate, and incorporate them into a "both corporeal and desiring mental space." In *WLM Demo Remix,* Kelly produces that space as a dissolve, a palimpsestuous, intergenerational haunting. In *Mimus* (2012), her most recent reflection on feminism's histories, she extracts and picks out—gleans, in Laura Mulvey's evocative phrase—the testimonies of witnesses to a Cold War feminist movement, Women Strike for Peace (WSP), and sets these passages into relief, inviting us to consider the dynamic of feminism and resistance to militarism in our own time of governmental mass surveillance and perpetual war.[12] Reviving a technique recommended by Virginia Woolf—thinking back through our mothers—*Mimus* takes up the question of what art informed by "the parallel existence" of multiple feminisms might offer us now.[13]

Lint

Produced in response to the first Gulf War, Kelly's 1992 installation *Gloria Patri* addressed the resurgent charisma of militarization by focusing on the newfound role of women in the military as agents of state violence. "I think the extent to which women have internalized the masculine ideal has been ignored," the artist noted at the time.[14] In *Gloria Patri,* the highly polished, coldly reflective aluminum surfaces of faux trophies, shields, and emblems signify the process by which militarism promotes participation in the abstracted violence of the state, instigating us to see ourselves in its shiny speculum.

With *Mea Culpa* (1999), Kelly then turned from women as perpetrators of war violence to the effects of war on civilians. Drawn from media accounts of atrocities against women and children examined by the International War Crimes Tribunal, the five text panels of *Mea Culpa* also inaugurate the medium of compressed lint in Kelly's body of work. Condensing the residues of countless cycles of laundry collected from the lint trap of a domestic dryer, she converted a material evocative of domestic labor—and security—into the ground of historical narrative, as crystallized in specific, subjective experiences of war. From the overlapping rhythms of the news cycle and wash cycle, both repeated ad infinitum, Kelly scavenged fragments, bits of stuff, to mold into historical vignettes, recounted in subjective voice. Compressed into undulating patterns resembling, by turns, sonic waves, radio and satellite transmissions, and brain waves, lint has become, in the artist's now-extensive cycle of work in that medium, an interface between the daily routines of a certain way of life and war violence. "My emphasis is not primarily on the real events," she explains, but instead on "the traumatic effect of their representation and the psychic residue that filters through the everyday."[15]

The official justification for the invasion of Iraq in 2003 was the threat that weapons of mass destruction could be used against the West. The specter of nuclear annihilation provided the pretext for an escalation of militarism that was soon accompanied, even on the Left, by a renewed "remasculinization" of politics—the term Susan Jeffords uses to describe the rehabilitation of militarism in the aftermath of the US war in Vietnam.[16] In *Gloria Patri,* Kelly exposes the psychic dynamics of that process, which reached a climax with the first Gulf War. *Mimus,* like a kind of prequel to that work, turns to the archives of Cold War anti-Communism, the precipitating situation of the war in Vietnam, to recall the role played by an emergent feminist pacifist movement, the WSP, in resisting nuclear militarism.

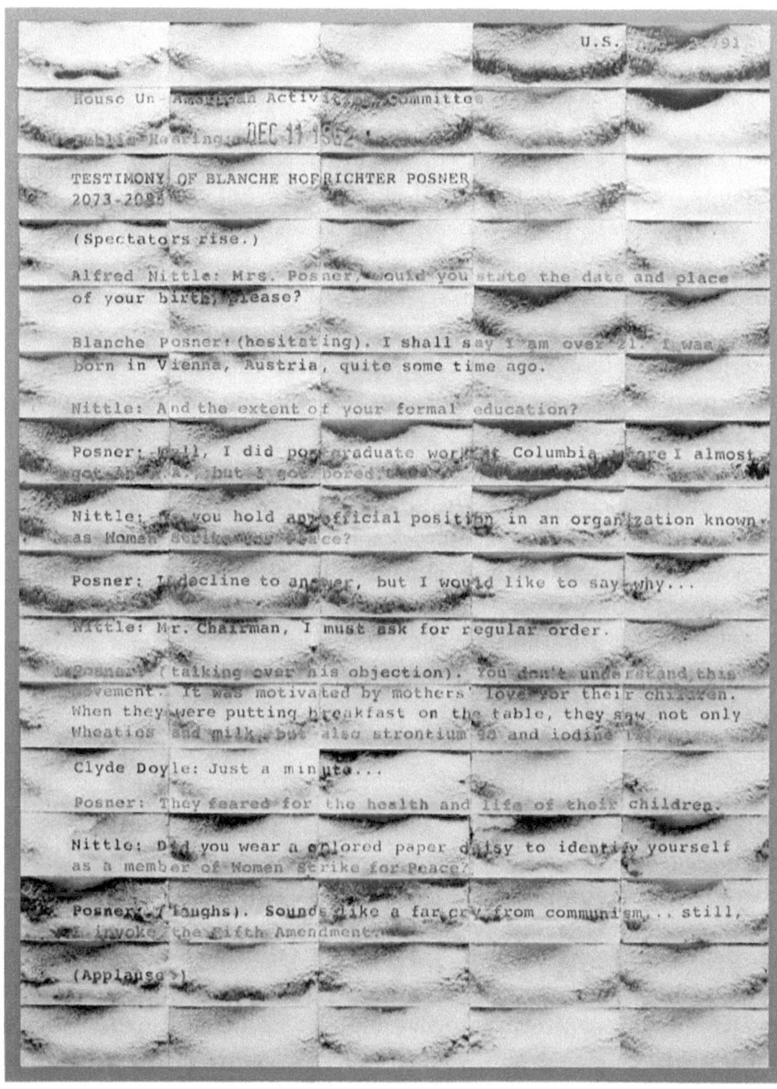

Mary Kelly, *Mimus, Act I (Posner)*, 2012. Compressed lint; 83½ × 61 × 2 in. Collection of Hammer Museum, Los Angeles. Courtesy the artist and Pippy Houldsworth Gallery, London.

Milk

On November 1, 1961, fifty thousand women in sixty cities across the United States came out for peace, walking off their jobs and "out of their kitchens" to demand an end to nuclear testing.[17] Overhead as they marched hung a radioactive cloud, the accumulated debris from a series of Soviet nuclear tests. Waving placards and carrying balloons that demanded "Pure Milk Not Poison," reflecting fears of contamination from nuclear fallout, the strikers launched a "motherist" peace campaign, as WSP activist and historian Amy Swerdlow has memorably described it.[18] Playing up the era's prescribed role of nurturing mother, the demonstrators protested the failure of Cold War containment policy to secure the nuclear family.

"Since the first nuclear explosions over Japan," Swerdlow observes, critics of US nuclear policy "had been dismissed or excoriated by most public officials."[19] Reawakening suppressed memories of the atomic bombings of the civilian populations of Hiroshima and Nagasaki in August 1945, the WSP claimed this as its "political primal scene," Kelly's term for a historical event whose psychic effects filter down to later generations.[20] The WSP marchers embodied the conventional, middle-class moral motherhood of the postwar era, brandishing this persona as a shield against state repression.[21] At a time when peace advocates were dismissed by the press, the public, and political leaders, remarks Swerdlow, "the image projected by WSP of respectable middle-class ladies ... helped to legitimize a radical critique of the Cold War and U.S. militarism."[22] Parading a conspicuous conformity to social convention in demeanor and dress, the carefully choreographed WSP marches and deputations to Capitol Hill disarmed the political establishment, garnering widespread, appreciative press attention. In an era of rampant anti-Communism, however, even the WSP's nonthreatening image did not prevent the group from becoming a target of red-baiting. In November 1962, a year after the WSP's first demonstration, fourteen activists received subpoenas to appear before the House Un-American Activities Committee (HUAC), which convened public hearings intended to expose the group as a Communist front.[23]

Mimus, "an installation in three acts," revisits the dramatic appearance of three of those women, Blanche Hofrichter Posner, Ruth Meyers, and Dagmar Wilson, before HUAC. Picked out in scarlet

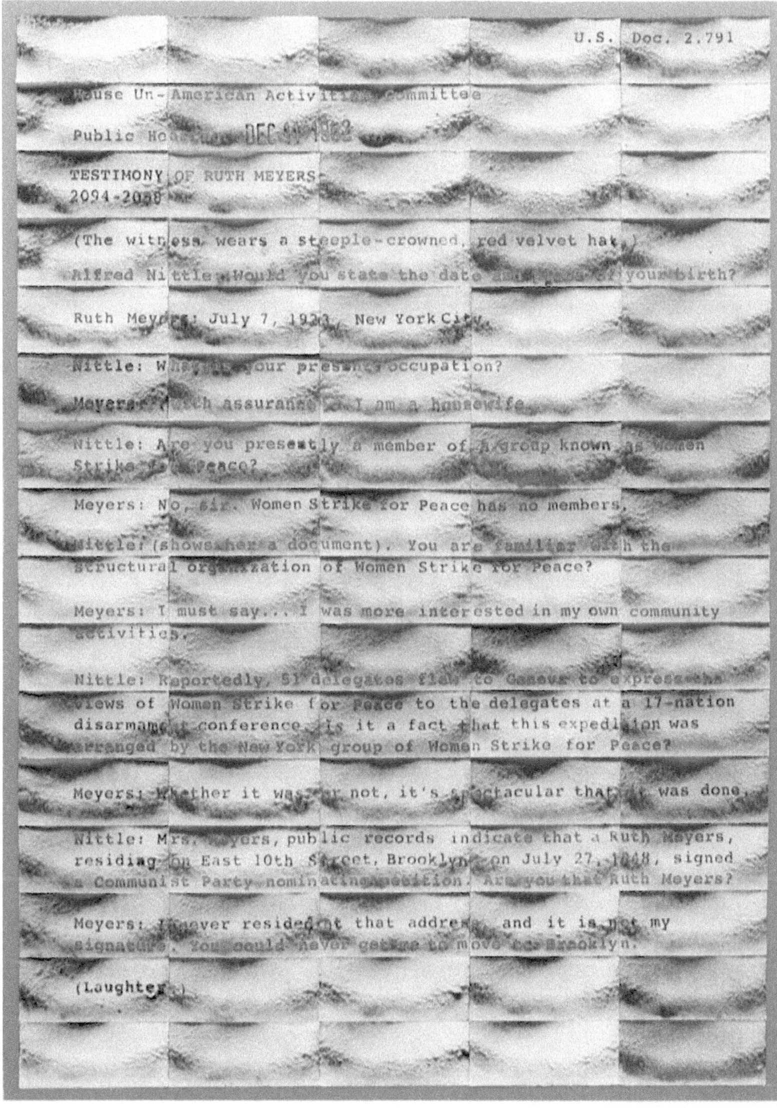

Mary Kelly, *Mimus, Act II (Meyers)*, 2012. Compressed lint; 83½ × 61 × 2 in. Private collection, New York. Courtesy the artist and Pippy Houldsworth Gallery, London.

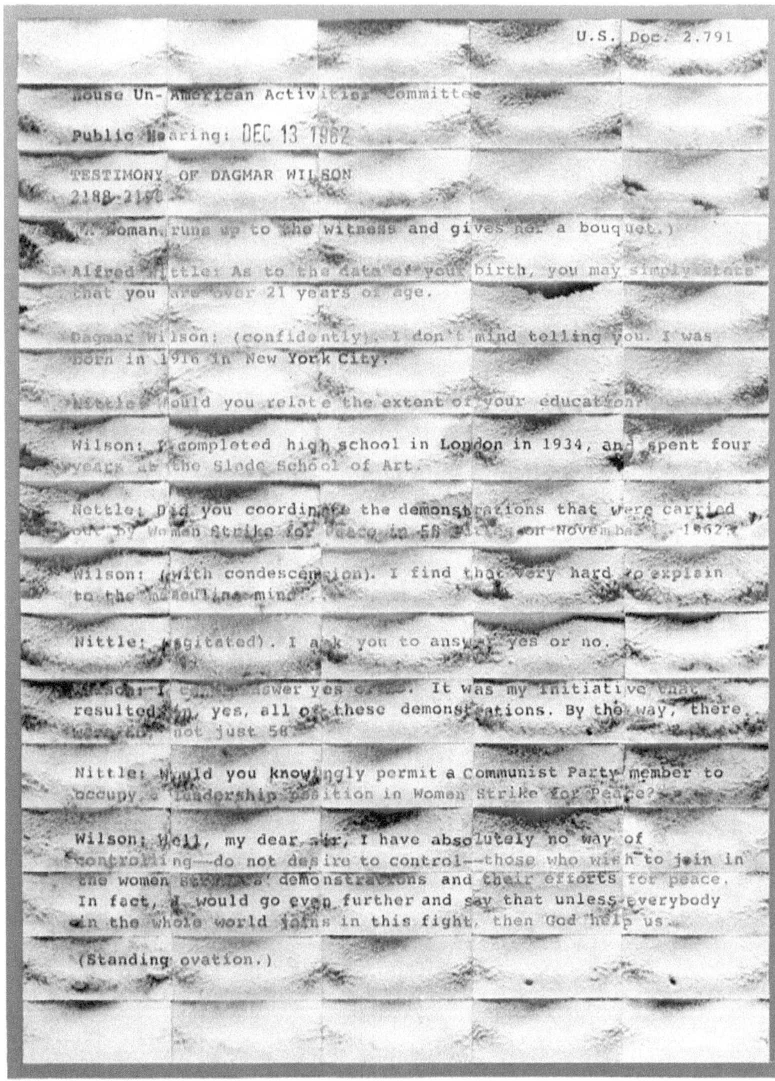

Mary Kelly, *Mimus, Act III (Wilson)*, 2012. Compressed lint; 83½ × 61 × 2 in. Collection of Margaret Morgan and Wesley Phoa. Courtesy the artist and Pippy Houldsworth Gallery, London.

letters on a bed of compressed lint harvested from a domestic dryer and molded into waves are extracts from the official transcript. Marked "U.S. Doc. 2,791," and stamped with the dates December 11 and December 13, 1962, the three large panels bear, under the heading "House Un-American Activities Committee Public Hearing," excerpts from the testimonies provided by Posner, Meyers, and Wilson under questioning by Alfred M. Nittle, chief counsel to the committee.

The ostensible focus of HUAC's investigation was the infiltration of peace organizations by the Communist Party, "with particular reference to Women Strike for Peace and its Metropolitan New York, New Jersey, and Connecticut section."[24] In response to the subpoenas, the WSP devised a distinctive strategy, "so ingenious in its exploitation of traditional domestic culture in the service of radical politics that it succeeded in doing permanent damage to the committee's image," as Swerdlow observes.[25] Before the committee had even announced its investigation, the WSP issued its own press release, proclaiming that "with the fate of humanity resting on a push button, the quest for peace has become the highest form of patriotism"[26] In a statement published in the *New York Times*, Wilson, the artist and children's book illustrator who had initiated the 1961 demonstrations, went further, dismissing the hearings as "an attempt to divert our attention from the most important issue women have ever faced, the preservation of our families in a world armed with nuclear bombs."[27]

On December 11, Chair Clyde Doyle of California opened the hearings with characteristic bombast, lacing his remarks with quotations from Vladimir Lenin, Joseph Stalin, and Nikita Khrushchev. "Peace propaganda and agitation," he declared, betraying familiar fantasies of impotence and emasculation against a ubiquitous enemy, "have a disarming, mollifying, confusing, and weakening effect on those nations which are the intended victims of Communism."[28] Some witnesses would be directly accused of being Communists, while the committee would cast others as Communist dupes—a strategy echoed in conservative newspapers: "There is nothing spontaneous about the way the pro-Reds have moved in on our mothers and are using them for their purposes," railed Hearst columnist Jack Lotto, while the *San Francisco Examiner* claimed to be in possession of proof that "scores of well-intentioned, dedicated women … were being made dupes of by known Communists."[29]

From the outset, the WSP was determined to resist bullying by HUAC. Uniting around the women who had received subpoenas, local groups organized delegations to attend the hearings, filling the five hundred seats in the caucus room of the Old House Office Building with "WSPers" from eleven states. Some attended with small children in tow, whose presence, spilling out of laps and patrolling the hearing room floor on hands and knees, was widely reported by newspapers. Posner, a retired high school teacher, was the first witness to appear (*Mimus, Act I*). When she was called to the stand, the audience rose to its feet, embodying a solidarity that would resonate throughout the proceedings in eruptions of laughter and waves of applause, an acoustic accompaniment to the women's testimonies that Kelly registers in the undulating rhythms of *Mimus*. Speaking over the chair and chief counsel, the indignant Posner immediately turned the tables on the committee, delivering a fiery peroration on motherism, which Kelly excerpts: "You don't understand this movement," she pointed out. "This movement was inspired and motivated by mothers' love for children." "When they were putting their breakfast on the table, they saw not only the Wheaties and milk, but they also saw strontium 90 and iodine 131. … They feared for the health and life of their children."[30] Countering Doyle's troika of Lenin, Stalin, and Khrushchev with motherhood, milk, and Wheaties, Posner demonstrated how readily the rhetoric of Cold War gender ideology could lend itself to an indictment of nuclear militarism.

A viewer familiar with Kelly's artistic history might detect in this passage an echo of the *Post-Partum Document*, a work that like *Mimus*, appropriates the typographic rhetoric of the document, and that as the artist has remarked, is devoted to questioning "the assumption that childcare is based on the woman's natural and instinctive understanding of the role of mothering."[31] *Mimus* returns to this cultural fantasy of the mother-nurturer, whose responsibility for the care of a child begins with filtering what that child ingests. Documentation I, the first substantial section of the *Post-Partum Document*, gives the serial treatment to a set of "analyzed fecal stains and feeding charts," investigating the indexical logic by which a baby's soiled diaper provides tangible evidence of parental—read maternal—competence in introducing solid food to its diet. Encapsulating a cultural contradiction by which maternal care is both naturalized in the portrayal of women as instinctive nurturers and

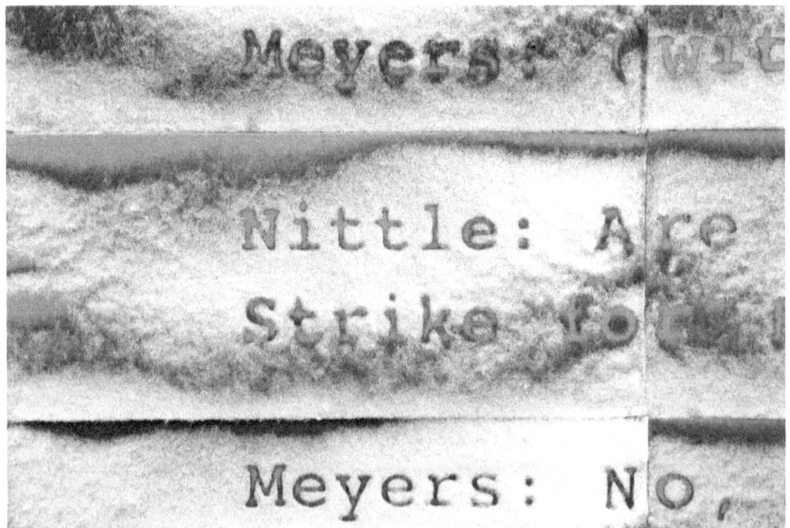

Mary Kelly, detail of *Mimus, Act II (Meyers)*, 2012. Compressed lint; 83½ × 61 × 2 in. Private collection, New York. Courtesy the artist and Pippy Houldsworth Gallery, London.

subjected to the authority of experts, the *Post-Partum Document* reveals a distinct ambivalence toward maternal knowledge. In *Mimus*, Kelly returns to this theme of maternal desire and knowledge, not only in the perspective of nuclear testing—which contaminated the food supply, making it impossible for mothers to perform their nurturing and filtering roles—but also nuclear-mentality culture. This is Hanna Segal's term for the dynamic of destructiveness established by the atomic bombings of Hiroshima and Nagasaki—a culture that, she also argued, persists into our own, post–Cold War era.[32]

Nuclear-mentality culture, by Segal's account, is infantile in a specific sense. The terror of nuclear war revives the vicious circle of paranoia and all-out destructiveness we all suffer in infancy. In nuclear-mentality culture, this primal terror returns in a militarism driven by anxieties of annihilation and fantasies of omnipotence. Building on Melanie Klein's theories of infantile anxiety, and in particular on Klein's concept of a "paranoid-schizoid position," in which the infant, in fantasy, risks obliterating its entire world (initially, the maternal body) to eradicate a perceived existential threat, Segal argued that the nuclear situation awakened primitive anxieties and defenses.[33] Only by considering

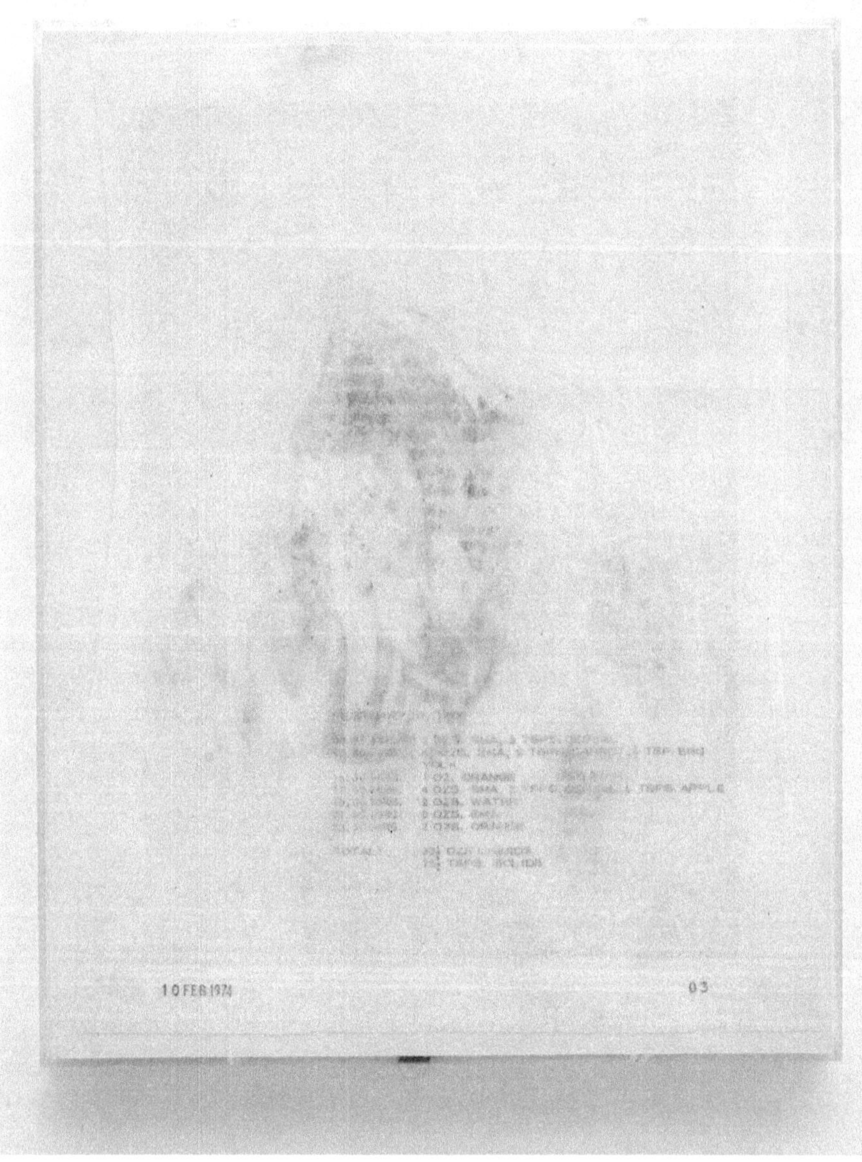

Mary Kelly, detail of *Post-Partum Document: Documentation I, Analysed Fecal Stains and Feeding Charts*, 1974. Perspex unit, white card, diaper lining, plastic sheeting, paper, ink; 14 × 11 in. Collection of Art Gallery of Ontario. Courtesy the artist and Pippy Houldsworth Gallery, London.

the psychic dynamics of the nuclear situation, she suggested, and acknowledging "our part" in it, could nuclear-mentality culture and its inexorable trend of escalation begin to be assuaged.[34]

For Klein, paranoid-schizoid anxiety, the psychic position of war par excellence, was alleviated by guilt, or the "depressive position." The dawning awareness that the destructiveness visited on "bad objects" in fantasy also threatens to extinguish good objects—notably the mother—represents, in Klein's theory, the opening for an adaptation to reality in which the figure of the mother as caregiver also plays a pivotal role. Kleinian psychoanalysis allows for the possibility that this process may fail—that destructiveness may prevail, or that in a crisis, it may be revived. The strategy of motherism that the WSP employed in resisting nuclear militarism touches on this unconscious trend of regression, or so Kelly suggests. Bringing "maternal thinking," in Sara Ruddick's helpful phrase, to bear upon anti-Communist paranoia, the WSP confronted the nuclear threat as a dangerous projection of infantile fantasies.[35] Its embrace of the Cold War imago of the mother was, Kelly implies in *Mimus*, not merely politically expedient. It represented a psychically astute political response to the nuclear threat.

A Paper Daisy

Writing in the mid-1960s, the Italian psychoanalyst Franco Fornari—like Segal, a Kleinian—argued that the threat of nuclear annihilation had made war itself obsolete. In *The Psychoanalysis of Nuclear War* (1964) and *The Psychoanalysis of War* (1966), he claimed that the prospect of nuclear destruction had precipitated a crisis that threatened the very institution of war.[36] For war, Fornari maintained, is a "system of security." Its ostensible objective is to defend against external threats. Its deeper purpose, however, is to abolish "illusory internal danger," the primal anxiety that attacks from within. War projects internal anxiety onto others, "finding, or … inventing, real enemies to kill." Turning illusory anxieties into real threats, it is a "cure for our madness." But "from the moment that war, as atomic war, becomes a potentially absolute external danger," Fornari contended, war as a system of security breaks down. The prospect of nuclear war, posing dangers out of all proportion to the "antianxiety functions" war has traditionally fulfilled, demands "new security organizations"—organizations that must disavow the sovereignty of the state, with sovereignty being "the attribute of the state that is most closely connected with the war institution."[37]

HUAC, by its very name, underscored the measure of identification with the sovereign state demanded of US citizens in the Cold War. Its raison d'être was to exact unquestioning identification with a state that was, in Fornari's terms, increasingly incapable of distinguishing "between nightmare and reality."[38] The WSP, by contrast, aligned itself with the efforts of "new security organizations" to restrain state violence. In April 1962, for example, Wilson led a contingent, including Coretta Scott King, to a seventeen-nation disarmament conference in Geneva.[39] That autumn, demonstrating at the UN Headquarters in New York during the Cuban Missile Crisis, WSPers carried signs advising President Kennedy to "be careful" and "let the U.N. handle it."[40] A commitment to disarmament under UN control was so fundamental to the group's thinking that any woman subpoenaed by HUAC, regardless of her politics or whether she was even active in the WSP, was to be embraced by the group if she shared this position.[41] For as one activist put it, "Each

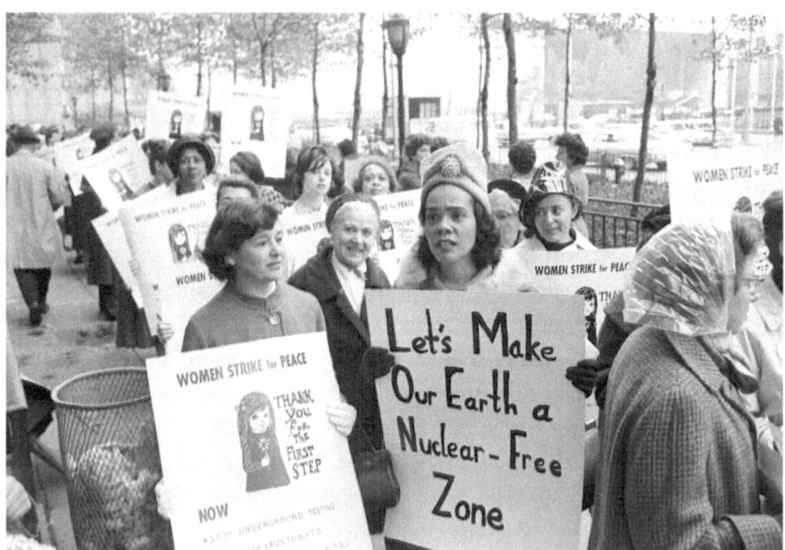

Dagmar Wilson and Coretta Scott King at a march on the UN Plaza marking the second anniversary of the original WSP, November 1, 1963. © Bettmann/CORBIS.

woman, regardless of her views, her goodness or her badness, is too precious to be violated for an abstraction like the state."[42]

In *Mimus,* the emblem of feminine resistance to "an abstraction like the state" is a kind of nonflag. In the McCarthy era, the time of HUAC, the flag became the national fetish it still is today. *Mimus* deconstructs this fetish, breaks it down, and recycles it into something else, namely, a screen. The units of *Mimus,* like all of Kelly's compressed lint pieces, are molded from fibers deposited into a filter, the lint trap of a domestic dryer. Here, these elements form another screen, another filter, but one on a historical scale. The immense grids of *Mimus* suggest a filtering of historical memory, a sifting out, a cycle of forgetting that leaves vast residues behind. In *Mimus,* these traces become the stuff of resistance. What the received history of the Cold War filters out, *Mimus* re-collects.

The ground of the WSP's dissent from Cold War anti-Communism was this: once "global survival was at stake," not only was the institution of war obsolete, but so was conventional politics.[43] The ethos of the WSP, Swerdlow observes, privileged "each woman's individual right to work for peace in her own way and according to the dictates of her conscience."[44] By offering apolitical maternal morality as proof of compliance with the gender ideology of the Cold War, the WSP had, in effect, exploited a loophole in the repressive culture of anti-Communism—an exemption that enabled some women to execute a strategy Fornari would later outline in *The Psychoanalysis of War* as the only viable response to the crisis posed by nuclear war: that is, to withdraw one's private violence from the state. Faced with the "pantoclastic prospect" of nuclear war, the individual had a responsibility, Fornari maintained, to reclaim "the aggressiveness saved by him [*sic*] and deposited into the state, as if into a bank." By withdrawing one's own share of this destructiveness from the sovereign state, he suggested, the individual might help to liberate it "from the accumulation of private violence which it has monopolized, capitalized, and finally increased to nuclear proportions."[45]

The testimony of the WSP witnesses before HUAC provided a dramatic, public demonstration of what it might mean, in practice, to reclaim "private violence" from the state. Unlike Fornari, however, the WSP perceived that it would fall to women, the era's custodians of individual conscience and private morality, to lead this effort. Pressed to subordinate their alarm about the prospect of nuclear war to the sovereign state's anti-Communist ideology, the WSP witnesses invoked maternal feeling, contending that a duty to protect children from annihilation overrode the claims of the state on private violence. Throughout, the women presented themselves as model private citizens: concerned mothers. Adhering to the conservative gender ideology of the period, they argued, in effect, that their role as mothers could not be reconciled with the demands for violence exacted by the nuclear state. Exploiting the gender norms of the Cold War itself, which conflated women with mothers, to whom innate propensities toward nurturing and protectiveness were ascribed, WSPers characterized resistance to nuclear war as an expression of women's "natural" concern for the welfare of children.

Having established motherhood as the Cold War bona fides of the WSP, Posner strove to shift the focus of the hearings from Communism to the dangers of nuclear annihilation, in the process exposing the foibles of the committee itself. In order to avoid being held in contempt for refusing to answer potentially incriminating questions about other women, she repeatedly pled the Fifth, including this surreal exchange a paper flower, which Kelly quotes:

NITTLE: Did you wear a colored paper daisy to identify yourself as a member of Women Strike for Peace?

POSNER: It sounds like such a far cry from communism it is impossible not to be amused. I still invoke the Fifth Amendment.[46]

Greeting each question as a further opportunity to display her own contempt for the proceedings, Posner repeatedly stirred the audience to boisterous laughter. It was a virtuosic execution of a strategy commended by Woolf in her *Three Guineas,* a 1938 polemic on the prevention of war. Woolf's advice to those who aspired to avert war was to rely on the "unpaid" teachers of women, in particular "derision and freedom from unreal loyalties." "Ridicule, obscurity, and censure," she asserted, could prove the most effective of tools.[47] Posner availed herself of all three.

"You must rid yourself of pride of nationality in the first place," Woolf counseled, but "also of religious pride, college pride, school pride, family pride, sex pride, and those unreal loyalties that spring from them." In her appearance before the HUAC, a notorious theater of "unreal loyalties," Posner, a native of Vienna and longtime schoolteacher, personified Woolf's model of educated women who "enter the professions and yet remain civilized human beings, human beings who discourage war."[48] Asked about the "extent of her formal education," she airily replied, in a passage Kelly quotes, that she had "done postgraduate work at Columbia, where I almost got an M.A., but I got bored." For Woolf, it is the responsibility of the individual to pursue knowledge, to "fight with the mind," but to forswear "college pride," the imprimatur of institutions, which, she holds, derives from the same sources of aggression as war itself.[49] In her distillation of Posner's testimony to a single page, Kelly encapsulates Woolf's argument that the prevention of war begins with ourselves.

A Red Velvet Hat

The second witness of the day (*Mimus, Act II*) was Ruth Meyers of Roslyn, Long Island. She stepped forward swathed in a red jersey dress and wearing a steeple-crowned red velvet hat—a piece of sartorial provocation to which the scarlet-tinged waves of *Mimus* pay extravagant tribute—and quickly proved herself "just as much of a headache to the committee as Posner had been," the *Washington Post* reported.[50] Asked to state her occupation, Meyers, in contrast to Posner, declared, "With assurance, I am a housewife."[51] "Are you presently a member of a group known as Women Strike for Peace?" Nittle demanded, to which Meyers retorted, "No sir, Women Strike for Peace has no members." When he attempted to draw her out on the "structural organization" of the WSP, she again rebuffed him, insisting, "I was more interested in my own community activities."[52] WSP groups were local. "The WSP method was characterized by a non-hierarchical, loosely structured, 'unorganizational' format that allowed autonomy to each chapter," Swerdlow explains.[53] Providing a blueprint for the future women's liberation movement, in which Kelly would take an active part, the WSP's decentered, egalitarian, individualistic, unorganizational ethos could not have been more incongruous with HUAC's characterization of it as a rigidly structured, externally controlled organization—or with HUAC itself.

Complementing its ethos of individual responsibility and community activism was the WSP's internationalist perspective, subsuming "pride of nationality" to potential peace. The group had drawn the attention of HUAC in part through the participation of the delegation led by Wilson to Geneva. "Reportedly," Nittle accused Meyers, as if on the point of revealing something nefarious, "51 delegates flew to Geneva to express the views of Women Strike for Peace to the delegates of a seventeen-nation disarmament conference arranged by the New York group of Women Strike for Peace." "Whether it was or not," Meyers replied, "it's spectacular that it was done."[54] When at last the chief counsel attempted to deliver the coup de grâce by demanding to know if Meyers was the same Ruth Meyers, residing at 175 East Tenth Street in Brooklyn, New York, who on July 27, 1948, signed a Communist Party nominating petition, the hearing devolved into farce: "I never resided at that address, and it is not my signature. You could never get me to move to Brooklyn."[55] A prolonged standing ovation accompanied her departure from the stand.

In part, the WSP's practice of not enrolling members was a pragmatic measure in a surveillance regime. Its unorganizational ethos, however, also exemplified the group's critique of organized pacifism. By rejecting the identity of a peace organization, the WSP questioned the radicalism of traditional pacifist groups. In this, it echoed Woolf's *Three Guineas,* a polemic prompted by a gentleman's dunning letter requesting a donation to a peace society. Over the essay's three long chapters, Woolf meditates on women's separate and unequal education; exclusion from the professions; financial dependency on fathers, husbands, and brothers; and above all, subjugation to the "tyranny of the private house." Rather than contribute to a pacifist group, she concludes, the aim of peace might be better served by supporting the education and public participation of women.

When the WSP reached the climax of its struggle with HUAC, many of the witnesses were obliged to confront their male adversaries without Woolf's voice ringing in their ears. Of the long history of women's peace activism, WSPers were, Swerdlow acknowledges, profoundly ignorant, "lacking any knowledge" and regarding "history as irrelevant." "As for feminist discourse, most of us had never heard of the first wave, and the second wave was only in formation," she admits.[56] No writer was more alert than Woolf to the ramifications of women's

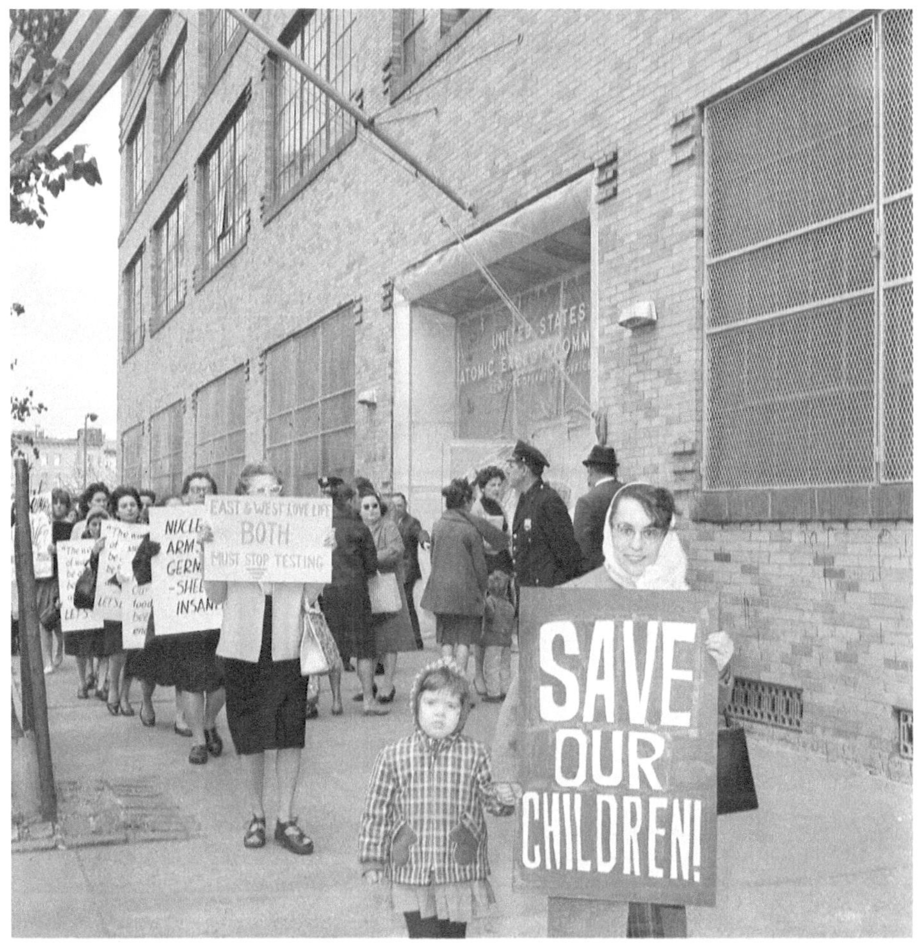

WSP demonstration at the US Atomic Energy Commission offices in New York City, November 1, 1961. © AP Photo/*PA Images*.

ignorance of history, which she treats extensively in *Three Guineas* as foundational to the architecture of militarism. Rigorously abridged into three acts, *Mimus* clearly echoes Woolf's polemic not only in structure but also in its cardinal themes. Woolf's advice to women, formulated earlier in *A Room of One's Own*—to think back through our mothers—remains, Kelly suggests, a timely recommendation: the history of the WSP is not well remembered today, and a pattern of segregating the histories of feminism and antiwar activism persists in our own time of war.

A red flag to our own lack of knowledge, our own propensity to regard "history as irrelevant," *Mimus* reminds us that feminism continues to be marginalized in war—and antiwar—discourse. It also signals the divisive trend of militarism that segregates us into distinct and mutually uncomprehending war generations—a partition that feminism, by "reimagining the past," still strives to resist. Like *Love Songs* and *Interim,* Kelly's previous meditations on feminism's generations, *Mimus* resonates with Kristeva's proposition that "generation" might imply "less a chronology than a *signifying space,* a both corporeal and desiring mental space." In particular, it broaches the possibility of an intergenerational dialogue about militarism, and one that embraces rather than disavows irreconcilable difference.

My Dear Sir

Emboldened by the success of a parade of witnesses in getting the better of the committee, the audience in the hearing room grew increasingly ebullient. By the timeWilson appeared on the third day, her supporters greeted her with cheers and a bouquet of flowers. An artist and 1937 graduate of the Slade School of Fine Art in London, Wilson had spent much of her life in Britain. Upon learning that Bertrand Russell had been jailed in London for his part in antinuclear demonstrations, she "decided that there are some things the individual citizen can do," as she explained to the *New York Times* in 1962.[57]

Meyers had claimed that the WSP had no members. Wilson now revealed that it had no leader. When Nittle demanded to know if she had coordinated the November 1, 1961 demonstrations opposing nuclear testing, Wilson declared the matter "very hard to explain to the masculine mind." Accepting that "it was my initiative that resulted in,

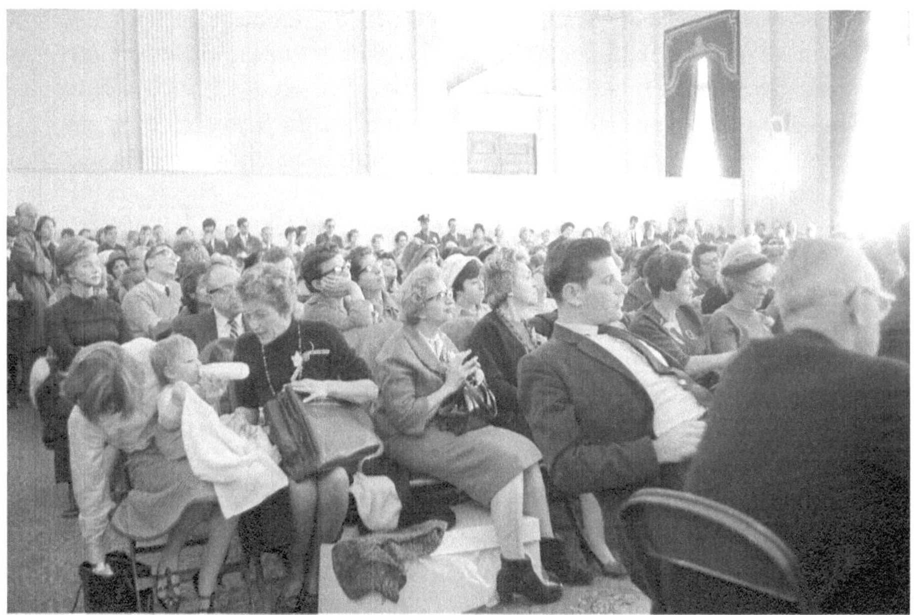

Hearing room during House Subcommittee on Un-American Activities investigation of the WSP, December 13, 1962. © AP Photo/Bill Allen/*PA Images*.

yes, all of these demonstrations that took place that day," she implied that this was not exactly to the point. "People like to call me leader," Wilson acknowledged, when pressed, adding, "I regard it more as a term of endearment, or, shall we say, an honorary title."[58]

Wilson's reference to the "masculine mind," which the official transcript fastidiously records was uttered "with condescension," nevertheless made a significant political point, implicitly linking HUAC and the Pentagon with the Communist enemy. Both nuclear powers, Wilson suggested, shared a mind-set, a "nuclear attitude," in Segal's terms. Asked in a moment of high drama, "Would you permit Communist Party members to occupy leading posts in Women Strike for Peace?" Wilson's reply was disarmingly direct: "Well, my dear sir, I have absolutely no way of controlling, do not desire to control, who wishes to join the demonstrators and the efforts that the women strikers have made for peace. In fact, I would go even further. I would like to say that unless everyone in the whole world joins us in this fight, then God help us."[59] Reprising a rhetorical technique perfected by Woolf in *Three*

Guineas, Wilson couched her testimony in the language of feminine politesse while making the hearing an occasion to present the masculine mind with a radically different perspective. The obsession with Communism, she maintained, betrayed a denial of reality. The McCarthy era was defined by intellectual repression. Its anti-Communist (male) hysteria, Wilson implied, was a defense against knowledge. The sweeping censorship, surveillance, and intimidation mobilized against the perceived peril of Communism served to deny the reality of the nuclear threat, an existential danger that compelled the whole world to be on the same side, rendering militarist thinking obsolete at the height of militarism. In the nuclear era, contended Wilson, a greater threat than that posed by any enemy resides in our own thinking—in our refusal or inability to think.

In 1963, President Kennedy publicly proclaimed the efforts of the WSP a decisive factor in the passage of the nuclear test ban treaty.[60] After his assassination, the WSP assumed a pivotal role in opposition to the war in Vietnam, translating its motherist antinuclear politics into resistance to the draft. Motherist politics, however, was also becoming the retrograde symbol of a repressive past, particularly for those younger feminists "who saw the WSP as an example of their own mothers' 'false consciousness.'"[61]

Mimus, like *Interim* and *Love Songs*, portrays feminism as "an event of love," a passionate project. *Sisterhood Is POW* ..., one section of *Love Songs* declares. Women's desire is a cardinal concern of Kelly's body of work, of her corpus, the name given to the opening section of *Interim,* in which the images of a black leather jacket, summer dress, and handbag are folded and knotted into a series of eroticized poses. In the corresponding handwritten text panels, derived from intimate conversations between women, passages highlighted in red find their echoes in enigmatic check marks, Xs, and arrows diagramming desires evoked by these articles of clothing, which figure in the text vignettes, everyday episodes in the lives of veterans of the women's liberation movement. That women dress, perform, and care for one another, Kelly has often suggested, is inextricably bound up with feminism's "personal" politics. Summoning the process by which feminists of different generations "reimagine the past" haptically, through tokens of desire, the dark red *tache* applied to the jacket in *Corpus* is transferred to *Mimus,* seeping into its thick, soft waves like a stain. The irreconcilable differences of feminism are also condensed, Kelly intimates, in the distinctions between a steeple-crowned velvet hat and the artist's "uniform" of the 1970s, a leather jacket. Thinking back through our mothers means, in part, standing in their shoes.

Notes

1. Sasha Archibald, "Care and the Psyche: An Interview with Mary Kelly," in *At the Mercy of Others: The Politics of Care* (New York: Whitney Museum of American Art, 2005).

2. Julia Kristeva, "Women's Time" (1979), in *The Kristeva Reader*, ed. Toril Moi (New York: Columbia University Press, 1986), p. 209 (emphasis in original).

3. Ibid. (emphasis in original).

4. Archibald, "Care and the Psyche," p. 26.

5. Rosalyn Deutsche, "Not-Forgetting: Mary Kelly's *Love Songs*," *Grey Room* 24 (Summer 2006): 29–30. Reprinted in this volume.

6. Ibid., 35, 36.

7. Ibid., 26–30.

8. Ibid., 36.

9. "Round Table: A Conversation on Recent Feminist Art Practices," *October* 71 (Winter 1995): 66.

10. For a discussion of Kelly's *Love Songs* as "written in the tense of the future anterior," the time of personal history as theorized by Jacques Lacan, see Deutsche, "Not-Forgetting," 35–36.

11. As Kelly remarks of *Love Songs*, in which she collaborated with her students, "I thought these women were really asking me, maybe in an unconscious way, 'Why didn't you do the job?'" Dominique Heyse-Moore, "'No Right to Speak without *Les Enquêtes*': Mary Kelly in Dialogue with Dominique Heyse-Moore," in *Mary Kelly: Projects, 1973–2010* (Manchester, UK: Whitworth Art Gallery, University of Manchester, 2011), p. 97.

12. Laura Mulvey, "Mary Kelly: An Aesthetic of Temporality," in *Mary Kelly: Projects, 1973–2010*, p. 91. Mulvey points that out while in the 1970s and 1980s, Kelly had drawn primarily on her own experiences and those of her immediate circle for her collections of material, "this close relationship between her experience and the material collected was disrupted in the early 1990s," when, turning to questions of war, she became "a 'gleaner' of emblematic stories" (ibid.).

13. Virginia Woolf, *A Room of One's Own* (1929), in *A Room of One's Own/Three Guineas* (London: Penguin, 1993), p. 69.

14. Mary Kelly, "On Display: Not Enough Gees and Gollies to Describe It" (1992), in *Imaging Desire* (Cambridge, MA: MIT Press, 1996), pp. 185, 181.

15. Mary Kelly, "Mea Culpa," *October* 93 (Summer 2000): 22n1.

16. Susan Jeffords, *The Remasculinization of America: Gender and the Vietnam War* (Bloomington: Indiana University Press, 1989).

17. Amy Swerdlow, *Women Strike for Peace: Traditional Motherhood and Radical Politics in the 1960s* (Chicago: University of Chicago Press, 1993), p. 15.

18. Swerdlow notes that "Pure Milk Not Poison" was the most effective slogan devised by Women Strike for Peace, perhaps because "mothers had to decide whether to let their children drink any milk at all during testing periods and worried whether milk products used later had been made from contaminated milk" (ibid., p. 83).

19. Ibid., p. 16.

20. Amelia Jones, "The 'Dispersed Body of Desire' in Mary Kelly's Practice: Amelia Jones in Dialogue with Mary Kelly about the Body in Feminist Art," in *Mary Kelly: Projects, 1973–2010*, p. 107.

21. Swerdlow, *Women Strike for Peace*, p. 3.

22. Ibid.

23. Ibid., p. 97.

24. Ibid., p. 108.

25. Ibid., pp. 97–98.

26. Ibid., p. 99. The fear of a "push-button nuclear holocaust," Swerdlow notes, was stoked by the Berlin Wall crisis and the resumption of nuclear testing after a three-year hiatus (ibid., p. 17).

27. Dennis Hevesi, "Dagmar Wilson, Anti-Nuclear Leader, Dies at 94," *New York Times*, January 23, 2011.

28. Quoted in Swerdlow, *Women Strike for Peace*, p. 109.

29. Quoted in ibid., p. 101.

30. Quoted in ibid., p. 111; *Mimus, Act I.*

31. Mary Kelly, preface to *Post-Partum Document* (London: Routledge and Kegan Paul, 1983), p. xviii.

32. Hanna Segal, "From Hiroshima to the Gulf War and After," in *Psychoanalysis, Literature and War, Papers 1972–1995*, ed. and introduced by John Steiner (London: Routledge, 1997), p. 167.

33. Melanie Klein, "A Contribution to the Psychogenesis of Manic-Depressive States" (1935), in *The Selected Melanie Klein*, ed. Juliet Mitchell (New York: Free Press, 1986), pp. 116–145.

34. Segal, "From Hiroshima to the Gulf War and After," p. 167.

35. Sara Ruddick, *Maternal Thinking: Toward a Politics of Peace* (Boston: Beacon Press, 1989).

36. Franco Fornari, *Pscicanalisi della Guerra Atomica* (Milan: Rizzoli, 1964); Franco Fornari, *The Psychoanalysis of War* (1966), trans. Alenka Pfeifer (Garden City, NY: Anchor Books, 1974).

37. Fornari, *The Psychoanalysis of War*, p. xv, xvi, xix, xviii–xix, xxvii.

38. Ibid., p. xix.

39. Hevesi, "Dagmar Wilson, Anti-Nuclear Leader, Dies at 94." Swerdlow (*Women Strike for Peace*, pp. 92–93) recalls Coretta Scott King's statement of support for the WSP and the test ban treaty in 1963: "Peace among nations and peace in Birmingham,

Alabama, cannot be separated." This position, she concedes, was significantly more progressive than that of WSP at the time.

40. Swerdlow, *Women Strike for Peace*, pp. 88–89.

41. Ibid., p. 98. Views were divided, Swerdlow notes, on unilateral disarmament.

42. Carol Urner, quoted in ibid., p. 105.

43. Ibid., p. 9.

44. Ibid., pp. 98–99.

45. Fornari, *The Psychoanalysis of War*, pp. xxvii–xxviii.

46. Quoted in Swerdlow, *Women Strike for Peace*, p. 111; *Mimus, Act II.*

47. Virginia Woolf, *Three Guineas* (1938), in *A Room of One's Own/Three Guineas* (London: Penguin, 1993), pp. 203, 205.

48. Ibid., pp. 205, 204.

49. Virginia Woolf, "Thoughts on Peace in an Air Raid," in *Thoughts on Peace in an Air Raid* (London: Penguin, 2009), p. 2; Woolf, *Three Guineas*, p. 204.

50. Swerdlow, *Women Strike for Peace*, p. 113.

51. Quoted in *Mimus, Act II.*

52. Quoted in Swerdlow, *Women Strike for Peace*, p. 113; *Mimus, Act II.*

53. Swerdlow, *Women Strike for Peace*, p. 3.

54. Quoted in *Mimus, Act II.*

55. Quoted in Swerdlow, *Women Strike for Peace*, p. 113; *Mimus, Act II.*

56. Swerdlow, *Women Strike for Peace*, pp. 106, 9–10.

57. Hevesi, "Dagmar Wilson, Anti-Nuclear Leader, Dies at 94."

58. Quoted in Swerdlow, *Women Strike for Peace*, pp. 116–117; *Mimus, Act III.*

59. Quoted in Swerdlow, *Women Strike for Peace*, p. 117; *Mimus, Act III.*

60. Swerdlow, *Women Strike for Peace*, pp. 95–96.

61. Ibid., p. 5. On the history of the WSP in resistance to the US war in Vietnam, see ibid., chapters 7–9.

Index of Names

Abraham, Karl, 103
Adams, Parveen, 79–98, 102, 107, 112
Aeneas, 89–90
Agamben, Giorgio, 153
Albert Hall, London, 158–159
Apter, Emily, 99–114
Aquino, Corazon, 107
Aragon, Louis, 69
Art and Language, 115

Badiou, Alain, 155–157, 160–165, 168
Balkans, 146
Barker, Barry, 115
Barthes, Roland, 132–133, 140
Baumgarten, Lothar, 78
Beirut, 134, 141, 143
Benjamin, Walter, 145, 153, 157, 164–165
Berger, Maurice, 133
Bhutto, Benazir, 107
Blum, Irving, 43
Bosnia, 141
Bourgeois, Louise, 15
Brecht, Bertolt, 36, 40
Breton, André, 69
Broodthaers, Marcel, 34, 78
Broude, Norma, 48n2
Brown, Wendy, 153
Bryson, Norman, 68
Buren, Daniel, 34
Burgin, Victor, 48n2, 115
Butler, Judith, 23

Canute, 54
Carson, Juli, 143–144
Cassatt, Mary, 99
Celan, Paul, 133
Chaplin, Charlie, 41
Charcot, J. M., 62, 67, 69, 74, 106
Chicago, Judy, 14, 23–24, 29, 32–36, 38, 40, 43–46, 50n28
Chomsky, Noam, 119–120
Clifford, James, 78
Cold War, 120, 169–170, 172, 176–182
Communist Party, 172, 175, 179, 182, 184, 187–188
Cornell, Drucilla, 46, 51n45, 158, 164–165
Cottingham, Laura, 48n9
Critical Art Ensemble, 153
Cuban Missile Crisis, 180

Dalto, Françoise, 17
de Lauretis, Teresa, 101
de Maupassant, Guy, 110
Deren, Maya, 57–58
Deutsche, Rosalyn, 34, 153–168
Dido, 89–90
Dora case-history, 62, 69, 74
Doyle, Clyde, 175–176

Drawing Center, 153
Duchamp, Marcel, 33

Ettinger, Bracha, 141, 148–149

Fanon, Frantz, 127
Ferenczi, Sándor, 69
Fifth Amendment, 182
Fisher, Jean, 101
Fornari, Franco, 179–181
Foster, Hal, 65–78
Freud, Sigmund, 1, 5n1, 6nn11,14, 15–19, 58, 62, 67, 69, 74–75, 82, 86–89, 101, 112, 143

Gagnon, Monika, 60
Garrard, Mary D., 48n2
Gatens, Moira, 25, 26–29, 36, 46
Géricault, Théodore, 75, 119–120
Godel, Ana, 101
Graham, Dan, 115
Greenaway, Peter, 133
Grosz, Elizabeth, 101
Gulf War, 116, 119, 135, 169–170

Haacke, Hans, 34, 50n33, 78
Habermas, Jürgen, 75
Hall, Stuart, 154
Hammons, Harmony, 48n2
Heath, Stephen, 121
Hiroshima, 172, 177
History Group, 16
Hitchcock, Alfred, 62
Holocaust, 145–147
Houghton Gallery, 151n1
House Un-American Activities Committee (HUAC), 172–173, 175–176, 180–181, 183–184, 187
Hunter, Alexis, 101

Institute of Contemporary Art (ICA), 5n1, 16, 115, 122
International War Crimes Tribunal, 170
Irigaray, Luce, 14, 69, 107
Iversen, Margaret, 115–129

Jakobson, Roman, 18
Jameson, Fredric, 75
Johns, Jasper, 43
Judd, Donald, 35

Kant, Immanuel, 149
Kelly, Mary, 1–7, 9–22, 65–78, 115–129
Kennedy, John F., 188
Kentridge, William, 145
Khmer Rouge, 141
Khrushchev, Nikita, 175–176
Kiefer, Anselm, 67, 121
King, Coretta Scott, 180, 190n39
Klein, Melanie, 17, 58, 177, 179
Kolbowski, Silvia, 48n2, 78
Korea, 146
Kosovan war, 136–138
Kosuth, Joseph, 50n33
Kristeva, Julia, 13, 58, 69, 71, 107, 149, 152n26, 155, 167–168, 186
Kruger, Barbara, 48n2
Kurtz, Steven, 153
Kwon, Miwon, 45, 49n21

Lacan, Jacques, 5n1, 6nn4,8, 10, 16–18, 68–70, 72–74, 80–89, 93–94, 105–107, 110, 112, 113, 126, 144, 149
Lacy, Suzanne, 48n2
Laforgue, René, 112
Laplanche, Jean, 82
Larsen, Ernest, 133
Latin America, 146
Laub, Dori, 145–146, 148
LeClaire, Serge, 82
Lefort, Claude, 155
Lenin, Vladimir, 175–176
Leonard, Sarah, 133
Levine, Sherrie, 76
Linker, Kate, 48n2
Lippard, Lucy, 48n2
Lotto, Jack, 175
Louvre, The, 75

Mannoni, Maud, 17
Marx Brothers, 40
Marxism, 2, 15–16, 31, 40, 42, 58, 65, 134–135
McCarthyism, 181, 188
Mendieta, Ana, 48n2

Meyers, Ruth, 172, 175, 183–186
Miller, Jacques-Alain, 87
Millot, Catherine, 69, 73, 106, 108
Miss World Contest, 158
Mitchell, Juliet, 5n1, 16, 58
Montrelay, Michèle, 17, 69
Mulvey, Laura, 48n2, 53–63, 73, 103, 169, 189n12

Nagasaki, 172, 177
Neshat, Shirin, 145
New Museum, New York, 81
Nine Inch Nails (band), 125
Nittle, Alfred M., 175, 182–184, 186
Nixon, Mignon, 167–191
Nyman, Michael, 133, 149

Old House Office Building, 176

Pane, Gina, 14
Pappenheim, Bertha, 75
Pataka, George, 153
Pateman, Carole, 34, 39, 48n16
Patriarchy Conference, 5n1
Phnom Penh, 141–142
Picasso, Pablo, 140
Pinochet, Augusto, 41
Piper, Adrian, 14
Plath, Sylvia, 162–163, 166n20
Plaza, Monique, 69
Pollock, Griselda, 24, 48n1, 49n23, 99, 131–152
Pollock, Jackson, 41
Posner, Blanche Hofrichter, 172, 175–176, 182–183
Postmasters Gallery, New York, 155, 160
Propp, Vladimir, 61

Richer, Paul, 106
Ringgold, Faith, 48n2
Riviere, Joan, 105–106, 108
Rockefeller Center, 122
Rollins, Tim, 78
Roosevelt, Eleanor, 145
Rose, Jacqueline, 75, 106, 135, 151n7, 163–164
Rosler, Martha, 15, 23, 29, 31–32, 34, 40–46, 50n38, 51n44, 78, 152n18
Ruddick, Sara, 179
Russell, Bertrand, 186

Sabra refugee camp, 141
Salpêtrière Hospital, 168
Santa Monica Museum of Art, 127
Santoro, Suzanne, 14
Sarajevo, 141–142
Sartre, Jean-Paul, 72
Schapiro, Miriam, 48n2
Schoenberg, Arnold, 155
Schor, Mira, 48n2, 103
Schor, Naomi, 101
Segal, Hanna, 177, 179, 187
Serbians, 136, 138, 141
Serra, Richard, 121
Shatila refugee camp, 141
Sherman, Cindy, 48n2
Silvestre, Michel, 88
Sirk, Douglas, 61
Slade School of Fine Art, 186
Smith, David, 121
Smith, Paul, 9–22
Sontag, Susan, 138, 151n13
South Africa, 141, 143
Stalin, Joseph, 175–176
Swerdlow, Amy, 172, 175, 181, 183–184, 190nn18,39

Taiwan, 146
Thatcher, Margaret, 56
Theweleit, Klaus, 119
Tickner, Lisa, 24, 48n2
Tillman, Lynne, 60, 73–74
Trippi, Laura, 67
Truth and Reconciliation Commission, 141, 143

Ukeles, Mierle Laderman, 23, 29–31, 33–34, 38–41, 43–46, 47n1, 49nn21,22

Vasari, Giorgio, 76
Vietnam War, 72, 143, 170, 188
Virgil, 89

Wadsworth Atheneum, 31, 45
Ward, Frazer, 36
Wiener, Lawrence, 115

Wilding, Faith, 24, 48n2
Wilke, Hannah, 14
Wilson, Dagmar, 172, 175, 180, 184, 186–188
Winnicott, D. W., 18
Wittig, Monique, 107
Womanhouse, 1–2, 14, 24, 48n2
Women Strike for Peace (WSP), 169–172, 175–176, 179–188, 190nn18,39, 191n61
Woolf, Virginia, 169, 182–184, 186–187
World Trade Center memorial, 153

Žižek, Slavoj, 94, 105

www.ingramcontent.com/pod-product-compliance
Lightning Source LLC
Chambersburg PA
CBHW020904180526
45163CB00007B/2619
9780262529327